PRAISE FOR A LINE IN THE SAND

"This remarkable book sends you into the boots of an infantryman in the Israeli special forces. Corey is a courageous young American who travelled 5,000 miles to put his life on the line to defend a country that stands on the front-line of a struggle for liberty and democracy that confronts us all. Read it to understand the dangerous day-to-day life of Israeli soldiers, and gain a unique insight into their relationship with the Arab population in a place that has been one of the world's most controversial flash-points for decades."

—Col. Richard Kemp,
Former Commander of British Forces in Afghanistan

"Corey Feldman's account of his IDF service is both a detailed handbook for a new recruit and a patriotic, passionate explanation of why it is that Israel has to fight. A candid, thoughtful memoir."

— David Horovitz, Founding Editor, The Times of Israel

"Many Israelis will tell you that the phenomenon of Jews from the United States abandoning all pleasures in the world and enlisting in the IDF (Israel Defense Forces) is the highest level of sacrifice on the part of our brothers and sisters from abroad. We call it Mutual Responsibility (Aravut Hadadit in Hebrew). Corey Feldman's story will touch your heart. It is a sensitive and accurate description of what a combat soldier sees and does while serving in the IDF."

—Dr. Colonel Moshe Elad (Res.), Former IDF Governor of Jenin, Bethlehem (West Bank), Tire (Lebanon) and Head of RSC to the Palestinian Security HQ, PhD Israeli-Palestinian Conflict

A LINE IN THE SAND

The events and conversations in this book have been set down to the best of the author's ability, although some names and details have been changed to protect the privacy of individuals.

An imprint of Astor Place Publishing LLC

Ordering information:
Special discounts are available on quantity purchases by corporations, associations, companies, organizations, and anyone that wants lots of copies of this great book. For details, email TheExaminedlifeNYC@gmail.com.

Written by Corey Feldman
Cover Design by Susi Clark

Title: A Line in the Sand
Description: First Edition. | New York : Astor Place Publishing, 2020.
Identifiers: ISBN 978-1-7347242-2-6 (paperback) | 978-1-7347242-3-3 (ebook) | 978-1-7347242-4-0 (hardback)

This book is dedicated to Danny Farahan Ben-David and Ayala Farber. Danny, a member of the anti-tank reconnaissance company within the Paratroopers, was a source of knowledge and inspiration to me before I joined the IDF. His advice was instrumental in my decision to enlist, and his memory will live on in all those he touched. Ayala adopted me like a grandson when I moved to Israel. During a period of my life when nothing was certain, she was a source of strength and stability and provided a home whose doors were always open. I miss her immensely.

"The true soldier fights not because he hates what is in front of him, but because he loves what is behind him."

—G.K. Chesterton

Phases of Love

I can't say it was love at first sight. I met her at an awkward point in my life, when I was still unsure of myself, and of the person I was supposed to become. I was on a family trip when we met for the first time. Though I felt an immediate connection to her, I was too young to make sense of my feelings. In the years that followed, I visited her several times, but back then it was all fun and games. As my teenage years melted away into my twenties, I gained a better sense of myself and a better understanding of what I wanted, and it was in that context, in late June of 2008, that I finally started seeing her seriously.

I strode into our relationship fearlessly; perhaps too fearlessly. I crossed her borders and flirted with her neighbors, but in the end, I always came back to her; or more accurately, I was pulled back to her by a force I couldn't quite explain. Our differences were many: she spoke a foreign language and came from a different culture. She was what strangers might call rude, but those who knew her well knew she wasn't rude—just brutally honest. Maybe even to a fault. But I admired that about her. As a 21-year-old with an eye for adventure, she was just what I was looking for. Toward the end of our first extended period together, we were still riding the high of our feelings for one another. And yet, even then, there was something more to our relationship than just hedonism. Her favorite song, "The Hope," brought tears to my eyes long after we had separated for the first time. The sight of the blue and white that she always wore brought back memories of late nights on the port, sunsets over the Mediterranean, and the pride of being associated with something as beautiful and dignified as her.

I took some time away from her, to make sure my feelings were real. It was during our time apart that I realized I was in love. She was all I thought about and all I talked about. She had become a part of me. As a young man in love for the first time, it seemed to me then that I was the first to feel this way about her. And so I came back to her. I was older, and just a little bit wiser. I had changed. I no longer had a backup. I no longer flirted with her neighbors. Now I was hers, and hers alone.

When I returned to her, I made a pledge to her and to myself, that I would love and honor her. I pledged to defend her, even if it cost me my life, and as a result, the nature of our relationship changed. It was no longer defined by candlelit dinners, dancing until sunrise, and lazy mornings spent recovering in bed. Now it was early mornings and hard work. In the first year and a half we spent together after we reunited, I worked harder than I'd ever worked in my life for her. We spent every moment together, and that can be taxing at times. A little bit of distance is healthy in a relationship, but I forfeited that luxury when I made a vow to defend her.

It's June 25th of 2011, nearly three years to the day from that afternoon in late June of 2008 when we first commenced our courtship. And yet, not everything has changed. While I now stand at attention when she plays "The Hope," it still brings tears to my eyes. Blue and white, especially when they're together, have become my favorite colors, too.

While Israel has been loved by many others before me, the connection I feel to her is my own. Like all relationships, it is not perfect. I don't always agree with her, but I believe in her. As I struggle at times to remember what first drew me to her so strongly, she rewards me with moments that I will never forget. Last month, she even rewarded me with a red beret. Our relationship continues to be a difficult one. Defending her takes more from me than I knew I had in me to give. But that comes with the territory. Nobody ever said love was easy. They just said it was worth it.

-Corey Feldman, Under the Tree Café, Tel Aviv.

CONTENTS

PART FIVE: ADVANCED TRAINING

PART SIX: LIFE AS A COMBAT SOLDIER

PREFACE

"Drive forward!" I shouted at the driver of our armored vehicle. We were parked in the no-man's-land between Gaza and our now-evacuated base. "Dekel told us not to move without permission," he fired back. The atmosphere was tense, and our words reverberated within the walls of the metal-plated truck. Several hours earlier, Hamas had declared war on Israel following the assassination of its chief in the Gaza Strip. I had just spotted movement near the Western gate of the Israeli settlement we had been charged with protecting—whether it was dogs or people I couldn't say. When the explosions started, our officer had sprinted to an embankment several hundred feet away to get a better view of the border, taking with him one of our teammates and our only working radio. The area between our truck and his embankment was completely exposed. Given our proximity to the border and the volume of rockets that had passed directly over us, we were quite certain that Hamas spotters were narrowing in our location. Running to him to get his permission would be dangerous, and driving there would expose him. Both would cost us precious time. Doing neither might cost innocent Israelis their lives.

October 2020 marked the seven-year anniversary of my discharge from the IDF. While my army service lasted only three years, I feel like I lived the better part of a lifetime within them. As I think back now on my service, it's hard to believe that the time I spent in the IDF can be quantified with a standard medium of measurement. There is nothing more believable than the movement of a watch hand, dutifully ticking away seconds and minutes of our lives. Yet, as I've grown older, it increasingly feels as though time speeds up and slows down as the pains and pleasures of life seem to multiply and divide it. In the army, days sometimes felt like weeks, and yet, almost inexplicably, months sometimes passed like weeks. Though there were long stretches of time during which I felt as if I had always been a soldier and would always be one, on a cool October morning in 2013, the day of my release arrived.

As my shift of guard duty came to an end that morning, I watched the sun cross the horizon for the final time as an active-duty soldier. A breeze from the west caught the Israeli flag that hung outside the gates of our base and stretched it against the backdrop of the colorful early morning sky. Though I had counted down the days until my release, excited for the adventures to come, I was suddenly overwhelmed by sadness. My future, I realized, would lack the obvious sense of purpose that had defined the last three years of my life, and would take me far away from the people with whom I had grown so close.

In the army, you are surrounded by people who truly know you. When you spend days, weeks, months, and years with the same small group of people, there are no secrets. Everything you are and everything you are not is revealed; the layers of depth are peeled back with time. The stories. The failures and the triumphs. The pride and the insecurities. It is easy to show your best side during good times, but when you are freezing cold, sleep-deprived, and hungry, your true self is revealed. It was in those moments, when every instinct in our bodies was shouting at us to attend to our own basic needs, that we were challenged to put the well-being of the team before ourselves.

The army, by design, forges deep connections among soldiers in a unit. These relationships are built and fostered during countless hours of executing mundane and, at times, miserable tasks as a team. This book tells the story of the training that transformed us from strangers into teammates and shaped us into combat soldiers.

In describing my journey through the IDF, it is impossible to exclude my perspective on the Arab-Israeli conflict. That perspective and my evolving relationship with Israel have been shaped by my experiences and values, which I recognize may not be shared by all. If I were born in Gaza, not New York, I'm sure I would see the world very differently.

F. Scott Fitzgerald once wrote that, "The test of a first-rate intelligence is the ability to hold two opposed ideas in the mind at the same time, and still retain the ability to function". Aspiring to Fitzgerald's intellectual challenge, I want to share a story about what it would be like to fight for the other side.

As a student in Seth Godin's altMBA, one of the assignments that I found most impactful was aimed at developing our capacity for empathy. The assignment challenged us to write from the perspective of someone with whom we wholeheartedly disagreed. The following piece was aimed at answering a difficult question: "Do suicide bombers go to heaven?"

I believe that some of them do.

If I were born in the Gaza strip in the late 1990s, some of my earliest memories might be of violence. I might remember that when I was seven years old, soldiers bulldozed our neighbor's home, and a piece of metal flew through the window and lodged itself under my right eye. I might remember touching my hand to my face, and the shock and fear I might have felt as I pulled my hand back, and saw it was covered in blood. I might remember my father running towards the soldiers standing near the bulldozer and begging them for help, and watching helplessly as he was beaten to the ground; they did not speak our language and believed that he was threatening them. I might not have known that Israel destroys the homes of suicide bombers as a means of deterrence and that our neighbor had blown himself up in a Tel Aviv café several weeks earlier, killing fifteen people. I might remember the fear and the anger I felt the following evening, when soldiers in black masks broke open the door of our home and grabbed my father from his bed. I might remember the blood-curdling screams of my mother as they dragged him away into the night and the deep, unsettling sadness that filled our home in the weeks that passed until they returned him. I might remember watching from the window of my house the next year as Israeli soldiers forcibly removed the Jews that had lived among us from their homes, and put them into trucks. I wouldn't have known it at the time, but in 2005, Israel forcibly removed all its citizens from the Gaza strip in an effort to trade land for peace. I might remember years later that our old textbooks were replaced by new ones which featured a map of an Islamic state that stretched from Gaza to the West Bank, and Syria to Egypt, in the area my teacher said was now occupied by the Zionists.

I might remember that life was hard and that there were many nights when I went to bed with a painful feeling in my stomach. I didn't understand why—I just knew that I wanted to eat, but we didn't have enough food, and my mother went to sleep crying a lot. I might remember that my father became much quieter after the soldiers brought him back. As I got older, he woke up earlier and came home later, often too tired from work to do anything but go right to sleep. I might remember missing the way his eyes used to light up when he smiled, and the way he used to play with me. I might have learned in school about Israel, by whose hand my people had been subjugated and occupied. I might have heard from my parents that all our problems were caused by the Jews. And I might have come to resent them. It was the Jews who had disturbed my happy existence and were the reason my mother cried each night. It was the Jews who took the food off our plates, and whose soldiers stole my father and brought back a man who was different. It was the Jews who locked us in an open-aired prison and prevented us from seeking better lives.

As I grew up, I might have attended Hamas' summer camps, since they gave my younger brothers extra food in exchange for me going. And I might remember the training, the crawling, the shooting, the long sleepless nights, and the bonds I developed with my friends there, as together we trained to take on the enemy of everything we loved, and the reason for all that we had lost. I might remember the camaraderie that formed, as together we learned how to be soldiers. I might remember the pride of being part of a movement that aimed to bring justice and honor to my people.

I might remember the day, when I was in the oldest group at camp, that I heard that Ismael, one of the boys in my group, had been shot trying to cross the border into Israel. I might remember our counselors explaining to us that Ismael had tried to sneak into Israel to find a better life and that he had been shot in cold blood by the Israelis, who killed him for sport. I might not have realized he was strapped with explosives.

And I might remember the pit that formed in my stomach, and the anger that pulsed through my veins, and eventually, as the adrenaline subsided, the feeling of helplessness that set in as I realized how powerless we were against our Israeli oppressors. And I might remember asking to speak to the head of the camp the following day, and telling him that I had to honor Ismael's memory, and asking him what I might do. He might have looked at me with sympathy and understanding and told me that he would let me know soon.

I might remember a time two weeks later when I was pulled out of our morning training session and led into a poorly lit room. I was addressed by three high-ranking military members of Hamas. I might remember feeling intimidated, but important. I was only eighteen, after all. And I might remember them telling me that they had a mission of supreme importance for me, one which would bring honor and wealth to my family. A mission that would ensure that there was always food on the table for my younger brothers and that my mother would no longer cry at night. A mission that would ensure me a place in paradise, as was promised by our prophet, Muhammad.

And I might remember going home that night, and being unable to sleep, excited but scared; I would not be told the details of the mission in advance, and once I was briefed, there would be no turning back. I might remember kissing my mother goodbye that next morning, without betraying the decision I was about to make, and the butterflies in my stomach when I told my counselor I needed to speak with the head of the camp. I might remember the pride of telling him I was ready to accept my mission, even as the fear of the unknown caused my hands to shake as I spoke the words.

I remember the weight of the vest they placed on me in the same room I had entered three weeks earlier. They told me I could never remove it in this lifetime. I remember the prayers we said together and the feeling of holiness and purpose that overcame me as they explained the plan. I would be climbing through a hole in the fence on the border with Israel, where I would be picked up by a Hamas sympathizer on the Israeli side, and taken to a bus stop. I would board the bus, and when I reached the fifteenth row,

I would press a button that would detonate my vest. Hearing the words, I felt as though I were in a dream.

I remember the drive to the border several hours after midnight, and the fear that I might end up like Ismael, who I now realized had tried to do what I was now going to do. I remember being relieved when I reached the other side and nobody stopped me. I remember being afraid that nobody would call, but that, as promised, the phone they had given me rang, and a man with palpable fear in his voice told me he would pick me up within ten minutes.

I remember thinking about my life as I waited; my struggle and all the hardships my family and my people had faced at the hands of the enemy I was about to kill in my final act on this earth. I remember pangs of fear that arose as I thought about how scary my task might be to carry out. But I also remembered my promise that once I accepted my mission, I could never turn back—and I could not risk shaming my family. To bring shame to them would be worse than death. I remember thinking to myself as the sun crossed the horizon that this would be my final sunrise on earth. As I looked at Israel spread out before me, I could see an Israeli flag waving in the distance, stretched out by the wind against the colorful backdrop of the early morning sky.

I remember riding in silence as the man with the twitchy eyes who kept staring down at my chest drove at exactly the speed limit. He looked relieved when we finally reached the bus station. He gave me a pill and commanded me to swallow it while he watched. I did as instructed, and several minutes later, a feeling of peacefulness came over me. To my surprise, the fear was gone. A deep feeling of satisfaction and calm had replaced it—I was ready to do what I knew I must.

When the bus arrived several minutes later, I moved intentionally towards the open door and walked up the three steps that brought me face to face with the driver. I smiled at him as he looked nervously back at me. They told me many times that I must remember to smile at the bus driver. Commitment replaced fear: the time to carry out my mission had finally arrived, and my mission was just. I remember stumbling forward, a bit off-balance from the pill, and looking around at the people in their seats. I saw their clothing in great detail, the colors of their eyes, and the expressions on their faces. When I reached row fifteen, I shouted "*Allahu akbar*!" (God is most great!), and pressed the button that ended my life.

In my three years in the army, I saw violence. Missiles fell within a hundred feet of where I lay pressed against the ground, praying not to become a statistic in the latest oversimplified *New York Times* graph documenting casualties in the Arab-Israeli conflict. Rocks the size of baseballs were thrown at my head, one of which knocked me to the ground. I saw hatred in the eyes of a young mother I directed to the side of the street as she walked with her child in Hebron. In prior years, several Jews had been attacked by Arabs as they traveled down that road on their way to prayer. As a result, the decision was taken that during prayer times, Arabs would walk along the side of the road on the route that Jews took to reach the temple. I remember looking into the eyes of that little girl, no older than six, and seeing confusion. When I looked up at her mother, I was met by her piercing stare, which was filled with anger and hatred. I wished she could see past my uniform and into my heart. While writing this book, I realized that if I have any lingering pain from the army, it is from being on the receiving end of such deep-seated hatred from other human beings.

INTRODUCTION

From 2010 to 2013, I served as a combat soldier in the Israeli Defense Forces. My life as a soldier was not glorious. At times it was incredibly difficult, both physically and emotionally. Often it was boring, and sometimes it was terrifying. It's now been seven years since I was released from my active-duty service, and I am still processing the things that I saw, did and felt as an IDF soldier. In writing this book, I've had to confront and relive many of the experiences that shaped my service which has, at times, been emotionally taxing. When I was a soldier, and a young man, the world seemed to be clearly divided between good and evil and right and wrong. As I've gotten older, I've come to agree with the Russian novelist and political prisoner, Aleksandr Solzhenitsyn: it is not individuals who are good or bad, but certain parts within each of us.

In the pages that follow, I have documented the things I saw, did, and felt while I was training and serving as a combat soldier in the IDF. The obstacles I faced and the challenges I overcame. I've done my best to explain what it means to be a lone soldier* in a combat unit, from training through my time spent guarding Israel's borders and carrying out missions. My story is unique to me, but serving as a lone soldier is an experience that I share with thousands of my Jewish brothers and sisters who move to Israel from all over the world to serve in the IDF.

Long before joining the IDF, I was fascinated by Israel's history and drawn to the heroic stories of soldiers who had died fighting for the young country's survival. From a young age, I loved to read, and I sought out literature that

*A lone soldier is an active-duty soldier without immediate family in the country, or whose family does not support them financially.

chronicled the wars that defined the country's early history. From within the pages of those books, and at the synagogue and after-school program I attended, my perspective on Israel was forged. I learned of six Arab countries that invaded Israel the day after the declaration of statehood in 1948, starting a war in which 1 percent of the population of Israel died. I learned of the 1973 Yom Kippur War, in which thousands of Israelis were killed when Syria and Egypt launched a surprise attack against Israel on one of the holiest days of the Jewish Year. I read the famous quote by Chaim Weitzman on the eve of independence: "The state will not be given to the Jewish people on a silver platter."

As Weitzman predicted, throughout Israel's seventy-year history, its existence has come at a high cost, a cost with which I became personally familiar as a soldier. Today, the dangers facing Israel are psychological as well as physical; many soldiers who stand guard over checkpoints in Judea and Samaria become desensitized, as I did during my service, to the plight of the Palestinians living under harsh conditions. Though checkpoints provide security, I fear that the type of interactions between Palestinians and Israeli soldiers necessitated by such checkpoints reduces the ability of both sides to imagine a future beyond the conflict. The palpable threat of invasion by Israel's neighbors was a reality for much of her existence. While that threat has been tempered in recent decades by the deterrent power of a strong IDF and U.S. support, other threats remain. A radical Iranian regime, that denies the Holocaust and openly calls for the destruction of Israel, continues to expand its regional power and influence, as well as its missile capabilities. Terror groups in the Gaza Strip, Judea and Samaria, and Southern Lebanon continue to threaten the lives of Israeli civilians.

Despite the high cost of Israel's survival throughout the years, I believe it is a cost worth bearing. To me, Israel is not just a place, but also a symbol of the persistence of the Jewish people. Years ago, a friend of mine attended a Hanukah party in the Old City of Jerusalem. The rabbi, from whom the guests expected to hear a long sermon about the significance of the holiday, asked only a simple question: "What would you fight for?" The discussion that followed challenged them to ponder questions of sacrifice and morality: "What would you risk life and limb for? Where do you draw the line?"

In October 2010, I enlisted in the IDF because I did not feel whole standing on the sidelines while terrorism threatened the right of Israel's people to live in peace. I discovered where I draw the line. I draw the line when bomb shelters must be built in playgrounds. I draw the line when guards must be placed outside of stores, restaurants, and movie theaters for fear of suicide bombers. I draw the line when schools are closed not because of incoming snow, but because of incoming missiles.

As I would learn over the course of my three years of military service, drawing a line is a lot easier than the follow-through required to uphold that commitment. Through the many trials and tribulations of the army, my military service separated my life irrevocably into two definitive periods. The naivety and unbridled idealism that defined me prior to enlisting were gone by the time I was released. Just as those changes within me came about over time, so too did the decision to enlist. Throughout my childhood, rich in Jewish history and pride for Israel, various choices led me down the road that would eventually result in my becoming an IDF soldier.

PART ONE:
THE EARLY YEARS

CHAPTER I: THE BEGINNING

In September of 1991, when I was 3½ years old, I was seen by a psychologist, who made the following observations:

> *Corey is a youngster in whom excitement frequently turns to tantrums, who frequently does not cooperate or handle situations as would be expected at his age. He gets easily overstimulated. When he gets angry, he drops to the floor and kicks and screams, has major difficulty in making changes and delaying gratification. His father tends to be more able to handle him, using firmness and his large size as a deterrent to Corey's behavior. (At that time, my father was six-foot-four and 220 pounds).*

As my psychological evaluation made clear, it was evident from a very young age that I was going to be a "challenging" child. At 2 years old, flying from California to New York, I delighted in running up and down the aisles of the airplane with my mother dashing after me. I joyfully tapped the heads of all the sleeping people, who would inevitably wake up just as my mother reached them. After a couple of years of my unbridled and uncontrollable energy as evidence of my attention deficit and hyperactivity, though I was not yet 5 years old, I was written a prescription for Ritalin.

School was hard for me. I switched kindergartens three times before my parents found a school that they felt was the right fit. With severe ADHD and learning disabilities, my educational future was very uncertain. Many doctors warned my parents that I had no hope of succeeding in mainstream education, and several prepared them for the reality that I might never attend college. Fortunately for me, the most surefire way to get me to do something was to tell me (or my parents) that I couldn't do it.

From first grade through fourth grade, I attended The Windward School, a school for children with special needs. There, I gained the skills that would allow me to overcome my learning disabilities. Without the privilege of attending Windward, I might have gone the way of many children in public schools who have learning disabilities and hyperactivity. They fall behind their peers and sink to the low expectations of teachers and mentors, who believe their poor academic performance stems from a lack of effort. The patient teachers and mentors at Windward saved me from such a fate. They supported and guided me, helping me develop the skills and confidence I needed to overcome my educational obstacles.

In the fourth grade, I made the switch to public school. Though mainstream public school was far from smooth sailing, I was better able to deal with my attention and processing issues thanks to the techniques I'd learned at Windward. My tendency to talk continuously to those around me during class led to the installation of what my friends called "Island Corey." While all the other students' desks were neatly pushed together into three rows, my desk was as far away from the other students' desks as possible in order to minimize my interference. So began my career in the Scarsdale Public School System.

Throughout my childhood, my parents were adamant that I face my problems head-on. If I had a disagreement with a teacher or an issue with a grade I received, instead of calling the school on my behalf, they insisted that I show up at that teacher's office. The same was true for sports coaches, friends and family members. If there were challenges in my life that needed to be resolved, my parents were supportive, but it was up to me to address them. The self-reliance that I learned during my formative years would ultimately prove immeasurably valuable when I entered the military.

As the only one of my siblings who didn't attend Jewish day school, much of my Jewish education and Zionism came from my home life and, especially, my grandparents. My father's mother, Lenore, served as the president of the National Council of Jewish Women, in which capacity she brushed shoulders with Shimon Peres, Yitzhak Rabin, and even Bill Clinton. My mother's parents, Sydell and Arnold, were strong figures in their local Jewish community. All my grandparents gave generously and consistently to causes that benefited Israel.

As a kid, like most kids who grow up in wealthy neighborhoods, I was sheltered from the suffering of the world by well-intentioned adults. Part of growing up includes coming to terms with the fact that the world is not perfect, and that suffering is a part of life. My introduction to that reality, and the pain of loss, was when my Grandpa George died from multiple myeloma at the age of 74. The cancer struck quickly and unexpectedly.

Though he passed away when I was only fourteen, my Grandpa George remains one of my greatest role models. At Shabbat dinner the night before my *bar mitzvah*, Grandpa George read me a piece of advice that his own father had written for him in his autograph book on the eve of his grammar school graduation in 1939. Grandpa George, like his father, was not big on long speeches or wasted words. When he spoke, it was short and to the point. And so too was his father's advice to him, written two decades before the civil rights movement, advice which he offered to me as I entered adulthood in the eyes of Judaism:

Dear George –
Be a man. How? –
Love your God, honor your and my native land, the good old U.S.A., cherish your parents and family, hold on to your true friends zealously, be continuous and efficient in your studies, strive for a worthy career, be honest in your dealings with man, without prejudice as to color, race or creed, and you will then measure up to my idea of a real MAN. – Dad

I have kept those words with me (literally, in my wallet) to this day, and have done my best to live my life in a way that would make both my grandfather and his father proud. Several years later, the bubble that my parents and my community had built around me to protect me from the pain of the world was once again punctured by tragedy.

****

Often, it is the role models who regularly surround us, like grand-parents, who most shape our characters and our perspectives. On rare occasions, however, there are people whose personalities are so magnetic, and whose beliefs are so strong, that even their brief intrusion into our lives can forever alter our trajectory. During the fall of my sophomore year at Scarsdale High School, I met such an individual. From time to time, our school held assemblies to which guest speakers were invited to discuss important topics. On a crisp fall day, the student body was addressed by Joe Opotowski, a 21-year-old representative from Free the Children. Joe began his talk by admitting that he had joined Free the Children because "there were more girls than guys, and I thought that would give me good odds." This immediately classified him as my kind of guy. As he continued, he spoke of genocide and injustice, child soldiers, factory conditions in less-developed countries, and poor families in Jamaica living in a garbage dump.

Joe possessed the unique ability to shape his speech, tone, and mannerisms to reach his audience; it felt at various points during his speech as if something or someone bigger than Joe was speaking through him. His talk awakened a sense of social justice within me that was dormant until that point. I had previously assumed that achieving good grades and getting accepted into an elite college was the path to greatness. That perception was dealt a severe blow by Joe's speech, which transformed me from a disimpassioned, grade-hungry high school student into someone who began to look at the larger picture. I began to see beyond my own needs. For the first time, I looked beyond the classroom to the school, the community, and ultimately, to the world. What I found in that picture were many things in need of repair.

Two days after Joe's address, our principal came over the loudspeaker to share the tragic news that Joe had been killed in a car accident while driving home from a speaking engagement. I immediately excused myself from class, ducked into an empty hallway, and burst into tears. In the hours, weeks, and months that followed, I could not shake the memory of my first and last interaction with Joe. After fighting through the crowd that gathered around him when he finished speaking, I stuck out my hand to shake his and began to thank him for his moving speech. Before I could finish my words of praise, he pushed my hand away and looked me in the eyes with a stare so intense that he seemed to be gazing into my soul. I was still stunned as he pulled me into a giant bear hug. Though he was significantly smaller than me, I felt strangely protected within his embrace. After a few seconds, he pulled back, looked me in the eyes, and said in the most sincere voice imaginable: "Have the best day of your life." Following Joe's untimely death, with his short but meaningful life as my inspiration, I got involved in my community. I ran for student government and ultimately became the vice president of the Scarsdale student body. Shortly before graduating, I interned with Facing History and Ourselves, an organization that seeks to promote tolerance by incorporating genocide into school curriculums. Through that organization, I traveled around New York City speaking to high school students about genocide and how they could take action to help stop it.

The summer after Joe's profound speech, I took my first trip to Israel with my family. Israel was in the midst of what is now referred to as the Second Intifada*. Our tour guide's ever-present pistol and watchful eyes were among the many signs that Israel was not at peace. The most powerful moments of that trip were visits to the monuments which memorialized civilians murdered in terror attacks and paid tribute to fallen soldiers who'd made the ultimate sacrifice for Israel. I felt a respect for and connection to those soldiers that I could not yet explain. As I approached the end of high school, those feelings grew stronger, as did my concern for Israel's safety as rocket fire from Lebanon directed at Northern Israel intensified throughout early 2006.

CHAPTER 2: THE END OF THE BEGINNING

I began my first semester of college at the University of Pennsylvania in the summer of 2006. I did the things I thought freshmen in college were supposed to do: I kept up decent grades, rushed a fraternity, played intramural sports, and drank too much and too often. I also served the community: I volunteered with Big Brothers and Big Sisters, worked as a not-for-profit speaker for the Darfur-Alert coalition, and coached a basketball team of local kids in West Philadelphia.

While I was participating in activities that seemed to serve the greater good, I felt at my core that I wasn't fulfilling any greater purpose than meeting my own needs and desires. I drank two-dollar beers at Smokey Joe's on college night while a substantial percentage of the world's population was living on less than two dollars a day. I spent dozens of hours studying for tests on theories of politics and international relations. In the real world, dozens of wars and conflicts raged, endangering millions of people's lives. While all conflicts are tragic, I was particularly moved

---

* The Second Intifada refers to the second Palestinian uprising, which began in September of 2000 and lasted until October of 2005. Approximately 1,000 Israelis were killed, 80 percent of whom were non-combatants, and many of whom were killed in suicide bombings. The Second Intifada was the third-highest death toll of any conflict in the country's history, surpassed in casualties only by the Yom Kippur War and the War of Independence. Thousands of Palestinians also lost their lives during this conflict. While most were killed by security forces while taking part in or planning hostilities against Israel, and by their own side as suspected collaborators, there were also innocent Palestinians who lost their lives to IDF security forces¹.

by the violence in Israel, given my personal connection to the country and its people. While my body lived in Philadelphia, my heart gravitated towards the people of Israel, who continued to suffer from acts of terror. My uneasiness grew with each report of fallen rockets and fallen soldiers.

The summer after my freshman year of college, I traveled to Israel to participate in the Hasbara Fellowships Program. Hasbara began in 2001 during the heart of the Second Intifada. It was created for the purpose of bringing college students to Israel to teach them how to advocate for Israel on increasingly anti-Semitic college campuses. Since my first trip to Israel, I dreamt of joining the IDF, but it was on that Hasbara trip that I realized definitively that my dream would one day become a reality.

We spent the first Shabbat in the Old City of Jerusalem. Evening set in and the dry, oppressive heat of the Israeli summer sun subsided. As the temperature dropped to a more comfortable level, the intensity of the bustling city softened as well. In Jerusalem, Sabbath is tangible. It can be felt in the motion preceding its arrival, and the stillness that follows its onset. We descended the cobblestone streets of the Muslim Quarter, making our way towards the Western Wall. Our ears were drawn to the sounds of Arabic music that played from dozens of speakers throughout the Quarter. As we continued to descend the narrow street, we passed by old men sitting outside of their shops playing checkers and smoking water pipes, filling the air with the sweet smell of flavored tobacco. A gentle breeze danced through the awnings of the shops that lined both sides of the streets, the same streets used by travelers, traders, and pilgrims thousands of years ago. I couldn't help but feel as though we had traveled back in time.

That Friday evening, after Shabbat dinner, Danny Farahan, the older brother of one of the program's participants, came to share his experiences as a lone soldier. Danny moved to Israel after graduating college and joined a special reconnaissance unit within the storied Paratroopers Brigade. After he finished his prepared remarks, a few of us hung around, partially to further pester him with questions about his army service and partially to get closer to his gun. He discussed the highs and the lows of life as a combat soldier and shared a few unclassified details of one of the missions in which he had participated while serving in Judea and Samaria. I was mesmerized by his stories and, as he spoke, I fantasized about what it would be like to serve as an IDF Paratrooper. When someone asked to try on his red beret, he happily passed it over. The beret went around the circle, and each person tried it on for a few seconds before passing it to the next person. When the beret was handed to me, I passed it immediately without trying it on. Danny looked at me, and as a slight grin formed at the edge of his mouth, he asked me why I hadn't tried it on. I hesitated as I contemplated the answer to his question, as I myself was unsure. Danny did not hesitate and quickly answered for me: "I know why you didn't try it on. You want to earn it." As his words sank in, the course I needed to take suddenly became clear to me, like the pieces of a jigsaw puzzle that had finally come together to complete a picture. My Zionism, my desire to fight for what I believed in, my longing to do something that mattered—it all pointed me towards the IDF. A path that had until that moment been fogged by indecision and self-doubt was suddenly illuminated. I lifted my eyes from the ground where I had been staring contemplatively since he spoke, and as my eyes met Danny's, an unspoken understanding passed between us. I knew that he was right: I did want to earn that beret.

A year later, in 2008, I wrote Danny a letter expressing some of the concerns I still harbored about enlisting. I shared the criticisms expressed by friends and family who insisted that I would go further as an activist than a combat soldier. Danny's response quelled my doubts and solidified my resolve:

You want to know where you would "be doing the most good." I think you are asking yourself the wrong question. The fact is this country needs fighters. Do you want to be one of them? It is easy to sit in America and go to conference after conference and talk about how important Israel is. The leaders in your community have made a conscious decision to put Israel second. I am not saying they don't care, but they are not living in America for our well-being here in Israel. If you come serve in the army, you are rejecting the foundation of their beliefs. The idea of finishing college and becoming a fighter instead of a lobbyist, lawyer, or grad student goes against their happy diaspora Jewish existence. I know why you want to be a fighter. Your country is under attack. You feel that you can help us fight the fight. It pains you to see missiles fall on Sderot. You would rather go into Gaza and shoot a gun then lament how bad things are in Israel while sitting on your sofa in America. You would rather go into Jenin and put the handcuffs on the bomb maker's hands than write a letter to your school paper. I know why you want to be a fighter. It is not very complicated. If you really want to do it, then do it. Tell your community it is what you have to do. Once you actually do it, your community will be behind you 100 percent. They will raise money for your unit, and they will do all they can to live vicariously through you. The road is long, it is hard, but it is worth it...All I can say is start running. The hardest thing is learning to run when you can't walk anymore. But it is all in your head.

I just finished my service last week. As I write these words my mother is sitting behind me. She told me to tell you that your mother will be worried and scared, but at the end of the day you don't even know how proud of you she will be..."

I will always consider Danny my first true inspiration for joining the IDF. He showed me that moving to Israel and enlisting in the IDF was not some distant fantasy but a dream that could be realized. When Danny spoke to our group about his experiences in the IDF, I saw in his eyes the pride of a man who had a dream and who followed it. That pride was notably absent from my life at that time.

CHAPTER 3: THE DECISION

Shortly before midnight on the eve of my twenty-second birthday, I clicked the "submit" button on my Israeli citizenship application, binding myself to military service in the IDF. With that single click, I solidified the commitment I'd contemplated making since my first trip to Israel nearly nine years earlier. It was both thrilling and terrifying.

During my final semester of college, I began attending monthly seminars for Garin Tzabar, the pre-army program created to help participants move to Israel and enlist in the IDF. It was originally open only to the children of Israelis living abroad but has since opened its doors to anyone who has lived in Israel for more than six months prior to applying for the program. Beyond helping young people enlist in the military, the program creates a framework that ensures lone soldiers have a network to support them during hard times. As a foreigner without connections to the army, and only basic Hebrew, I relied on Garin Tzabar to help ease my transition into Israeli society. They also guided me through the enlistment process and the tryouts as I pursued my dream of serving in an elite combat unit of the IDF.

As the date of the first seminar approached, I grew anxious. Of the twenty-four participants that began the 2010 East Coast seminar, I was one of only five over the age of 18, and I worried about the maturity levels of the other participants. Fortunately, I would quickly learn that while most high school seniors are happily preparing to spend four years having fun, making friends, and discovering themselves as I did at that age, those who came to that seminar were different. They had made a conscious decision to forfeit, or at least postpone, that period of their life in favor of serving the state of Israel.

The first Garin Tzabar seminar was conducted entirely in Hebrew. While this was unexpected, it gave me a much-needed opportunity to practice, and more importantly, a wake-up call. Despite the four semesters of Hebrew classes that I'd taken at Penn, which according to the university had qualified me as "fluent", it was quickly apparent that my Hebrew lagged far behind that of the other participants, all of whom had at least one Israeli parent.

Over the course of the next several months and six seminars, as the move to Israel grew closer, we also grew closer to one another. Despite each of us being told by some combination of friends and family that we were crazy for wanting to join the IDF, we all maintained our resolve to enlist. When the time came to say goodbye after our final seminar, we were nervous and excited. The next time we would all meet would be in Israel. There, we would begin our new lives preparing for our service in the IDF.

PART TWO:
THE MOVE
TO ISRAEL

CHAPTER 4: A NEW HOME

After weeks of tying up loose ends and saying goodbye to friends and family, the day of my move to Israel finally arrived. It was a day I had been anxiously awaiting and simultaneously fearing. I remember the details of that day with great clarity. It was especially hot, and the nearly 100 pounds of bags I had to load and then unload from the family minivan left me drenched in sweat. As I swung the bag out of the trunk and onto the curb outside the terminal at JFK airport, I wondered if the bag I would have to carry in the army would be as heavy. I was overcome by the sensation that one gets on a roller coaster as it nears the end of its initial climb, right before the imminent descent. While your anticipation of the ride fills you with excitement, some small part of you, one that you would be too embarrassed to verbally acknowledge, wants very much to get off and go back to a place where you were comfortable and safe.

Before walking towards the security line, I embraced my parents one final time. As I did, I was overwhelmed by the familiar scents of my mother's perfume and my father's deodorant. Over the years, these scents had come to symbolize the comfort, protection and love of my parents.

Just before I rounded the corner to pass through security, I turned around to take one final look at my parents. Though my mother had been composed when we'd said goodbye, I could see that she was now sobbing uncontrollably in my father's arms. Knowing that I was the cause of her pain was a terrible feeling. I wanted so badly to tell her that everything would be OK and that she had nothing to worry about. But I knew that was a promise I could not make. Though every fiber of my being wanted to run back and embrace her, I knew that it would only prolong the inevitable separation. So I took a deep breath, and willed myself to keep walking: away from my parents and my past, and towards my gate and my new life. The next time I saw them, I would be a soldier in the IDF.

When I reached my gate I collapsed into the first chair I saw, physically and emotionally exhausted. An hour later, the boarding announcement pulled me from daydreams of my imagined future. I rose from my seat and boarded the flight. Fellow passengers, like hamburgers, come in many shapes and sizes. Among these sizes are super-sized, which would accurately describe the size of the man whom I had the misfortune of unintentionally sharing half of my seat with on the ten-hour plane ride to Israel. Given my combined fifteen hours of sleep in the prior five days, neither the sharp blow to my right side each time the goliath collapsed back into his seat, nor the ramming of my left leg by the heavy cart wielded by impatient El-Al stewardesses, nor the dozens of crying children, could prevent me from sleeping relatively peacefully.

Ten hours later, the plane's wheels touched down on Israeli soil at Ben Gurion International Airport, and 204 passengers erupted in applause. The flight attendant came over the PA to welcome us in Hebrew and English to "*Eretz Yisrael*," the Land of Israel. Her announcement sent chills down my spine. As we taxied toward the gate, I felt a rush of uncertainty; I wondered how I would adjust to linguistic shortcomings and cultural differences that distinguished me obviously and significantly from the average Israeli. I descended the stairs to the tarmac, and walked towards the airport, basking in the warm glow of the morning sun. I felt a pang of loneliness mixed with the excitement of the unknown. That sensation would become a familiar one in the months to come.

As new immigrants to Israel traveling with Nefesh B' Nefesh, we were ushered immediately from passport control to the Ministry of Absorption where we received 1,250 Shekels (roughly $400), and a voucher for a free taxi ride from the airport to anywhere in the country.

When we finally emerged from the border control area and entered the main terminal, we were greeted by dozens of singing and dancing Israeli teens who had come to the airport to welcome us to Israel. One girl with thick glasses and braces, who looked to be about 13 years old, held up a sign that summarized the collective feeling of that moment—in both Hebrew and English, in big block letters, were the words "Welcome Home."

After leaving the terminal, I jumped in a taxi headed to Tel Aviv. I had a week before the Garin Tzabar program began, and would be staying with my friend Josh, who had graciously offered to host me. We had met while I was studying abroad at Tel Aviv University during my junior year of college. He had graduated a year before I did, moved to Israel, and enlisted in the IDF.

Earlier that day I had become a citizen of the state of Israel. As I reflected on the implications and responsibilities that Israeli citizenship carried with it, I began to see the country through a different lens. I'd walked the streets of Tel Aviv dozens if not hundreds of times. I'd eaten the food, I'd met the people, I'd experienced the bars and the restaurants. Yet in that moment, everything suddenly felt different. No longer was I an outsider looking in through the window. I was a member of the club, an Israeli citizen by right of the "law of return." Enacted in 1950 by the Israeli Knesset, the law grants citizenship to anyone with a single Jewish grandparent, which was considered by the Nazis to be "Jewish enough" to be sent to the concentration camps.

The next morning, though I hadn't slept a full night in nearly a week, I woke up early. It was a day I had anxiously waited for some time...the day of my lunch date with Raz.

CHAPTER 5: YOUNG ROMANCE

While studying at Tel Aviv University, I was required to take Hebrew language classes in addition to the regular curriculum. In December, after classes had ended, and following several months of Josh and me nagging her, our Hebrew teacher Ronit finally agreed to meet us for a drink. When she arrived at the bar on the chosen night, my eyes were immediately drawn to the friend she'd brought along. Raz had dark skin and brown eyes and, as I would soon find out, spoke English fluently. We caught each other's glance several times, and when my friend got up to go to the bathroom, I made up a reason to take his seat so I could sit next to her. Raz had a sass to her that was both familiar and foreign, and I found her mysterious and attractive. We spent the rest of the night talking and flirting, and just before she left, I worked up the courage to ask her for her number. Testing my confidence, she asked me why I wanted it. Thinking quickly, I told her I planned to cook her a magnificent chicken dinner in my unheated, three-walled apartment. She laughed and told me she would be honored.

On the night of our date, being the entitled, completely useless college kid that I was, I bought pre-cooked chicken. After disposing of the box, I strategically placed the chicken on the frying pan just as she called to tell me that she was outside. When I brought her back to the room, I pretended that she had "caught me" in the act of cooking. As we ate, drank, and laughed together, the hours flew by, and before she left that night, we had already made plans to see each other the following night. Over the next few weeks, we saw each other as often as her work schedule would allow until the day I left Israel. And yes, I eventually admitted to her that the chicken was pre-cooked.

Far too quickly came the night of my flight back to New York. We knew it would be a long time before we would have an opportunity to give what we had started a real chance, but we promised we'd try to stay in touch. It was a cold December evening when we said goodbye outside of the dorms I had called home for the past six months. Not wanting to cause a scene, I kissed her one final time, spun on my heels, and jumped into the backseat of the taxi that was waiting to take me to the airport. I hoped that she hadn't seen the tears that were now freely streaming down my face.

After I returned to America, weeks turned to months, and we did our best to stay in touch. We Skyped often, and she would laugh out loud as she recalled the spelling and grammatical mistakes in the latest letter I had written her in Hebrew. Though time and distance took their toll, and we both saw other people, we managed to maintain our connection.

Nearly a year and a half had passed between the cold December night when we'd said goodbye and the warm summer afternoon that we met again when I moved back to Israel. Raz and I met for lunch at La Mer, a restaurant on the beach adored by Americans for its American vibe, and hated by Israelis for precisely the same reason. Raz laughingly told me I was off to a bad start in my restaurant choice, but ultimately, lunch turned into dinner, and dinner into a night out. As we reminisced and caught up on all that had happened in our respective lives over the previous year and a half, time seemed to stand still. In what felt like the blink of an eye, thirteen hours went by, and suddenly it was 2 a.m. I walked Raz to her car, and as I opened the door for her, our eyes locked. We kissed passionately under the dim lights of the deserted parking garage, confirming that lingering feelings from the past were still present, even if hidden under layers of distance and time.

In the weeks and months that followed, we saw each other often. Raz was understandably guarded with her feelings, knowing that I would soon be a combat soldier confined to base for twelve, twenty-one, and on occasion, twenty-eight days at a time. In the period of uncertainty before being drafted and through the start of basic training, without close family or friends in Israel, Raz became my confidant. While my teammates went home on the weekends to their families and their high school girlfriends, I often went home to an empty apartment. I longed for a romantic connection and for the love of family, and perhaps unfairly, Raz became somewhat of a combination of those two things. I ate Shabbat dinner at her home with her family and called her in the evenings during my hour of free time after training.

As time progressed, neither of us was as certain as we once had been about our compatibility. Our time apart accentuated our cultural differences, and no longer being bright-eyed 20-year-olds blinded by infatuation, we both viewed our connection more pragmatically. In time, we realized that it wasn't as perfect as it once seemed. Looking back now, I recognize the many parallels between our relationship and my initial relationship with Israel. In the months following my *aliyah** (immigration to Israel), while I sought to understand and adapt to Israeli culture, part of me still embraced my American identity. It felt familiar and safe but, in many ways, it clashed with Israeli values. The more I clung to my old identity, the more I pushed Raz away, and the more disconnected I felt from my new home.

In late December, after I had been in the army for two months, we decided it was best that we not see each other. Our trajectories were aimed in different directions, and though it hurt, we knew parting ways would ultimately be for the best. Eventually, our romantic feelings for each other subsided, and we became friends, as we've remained to this day. But on that warm July night, when we kissed again for the first time, all I knew was that the butterflies I had felt in my stomach when Raz and I were together in 2008 had returned. As I crawled into bed that night, I lay my head on the pillow and shifted my face towards the small bedside fan, which was trying with all its might to clear a path through the stuffy summer air. I too was trying my best, with little success, to clear away all the thoughts, fears, and feelings running through my mind long enough to fall asleep. Eventually, lost in my thoughts, I drifted into a soft, lonely slumber.

Aliyah is the immigration of Jews from the diaspora to Israel. It translates to "going up," implying increased proximity to Jerusalem. Moving to Israel is one of the basic tenets of Zionism.

CHAPTER 6: KIBBUTZ YIFTAH

In the late summer of 2010, I moved to Israel with Garin Tzabar in preparation for the November 2010 IDF draft. I was one of 215 boys and girls from all over the world who had chosen to move to Israel and enlist. On the official start date of the program, we all attended the induction ceremony at Tel Aviv University. From there, we were split up into twenty-two kibbutzim based on the locations of the seminars we attended in the previous six months before moving to Israel.

The kibbutz movement* in Israel began at the turn of the 20th century. It was advanced by young Jewish pioneers, mainly from Eastern Europe, who had come to Israel to reclaim their ancient homeland and create a new kind of community. Prior to the Jewish migrations that coincided with the start of the kibbutz movement, Israel, according to many who visited, was a barren wasteland. In 1857 the British consul in Palestine, James Finn, reported back to England, "The country is in a considerable degree empty of inhabitants and therefore its greatest need is that of a body of a population."[2] Mark Twain wrote of the country as a whole: "Palestine sits in sackcloth and ashes. Over it broods the spell of a curse that has withered its fields and fettered its energies...Palestine is desolate and unlovely...it is a hopeless, dreary, heartbroken land."[3] Eminent English cartographer Arthur Penrhyn Stanley wrote in 1881 that, "In Judea, it is hardly an exaggeration to say that for miles and miles there was no appearance of life or habitation."[4] By the third quarter of the 19th century, the total population of the entire country, Arabs and Jews, was 400,000-less than five percent of the population today.[5] The land that the young pioneers found when they arrived to build the kibbutzim was hostile and desolate. Water, funds, and knowledge of farming practices were scarce. Still, despite these hardships, the early *kibbutznikim* (kibbutz-dwellers) ultimately

The kibbutz movement was an experiment in communal living. Property and other needed items on the kibbutz were distributed freely, or in accordance with the Marxist principle, "from each according to his ability, to each according to his needs." Meals were eaten together in the central dining hall. The kibbutzim had weekly meetings at which important topics were voted on. All income generated by the kibbutz went into a common pool, and all members received the same budget based on family size, regardless of their job or position.

succeeded in building thriving communities that played an instrumental role in the establishment of the State of Israel. Garin Tzabar builds upon the ethos of those early settlers by sending new immigrants to Israel directly to kibbutzim. Like those who came before them, they work for the benefit of the community. In so doing, they earn a place within it, and within Israeli society.

As the beginning of the ceremony approached, we trickled into the auditorium, where we mingled and chatted nervously with one another. Some were friends, some would become friends, and some would never meet. Yet we all shared an undeniable bond, with each other and with Israel, as a result of the decision we had made to enlist. Also present at the ceremony that morning were lone soldiers from previous Garin Tzabar programs who were actively serving in the IDF. Though they wore different colored berets and different unit insignias, all were bound together in their service to Israel.

When the ceremony ended that afternoon, I boarded a coach bus with the twenty-three other participants in my Garin and began the long journey north to Kibbutz Yiftah. As we escaped the commotion of Tel Aviv, crowded streets and tall buildings melted away into cattle pastures and rolling hills. Gradually, afternoon gave way to evening. We watched out our windows as the sun set over Northern Israel, and the bright orange hues it threw across the sky meshed with the green landscape to create an incredible vista. By the time the buses rolled through the gates of the kibbutz, it was well after dark. Our living area was only partially visible under the dimly lit lamp posts whose bulbs seemed not to have been changed in several decades.

As the days passed, I grew acquainted with my new home. The two-mile gravel path that circled the diameter of the kibbutz; the obsolete guard towers used to defend the kibbutz from attackers and cross-border reprisals in the years before and after the war of independence; the chicken coup; the factory; the various personalities and families that together formed the essence of the kibbutz. The entire kibbutz was built on a hill, which climbed progressively upwards until it reached its peak at the dining hall. From there, a quick walk out the gate and across the street brings one to a breathtaking view of the Emek Israel valley. At night, dozens of kilometers from the nearest city, the vantage point affords an unobscured view of thousands of stars that shimmer like diamonds over the sprawling valley below. I spent a lot of time by myself at that overlook during my first few weeks on the kibbutz, reflecting on my decision to enlist, all that I had left behind, and the challenges that remained before me.

On the fifth morning of our new life on the kibbutz, we woke up early to beat the sun and set out on a hike to familiarize ourselves with the surrounding area. At approximately 3:45 a.m., we began our walk through the trails of the Upper Galilee. The stars were still high in the sky with no sign of the approaching day. Walking across the mountain pass, I took in the serenity of the predawn hour and the natural beauty that surrounded us. As the sky began to lighten, our eyes were drawn to the glimmering green of the Beit HaKerem valley below us, all of which was once submerged underwater. Above us towered the majestic mountains of the Golan Heights and the Hermon. Scattered throughout the barren landscape were remnants of imperial occupation of the land—British lookout towers, French forts, and burned-out Israeli armored vehicles that were destroyed during Israel's War of Independence.

There is an hour before the sun rises where the pink hue of the approaching sun blends with the soft blue of the distant mountain ranges, such that it is impossible to tell where one begins and the other ends. It was a time of day that I did not see often in college, but one I would become very familiar with during my three years in the army. In the days and weeks that followed, I became certain that joining Garin Tzabar was the best decision I could have made. As a lone soldier, particularly one who did not speak fluent Hebrew or fully grasp the cultural differences between Israel and America, Garin Tzabar proved to be incredibly helpful in easing my transition. Within a single week of beginning the program, my Israeli bank account, phone plan, and healthcare enrollment had been set up. I'd been given my national identity card, a date for the driving test required to convert my license, coached on the proper way to fill out the paperwork required for the Ministry of Absorption's funding, and received my First Notice. Doing all of those things on my own would have likely taken six months or longer.

Despite the ease that Garin Tzabar contributed to our transition into Israeli society, the program could only take us so far; ultimately, we would have to forge our own destinies in the tests and tryouts. The results of these would determine the units in which we would serve for the next three years or longer. Just as the mountains appear small when observed from a distance, and grow in perceived size as one approaches them, so too did the grandiosity of the task that lay before me reveal itself ever more as my draft date approached. The closer that day came, the clearer it became how much my Hebrew and physical conditioning needed to improve if I were going to stand a chance in the tryouts for the special forces. When I wasn't in Garin Tzabar programming,

I devoted most of my time to studying Hebrew and training, leaving myself very little time to ruminate. Inevitably, though, as I sought a few minutes of respite from my studies, or caught my breath between sprints, my thoughts would gravitate towards my loved ones. No matter how much I studied, nor how far or fast I ran, the loneliness I tried so hard to ignore caught up with me. Despite my conviction and dedication to the path I'd chosen, I missed my family and friends tremendously.

By a stroke of luck, my randomly assigned kibbutz roommate, Eitan, became one of my closest friends, as he is to this day. Eitan was one of four college graduates on the kibbutz and was someone with whom I felt I could have real conversations about the emotional challenges of being a lone soldier. After his college graduation, Eitan had decided that service in the Israeli Defense Forces was an integral part of Israeli society, and thus a necessity for anyone who was considering living in Israel. Together, Eitan and I navigated the bureaucracy of the army. I relied on him often for help, as he spoke Hebrew fluently while I continued to struggle to learn and understand the language. While chance had made us roommates on the kibbutz, we roomed together by choice in Tel Aviv and New York City after completing our service. Eitan broadened my intellectual horizons and my friend group, and greatly contributed to my increased self-awareness—not bad for a (once) randomly selected roommate! In the lead-up to the draft, we were equally anxious to be accepted into top units, and so together we sought out a training program that would get us into fighting shape.

Many of the Israelis who try out for elite units have known since childhood where they want to serve, and prepare accordingly. As teenagers, they join programs that meet up to three times a week for several years, where they train on the sand dunes in preparation for the tryouts known as *gibbushim*. During the five-day tryouts for Israel's top units, everyone eventually reaches their breaking point; only those who are deeply committed to success find the mental strength to persevere. But even those who fight past their breaking points are not guaranteed a spot. Most of the candidates have already been through significant mental and physical testing before arriving at the tryouts. Determination is the norm rather than the exception, so perseverance is not always enough. The candidates who are ultimately accepted into the training regimens for the top units are those who arrive in excellent physical condition—a result of having pushed themselves in the weeks, months, and years before the tryouts.

There is a saying in Israel: *"Hacole be rosh"* (It's all in your head). In reality, that's a half-truth. If you haven't trained on inclined surfaces, lactic acid will build up in your legs after an hour of running up sand dunes. When that prevents you from summoning the explosive power you need to come in first, that is not a problem of motivation. The difference between winning and just finishing is also in your lungs and in your legs. Archilochus, the Greek soldier and poet, put it best: "We do not rise to the level of our expectations. We fall to the level of our training."

Lone soldiers who grow up without Israeli relatives who served in the IDF lack the benefit of forehand knowledge about the tryouts. Realizing that this would be an inherent disadvantage for us, Eitan and I sought to bridge that gap by finding a training program that would properly prepare us for the challenges to come. Thanks to a lucky Google search, we discovered a pre-army training academy called Tsevet Lohamim. Though I couldn't have known it then, that program would alter the course of my life, providing me with the training which I credit for my acceptance into the special forces and the friends who became my family in Israel.

CHAPTER 7: THE BONDS OF TRAINING

On our first free weekend from Garin Tzabar's programming, Eitan and I took the three-hour bus from the kibbutz to Tel Aviv, where we participated in our first training session. Pushing ourselves well beyond our assumed physical limits was an eye-opening experience, but it was an important lesson in the level of mental fortitude that would be required to be accepted into a top unit. Throughout that morning, my body went into spasms several times from the weight of the stretchers, the frequency of the sprints, and the strength of the summer sun. I threw up twice, despite not having eaten in twelve hours, but I left the training that morning with a newfound feeling of confidence, proud that my willpower had endured the physical demands of the training session that had been designed to break me. We returned to the kibbutz with a new understanding of the tremendous challenge we would face in seeking to cram years' worth of tryout-specific training into the two months that remained before our tryouts. As the bus pulled out of the central station in Tel Aviv, bound for Rosh Pina, I closed my eyes and sank into the plush fabric of the coach bus seat. The journey was just beginning, and a long road lay ahead, but I was one step closer to achieving my goal.

In times of war, it has often been said that soldiers fight not for their country but for the men and women next to them. As I would come to learn, training is similar in that respect. Over the course of many training sessions, while preparing for the tryouts to come, Eitan and I grew increasingly close to each other and the other trainees. Trainers turned into mentors, and ultimately, trainees and trainers alike became like family, all of us united by our desire to serve Israel.

Two of those trainers, Daniel and Bernardo, would eventually become my roommates and among my closest friends in Israel. When I met Daniel at that first training session, he was already in training for Duvdevan, an elite counter-terror unit within the Paratroopers specializing in infiltrations, arrests, and undercover operations. Despite his limited free time, Daniel chose to volunteer during his infrequent weekends off base to help train future generations of lone soldiers to be successful in their own tryouts. At the age of nineteen, he moved to Israel from Miami to join the IDF and ultimately received various awards for marksmanship and professionalism. As I struggled through my first year in the army, Daniel assumed the roles of friend, roommate, and mentor all in one. I called him whenever I felt my motivation waiver, or my resolve weaken. He picked me up, and when I needed it, kicked me and told me to keep going.

Equally impactful on my preparations for the tryouts was Daniel's roommate, Bernardo. Bernardo founded Tsevet Lohamim in 2009 to help lone soldiers develop the skills necessary to succeed in the IDF, both in the tryouts and during their service. Bernardo has a burning intensity to his personality that he channels into the fulfillment of his one true mission— the defense and security of the state of Israel. To this day, sixteen years after he drafted, he continues to play an active role in Israel's defense. Tsevet Lohamim boasts the highest special forces acceptance rate of the pre-IDF training programs, and the story of his own service sets a high standard of commitment for everyone he trains. Bernardo had originally volunteered for eighteen months of service, but months after being released, the Second Lebanon War broke out in 2006. Bernardo not only reenlisted but also fought his way into the special forces, which required him to voluntarily complete an additional eight months of training.

During the first and hardest part of my service, Daniel and Bernardo became my older brothers and toughened me up so that I might measure up to the challenge of special forces training. Out of the kindness of their hearts, without requesting that I pay rent, Daniel, Bernardo, and their third roommate, Rachel, allowed me to spend my four to five days off a month in their Tel Aviv apartment. I was a newly drafted soldier making less than $5,000 a year. My housing stipend went directly to the kibbutz for the first year of my service, so I could not afford to pay them. On many occasions, Daniel insisted I take his bed, and he slept on the living room couch. Having previously experienced the grueling training regimen in which I was currently engaged, he decided I needed the bed more than he did. At times, our vastly different definitions of the word "clean" and my bachelor's lifestyle caused them stress and hardship, but they rarely complained and never asked me for a dime. Daniel, Bernardo, and Rachel gave selflessly and without expectation of receiving anything in return. During my time in the IDF, I came to learn that this was a characteristic common to all great soldiers.

Just as trainers became mentors and friends, so too did fellow trainees. Each of us had experienced some degree of anti-Semitism in our home countries, and each of us felt a calling to IDF service that we felt compelled to answer. Rafi was one such friend. Before he moved to Israel, Rafi was a sheltered Australian Jew who'd attended a prominent Jewish day school. At thirteen, after his *bar mitzvah*, Rafi decided to leave the comfortable enclave of a Jewish day school to attend a public middle school. At his new school, it was quickly apparent that it wasn't just his status as a newcomer that set him apart.

Among 1,000 students, Rafi was one of three Jews. At first, the anti-Semitism was subtle. Rafi was excluded from social gatherings and made to feel like an outsider. The unspoken, and then spoken, reason for that exclusion was his Jewish faith. In 2006, the start of Holocaust studies in Rafi's history class coincided with the start of the Lebanon war in Israel. At a school with a large Lebanese population, being the only male Jew made Rafi an obvious target. Classes on the Holocaust became tutorials for Rafi's classmates. They learned about how Jews had been treated in the years leading up to the Holocaust, and in a quite opposite than intended effect, began to emulate the behaviors they'd learned about in class. Rafi often returned from trips to the bathroom to find swastikas drawn on his notebooks and assignments. As the war in Lebanon picked up, so did the aggression of Rafi's classmates. What started as verbal assaults turned into physical ones. People would trip him in the hallways and slam him into lockers. Eventually, things reached the point where Rafi woke up in the morning afraid to go to school.

As a result of his involvement in pro-Jewish organizations, Rafi saw firsthand the rampant and often unpublished anti-Semitism in Australia. He witnessed increasing violence against Jews in his community, anti-Israel protests, and even the razing of a Jewish store—activities that one might expect to see in the 1940s, but certainly not in the twenty-first century in a democratic nation. Rafi's first trip to Israel at the age of 18 changed him profoundly. There, he saw that people didn't have to hide their Judaism. They hung Israeli flags on the balconies of their houses and apartments. Religious Jews walked home from temple at night without armed escorts. And Rafi saw something else in Israel: a strong army dedicated not only to the defense of Jews in their homeland but around the world. As soon as he finished high school, Rafi left his old life behind him, boarded a one-way flight bound for Israel, and enlisted in the IDF. On the first day of the tryout for Maglan, a special unit within the Paratroopers, he twisted his ankle. Though the commanders urged him to quit, he refused and used a stick he had found as a makeshift cane. Each time the eighteen soldiers in his tryout team were ordered to sprint, a single figure could always be seen hobbling methodically behind the chaotic cluster of seventeen, always finishing last, but always finishing. His antics earned him the nickname "Moses," but more importantly, a spot on one of the teams in Sayeret Maglan.

Another lone soldier with whom I trained, Rudy, had made *aliyah* from France. Like Rafi, Rudy had experienced anti-Semitism growing up. He told me stories of kids in school drawing swastikas on his notebook and people spitting on him on his way to shul. Rudy and I met in the Garin Tzabar program and became fast friends during tryouts and the training that followed. We were two of only three college graduates in our company, and we often spent our free time together discussing our old lives and our post-army aspirations.

When meeting Rudy, one immediately senses his conviction, work ethic, and integrity, all of which contributed to my immediate and prevailing admiration for him. Rudy, like Rafi, was loyal, generous and selfless, which made them both favorites among their fellow soldiers and commanders. As lone soldiers, without immediate family in the country, we turned to each other during hard times.

As the tryouts approached, Eitan and I continued to attend Tsevet Lohamim's training sessions. The hours I spent carrying stretchers under the punishing Tel Aviv sun during those sessions dramatically increased my confidence, as well as my physical and mental preparedness for the challenges ahead. A few shorts weeks after that first training session, I faced my first test. Though it was a test of neither strength nor endurance, the results would either bring me closer to my dream of serving in the special forces or forever block that possibility.

CHAPTER 8: THE FIRST NOTICE

On Thursday, August 12, 2010, my alarm went off at 7:05 a.m. I walked sleepily to the bathroom and splashed cold water on my face. As I thought about the day ahead, I smiled remembering that it was the date of our First Notice. From that day forward, we were the property of the Israel Defense Forces—it was the first step towards becoming a soldier. Thereafter we would be subject to travel restrictions and legally obliged to be accessible to the army at all times until the day we drafted, which was set to be sometime in early October. The First Notice instructs recipients to arrive at one of Israel's draft centers for a day of intelligence tests, medical examinations, and a psychological evaluation. The results of these tests play an instrumental role in determining where the soon-to-be soldier will serve in the military. While friends who joined the IDF without assistance spoke of waiting half a year or longer to receive their First Notice, thanks to Garin Tzabar, we received ours only three weeks after landing in Israel.

The day was divided into five parts: the initial background interview, the Hebrew test, the intelligence test, the physical exam, and waiting, the latter of which consumed nearly six hours of my day and allowed me to start and finish a 280-page book. The initial interview allows the army to record some basic information about the soon-to-be-cadet (date of birth, any family he or she has in the country, passport numbers, etc.). Following the interview, the same soldier administers a Hebrew test, the results of which determine whether or not the soon-to-be soldier will spend the first three months of army service on the Michveh Alon base in an intensive Hebrew language course (also known as army *ulpan*). My Hebrew was good but not great. Still, I was certain that the chemistry between me and the female soldier that administered my interview would serve as a deterrent to her sending me to Michveh Alon, which I told her very clearly and very often I did not want to attend.

Ultimately, it was decided that because of my Hebrew level, though my score was not yet calculated, I would take my intelligence test in English. The language test was a bit of a catch-22. If you performed too well on the Hebrew test, you were forced to take the intelligence test in Hebrew, a huge disadvantage to a non-native speaker. But if you scored too low on the Hebrew test, you were sent to Michveh Alon, which disqualified you from the tryouts for elite combat units until after you completed the three-month language course. There was a happy middle ground where you were considered fluent enough to avoid the ulpan but still entitled to take the intelligence test in English, which is where I optimistically assumed I had landed. Your score on the test and the interview with the psychologist determine your KABA[6] score (an aggregate assessment of your intellectual and psychological qualifications for combat). This, in turn, determines the kinds of units for which you will be invited to try out, and whether or not you are qualified for Officer Training School. It is the Army's policy not to share KABA scores with candidates. However, I managed to find out mine by flirting with one of the cute girls in the office where the results were processed.

The final part of the day was the physical examination. Given the extent of my scoliosis, the physical exam was my biggest fear as I approached my draft date. While Hebrew can be learned, and the body can be trained, no amount of willpower was going to straighten my back, and the flick of a single doctor's pen could forever prevent me from achieving my dream of serving in the Israeli special forces. After a standard battery of tests, I was brought into a private room where an overweight, slightly disheveled Russian doctor asked me in English all about my medical and psychological history. After the questioning segment of the exam, the doctor ordered me to strip down so he could, "see chwat is going on down there." This was rather uncomfortable for many reasons, not the least of which was how he phrased the already awkward request. The score you receive on your physical exam determines your eligibility for the various combat units within the military. The following are the potential results of the IDF's physical:

- 97: Physically eligible for all combat units in the army—97 is the highest score you can achieve on the physical, the running joke being that since every Jew is circumcised, nobody has a full package, thus the three-point deduction.
- 82: Physically eligible for most combat units except for pilot's course and commando units.
- 72: Physically eligible for combat service in the Armored Corps, Artillery Corps, and Combat Engineering. Ineligible for infantry and commando units.
- 64: Physically ineligible for combat duty.

The physical exam was extensive. As the doctor ran his hand along my back, checking the extent of my scoliosis, my heart rate quickened, and perspiration began to form across my brow. I knew this would be the moment of truth. I had made my intentions to join the special forces quite clear to him, which we both knew would require me to have a 97 profile. While I will never know if my pleas played a role in the result, when he tallied up all the points that go into calculating the profile, he lifted his head and, in a thick Russian accent, said, "Chwell, I am happy to tell you, Mr. Feldman, that you chav received a 97." Fortunately, there was a table in between us, because if there hadn't been, I might well have embraced him, which would have been very awkward given that my pants were still around my ankles.

With the intelligence tests and my physical exam out of the way, I could direct my focus towards the first major physical challenge I would face in the IDF: Yom Sayarot, the one-day tryout for the five top (known) special forces units in the army: Shaldag, 669, Sayeret Matkal, Shayetet 13, and Hovlim. The unit in which I aspired to serve, Duvdevan, was accessible without attending Yom Sayarot. When I arrived in Israel, I learned that as an Israeli citizen, I was eligible for any unit in the IDF. With that information, I immediately set my sights on Sayeret Matkal. Acceptance would require that I attend Yom Sayarot and excel above my peers. Though much was still uncertain, I left the base that day content in the knowledge that, having received a 97, I would be physically eligible for the tryouts that would occur in a few short weeks.

CHAPTER 9: THE FIGHT FOR THE TRYOUT

In the weeks following our initial evaluations, I became increasingly nervous about the results of my Hebrew exam. I had received a perfect score on my physical examination and scored well on the intelligence test, qualifying me for the top units of the IDF, but I had still not been informed about the results of the language test. Each day I nervously checked the mail, the IDF's preferred means of communication, to see if I had received anything that might hold the answer to my burning question. Finally, one morning, as I was sifting through the mail in the clubroom, I came across an important-looking envelope from the IDF that was addressed to me. I sat there holding the envelope for a few moments before my fear succumbed to my curiosity. Gripping the letter tightly, I took a deep breath, rose quickly, and exited the back door of the club. My face was immediately enveloped by the warm sun, and my ears registered the sounds of birds singing their late-morning melodies. I walked nervously towards the towering oak tree outside of our rooms, where I had spent dozens of hours with friends from the kibbutz discussing our collective futures. This seemed like a fitting place to find out the answer to the question that would most greatly impact my immediate military future. I sat down on the bench beneath the tree and looked around to make sure I was alone. With my heart pounding, I tore open the envelope, took a deep breath, and began to read the letter. At first, I was sure I had misunderstood the words I was reading, but as I read them again and again, reality began to sink in: I had failed the Hebrew test. I would have to attend army ulpan, a three-month intensive Hebrew language course that would delay me from the special forces tryouts and significantly reduce my chances of acceptance. This was the first of many occasions when I learned the hard way that Israeli women, in this case the one who'd conducted my Hebrew test, do not buy my bullshit.

People who had been in the position in which I now found myself told me that there was no way out of the ulpan—the best I could hope for was an opportunity to participate in the tryouts after the three-month language course. As is usually the case when people tell me I can't do something, this only strengthened my resolve to prove otherwise. I made it my mission over the next month to ensure that the highest-ranking officers that I encountered on every army base we visited remembered my name and my story.

My first opportunity came a few weeks later at the Bakum, one of the largest bases in Israel. We were brought to the base that day to learn about what we should expect on Draft Day, which would happen a few weeks later. Many officers addressed us, including a colonel who was a brigade commander in Nahal, responsible for more than 5,000 combat soldiers. We were also addressed by a lieutenant colonel who was responsible for the planning and implementation of Yom Sayerot, the one-day tryout for the top known special forces units in the IDF. I chased down both officers after they had concluded their remarks and explained my predicament.

The colonel told me to fax him a letter with a full explanation of my situation, and that he'd see what he could do to help. The lieutenant colonel, whom I deemed to be in a better position to help me, told me to speak to her soldiers. Unfortunately, her soldiers were not sure what to do with me. Their job was to inform people where they were qualified to serve, not how to qualify for those units. I returned to their table intermittently throughout the day and asked them repeatedly to speak with their commander. Finally, at 3 p.m., after the last speech, I wore down their resolve. They called their commander and put me on the phone with her.

I explained to her in Hebrew that my grasp of the language was very good, and that I had understood everything that had been said to us that day. There was no reason, I pleaded, that one soldier's opinion of my Hebrew language skills should prevent me from pursuing my dream. When I finished speaking, there was a long silence on the phone, and I cringed in silent, fearful anticipation of the words to come.

When she finally spoke, she did something completely unexpected: she agreed with me. She told me that she also thought my Hebrew was strong enough to attend the tryout and that she would try to push my name through the system. Shocked by her response, I stammered my way through a few sentences of thanks and gave the phone back to the soldiers. Though it seemed I had achieved my goal, I had already learned to never put all my eggs in one basket when dealing with IDF bureaucracy. I faxed the colonel a letter the next day explaining my situation and begging for the chance to attend Yom Sayarot. A week later I was informed that my pursuit had been successful and that my name had been placed on the list.

Without ever firing a weapon or even donning an IDF uniform, I had already learned an invaluable lesson from the IDF: If you reallywant something, never let somebody tell you that you can't have it, or that it can't be done.

CHAPTER 10: OFFICIALLY A SOLDIER

On the morning of October 3rd, less than three months after we had arrived in Israel, we were bussed to the Bakum, the army's drafting center, and officially became soldiers in the Israeli Defense Forces. As lone soldiers on the Garin Tzabar program, we still had several weeks before we were to report to our respective bases. Many of us, myself included, still had tryouts and interviews to undergo before finding out in which unit we would ultimately serve. Despite this reality, as soon as we arrived, our phones were taken away, and the commanders of the base lined us up and began yelling at us, seemingly to drive home the point that we were now "technically" in the army. Over the course of the day we were brought to various stations where we underwent logistical tasks that changed us from civilians into soldiers— at least according to the army's database. At the first station, I was placed in front of a white wall, and a girl who was furiously texting decided at some arbitrary moment, without any warning, to take the picture that would be on my army ID for three years. Unsurprisingly, as I was staring blankly at the wall, waiting for some indication that I was supposed to smile, I looked like a serial killer in the picture, which she refused to retake.

At the next station, my mouth was X-rayed by a soldier who still had braces, yet another reminder that I was significantly older than nearly all the soldiers with whom I was drafting that day. After setting up our bank accounts and receiving our mandatory shots, we were taken to a window where we picked up our military IDs and dog tags. As I looked down at my own dog tags and saw my name imprinted on the metal disk, I was overcome with pride. I felt a deep connection to both of my grandfathers and my great uncle, all three of whom served in the U.S. military. I'd worn my Grandpa George's dog tags for years and had always looked forward to the day when I would have my own. I felt very close to him at that moment. After finishing at all of the stations, I boarded the bus bound for my kibbutz, officially a soldier in the IDF.

As the date of the tryouts approached, I progressively intensified my training until a week before the big day when I ceased all but the lightest of workouts to prevent injury and fatigue. As difficult as training was physically, it was equally if not more challenging emotionally. The exhaustion that came with such intense physical exertion was exacerbated by the loneliness of not having my family to turn to for comfort. As a result, I was particularly excited to spend the week before the tryout with my distant relatives, Ayala and Natan. They were cousins of my grandparents and, during my time in Israel, Natan and Ayala became like grandparents to me. Their apartment was on the nineteenth floor of a building that afforded a breathtaking view of the city. As the sun retreated behind the taller buildings on its path towards the Mediterranean, a gentle breeze from the west whispered through the open windows of the apartment, keeping it just cool enough to be comfortable without being cold. In the evenings, Natan often smoked his pipe while he carried out his research, and the sweet smell of tobacco blended with the scent of the fresh coastal breeze. Ayala and I would sit together in the kitchen and drink tea as we spoke of our shared love for Israel and our plans for the future. I loved to listen to Ayala tell stories; her passion and energy were so captivating that it was as though she physically took you to the place she was describing. Unlike most captivating speakers, Ayala was also a fantastic listener. In a world of short attention spans, Ayala would stare at you when you spoke with the most passionate, focused expression, and you understood that in that moment, what you were saying was the only thing in the world that mattered to her. She was undeniably present. We spoke often of the Israel of old - the Israel born of a generation of dreamers who willed her into being. I had learned from books, songs, poems, and movies, about the Israel in which Ayala had grown up. It was the stories of the Israel of old that had first drawn me to the country. As time passed, I struggled to reconcile that idealistic vision of Israel with the Israel that I came to know during my military service. In an interview shortly before his death, Amos Oz summarized the disappointment inherent in the realization of dreams:

The moment you carry out your dreams, it's always, by definition less perfect and rosy than it had been as a dream. This is the nature of dreams. And Israel—let's not forget it—Israel is a fulfilled dream. Nothing that exists here existed here a hundred years ago...Now, dreams fulfilled are imperfect. And, Israel is imperfect, of course it is—a far cry from the monumental dreams of the founding fathers. One of the reasons is that their dreams were unrealistic. They were bigger than life. These were messianic dreams, dreams about total redemption for the Jews, for the world. Such dreams do not come true, not in their entirety....

At times I became disillusioned by the dichotomy between the Israel of my dreams and the one I came to know. Nonetheless, my belief that she is worth defending has never wavered. The night before the tryout, after I said goodnight to Natan and Ayala, I lay awake in bed preoccupied with thoughts of the following day. One five-hour tryout had the potential to determine the course of the next five years of my life. I thought of the years of anticipation and the countless hours of training that had led me to that point. In a few short hours, it would begin. As I finally drifted off to sleep, I dreamt of sandhills and stretcher marches.

Learning Hebrew on
Kibbutz Yiftah.

Garin Tzabar Welcome Ceremony,
August 2010.

Headline reads, "21 young men from abroad draft into the Paratroopers after integrating into kibbutzim."

Gadna with Garin Tzabar.

Team breakfast after a Tsevet Lohamim training session.

Raz and I sharing a drink.

Visit TheExaminedLife.NYC/ALineInTheSand or
scan here for HQ color photos.

PART THREE: SPECIAL FORCES SELECTION

CHAPTER II: THE TRYOUT

Wingate, Israel's national center for physical education and sport, is among the most beautiful places in the country. The institute, founded in 1967, is dotted with dozens of sandhills, all of which afford breathtaking panoramic views of the city of Netanya and the Mediterranean Sea.

Shortly after noon, I exited the doors of bus 601 from Tel Aviv with dozens of Israeli teenagers, all of us dressed in plain white T-shirts, shorts, and running shoes. The candidates who gathered that morning came from vastly different cultural backgrounds. While most were Israeli's, the rest of us came from over a dozen different countries. We all shared a singular goal: to ace the tryouts. When all 350 of us had checked in, we were broken up into four groups of roughly ninety candidates.

Yom Sayarot is the day of tryouts for the five commando units in the IDF. Successfully completing that tryout can earn you a spot in one of three succeeding tryouts: Matkal (somewhat comparable to the U.S. Delta Force), Shayetet (the Navy Seals), or Hovlim (the naval submarine captains). If a candidate passes through the second round of tryouts for those three units but is not accepted, he can earn entrance into the training programs of two more elite units. The first is Shaldag, an air force unit that deploys into hostile environments to conduct special reconnaissance and establish assault zones. The other is 669, the search and rescue unit that specializes in the extraction of pilots downed behind enemy lines. Though one is never given an official "ranking" at the end of the tryout, those who perform the strongest are typically sent on to the Matkal or Navy Seals tryouts.*

We began the tryout with a timed run. This is the standard first activity of every IDF tryout and is used to help the commanders gauge where everyone's fitness stands in relation to one another. I was relieved that I finished in the top 20 percent of my group. After eating a quick dinner, we were sent to bed. The next day we would be awake long before sunrise. Under a giant tent, 350 hopeful candidates full of anticipation for the following day's tryout crawled into sleeping bags. Every Hebrew lesson, every sprint, every push-up, and every pre-dawn wake up on Friday mornings to run with stretchers up sand dunes was meant to prepare me for the following day. Five hours would be

*To get an invitation to the Yom Sayarot tryout, you must have a physical profile of at least 82 and a high enough KABA, or intelligence score, to qualify you for the commando units. You can speak to Liskat HaGius (the draft board) or Mador Sayerot in order to get an invitation.

used to evaluate my previous three years of preparation; there was no room for error. People began to stir around 3:45 a.m., and at 4:00 a.m. came the official wake-up call, after which we were hurried out of the tent and briefed on the schedule for the morning.

Our group began with eighteen candidates. We were lined up in front of our three commanders, each of whom came from one of the units for which we were trying out. We were ordered to bring three chairs, eighteen shovels, two jerrycans, eighteen empty sandbags, and two stretchers to the top of a distant sandhill. By 5:00 a.m., we were on top of that no-longer-distant hill, our commanders were sitting comfortably in their chairs, and we were stretched and ready to go. The head commander pointed to a bucket some distance down the hill. He gave us an unreasonable amount of time to get there and back, and with a command of "*Tseh!*" (Go!), sent us sprinting down the hill, around the bucket, and back up the hill, where we lined up in front of him in the order in which we had arrived. Each time we returned he would ask the candidate who had been the designated timekeeper for that sprint how long it took us, shake his head at our time, and send us off again.

Each sprint took between fifteen and twenty-five seconds. At times, I was so exhausted between the sprints that I struggled to find the strength to stand upright. On one occasion, I stood hunched over the finish line, trying desperately to catch my breath before the next sprint. Though I was slightly disoriented from the lack of oxygen, my eyes registered the Sayeret Matkal logo prominently displayed on my commander's shirt. I knew that the men who wore that insignia gave their blood, sweat, and tears to earn the right to do so, and if I had even the slightest chance at following in their footsteps, I would need to do the same. I drew strength from the rationalization that if men had done it before me, it could be done. I willed myself to stand up straight, bringing me face to face with the commander whose shirt had caught my eye. He looked at me, and I back at him, neither of us breaking eye contact for several seconds. Though I sensed compassion in his eyes, his demeanor betrayed no such emotion. When the last of us had reached the starting line, he looked down at his watch, shook his head, and yelled only a single word, "again," which sent us barreling back down the hill.

I learned before the tryout from Tsevet Lohamim that regardless of how fast you run during the sprints, you will not beat the given time. During this phase of the tryout, as was its intention, many candidates voluntarily withdrew. When I went through the tryouts in 2010, nobody was sent home halfway into Yom Sayarot; the only early departures were for medical reasons or a candidate's voluntary withdrawal.

After about forty minutes of sprints and several voluntary withdrawals, we were given a ten-minute water break before once again lining up in front of our commanders. I used one of the precious minutes of our break to pour the sand out of my shoes, which by that point felt several pounds heavier. Following the break, we found ourselves standing in front of two stretchers, each with four sandbags strapped to them, weighing about 120 pounds each, and two fully filled twenty-liter jerrycans alongside the stretchers. Each exercise consisted of two sprints; your position in the first determined your level of hardship in the second. After the first lap, the first eight candidates to arrive did a second lap carrying the stretchers, the next two to arrive did a lap with the jerrycans, and the remaining eight candidates did another lap like the first one. To be among the first eight men to finish the sprint meant you ended up under the stretchers. This was by far the hardest of all the options, which the commanders used as a gauge of who wanted to win the most, even when winning meant more work. After a half-hour, the commanders announced that they would only record the names of those carrying the first stretcher to arrive, so the two stretchers raced down the hill and back up against one another. As a result of my training under the guidance of the extremely qualified instructors in Tsevet Lohamim, I was under the stretcher nearly every time.

The end of that exercise marked the end of the first phase of the tryout and with it the frantic intensity that had defined the various crawls, sprints, and stretcher drills we had carried out up until that point. In the second phase of the tryout, that intensity was replaced by the dull, disheartening pain of repetitive, uncomfortable exertion. Though we didn't realize it at the time, the latter resembled the army much more than the former. When our second water break concluded, we returned to the start line as ordered with our sandbags filled. With the sandbags resting on our shoulders, we were told to walk in a large circle around the bucket and call out the number of laps we had walked each time we passed the commanders. We were told to walk "at our own pace," but were not told how long the drill would last.

This was a test of motivation as well as integrity, to see who would cut corners and who would report back with the right number. Our commanders really wanted to assess who was going to pull their weight day in and day out, even when nobody was watching—especially when nobody was watching.

After about forty minutes of circling in silence, each man absorbed in his thoughts, we were given shovels and instructed to dig a hole as wide as the shovel, as deep as the shovel, and as long as possible. Unfortunately, my sub-par Hebrew led me to understand that the hole was supposed to be as long as the shovel, as wide as the shovel, and as deep as possible, which I had to work at a frantic pace to fix when I was corrected halfway into the exercise. The shovels we used were standard-issue U.S. Army shovels from the Vietnam War era. Just about the only thing they were capable of doing effectively was jamming on us and cutting up our hands when we tried to fix them.

After we had filled in our holes, we were informed, to our collective relief, that the physical segment of the tryout was over. After taking a few minutes to stretch, we sat in a circle, and each of us was asked to share our name, where we were from, and how we had prepared for that morning's tryout. I believe that what we said wasn't as important as how effectively we expressed ourselves to our peers.

When we had all spoken, we were brought together into one large circle with all of the candidates who had finished the morning's tryout. There we were addressed by a lieutenant colonel, who congratulated us on making it to the end of the day. At the close of his brief remarks, he began to read the numbers of those who had graduated to the next phase of tryouts.

The list of numbers (each corresponding to a name) of those who made it to the Sayeret Matkal tryout was about a page and a half long and contained forty numbers, organized in no particular order. When he turned the first page and my number had not yet been read, my pulse quickened. Each number called that wasn't mine struck at my confidence and increased my doubts as to whether I had performed to the level required to move on to the next stage. Finally, seven numbers into the second page, I heard mine called. The feeling of excitement was overwhelming. Out of respect for those who had not made the cut, I tried to repress any outward expression of joy as I ran to sit with the other candidates who had been selected. We sat quietly, each lost in our thoughts, while the remaining numbers were read. The lieutenant colonel walked over and began to speak, shattering our silent contemplations and daydreams of grandeur. "Congratulations on successfully passing Yom Sayarot. You have been selected based on your fitness, your motivation, and your leadership potential. These attributes will serve you well in any unit where you ultimately serve. Most of you will not make it past the next tryout. However, those of you that do will be training for the most interesting and important jobs that the IDF has to offer."

After some handshakes, laughs, and congratulatory back slaps, we disbanded and went our separate ways. As I walked towards the entrance to the base, I saw a group of colonels speaking in the distance. Among them was the woman in charge of Yom Sayerot who helped me fight through the IDF's bureaucracy so I could attend the tryout. I waited patiently, keeping a respectful distance from her conversation. When she finally turned towards me, I reminded her who I was and thanked her profusely for her help along the way. She told me she was happy to have seen my name on the list for the Sayeret Matkal tryout and wished me the best of luck going forward.

While most people had passed one test, I had passed two. I had fought as hard to get to Yom Sayerot as I had to successfully complete it. As I approached the third and final tryout, I did so with the knowledge that, statistically, my chances of success were very slim. It wasn't that anyone wanted it more than me, or that I felt I wasn't smart enough or strong enough. Of the few hundred cadets who would begin the tryout, only thirty would earn the opportunity to start the infamously rigorous training regimen of Sayeret Matkal. Of those thirty, nearly half would be dropped from the training process along the way due to screening, injuries, and various other reasons. Nevertheless, I counted down the days until the tryout with excitement and anticipation. I welcomed the challenge and my chance to prove to myself and to the commanders that I could measure up to the high standards of the unit referred to simply and tellingly as "The Unit."

CHAPTER 12: THE ALMOST TRYOUT

A few short weeks after Yom Sayerot came the five-day tryout for Sayeret Matkal. All the candidates invited that day had passed through rigorous physical and psychological screening, and all had proven to be intelligent individuals in top physical condition with the motivation to back it up. Like everyone else who arrived for the tryouts that morning, I filled out the required forms and lined up to see the doctor. Unlike everyone else, however, thanks to my poor understanding of written Hebrew, I did not have the doctor's note required for participation in the tryout.

I was told to wait with nine other candidates who had also forgotten their forms at home. I quickly realized that I didn't have the form they wanted, but I was not yet ready to reveal that. I called my kibbutz and waited impatiently for them to fax copies of the medical forms from America they had on record. Though I knew they were not the forms the army wanted, they were the closest things to those forms in my possession. It has been said that misery loves company, but my company was dwindling quickly. The knot in my stomach tightened as each candidate received his form, either by fax or from his parents who showed up in person to bring the needed form to their son. Soon I was the only candidate left without the needed medical forms. I waited helplessly as the commander in charge declared that she would need to close the tryout shortly. Silently, I watched and prayed as the soldiers from Mador Sayerot*, with whom I had become friendly after so many battles with the Army's bureaucracy, begged and pleaded that she wait for my forms to arrive. I paced back and forth nervously, unable to sit, as those helping me on my kibbutz insisted that they had faxed the forms while the officers on-site claimed they had received nothing from them. With one minute remaining before the commanding officer closed the tryouts, my kibbutz succeeded in sending an email with my medical forms attached. I breathed a sigh of relief... until I realized that the forms did not contain a doctor's signature. As I watched the officers pass my form back and forth and speak to one another in muffled whispers, it was clear from their expressions and their refusal to look me in the eyes that this form was not going to cut it.

Realizing I was out of options, I reached into my bag and pulled out my emergency last option: a note from an American doctor. It said, in more and fancier words, that my scoliosis would not prevent me from fulfilling all of my duties as a combat soldier in any unit in which I served, regardless of its demands. I feared this might lead the on-site doctor to misgivings about my back, which is why I had kept it hidden until then. But having no other options left, I presented the two forms together in the hopes that the signed doctor's note would legitimize the unsigned medical exam as well.

The doctor on-site told me that he would consider accepting this as sufficient documentation, but that he wanted to evaluate my scoliosis for himself. We walked away from the group of officers that had gathered so that he could examine me in relative privacy. With my heart racing, I pulled up my shirt, extended my arms, and stretched forward. He ran his hand along the small of my back, and within seconds he pulled me back up and put his arm around my shoulder. The look in his eyes betrayed the difficulty of the

---

*Mador Sayarot is the office in charge of the acceptance into and administration of Yom Sayarot.

message he would soon need to deliver. When he finally spoke, he informed me that, in his opinion, were I to enter the unit's training with my degree of scoliosis, I would be permanently crippled within two years. He could not in good conscience allow me to participate in the tryout. My protests fell on deaf ears, and it was clear that no amount of pleading on my behalf by the soldiers who had sought to help me all morning was going to change his mind. I asked for a second opinion, but his second-in-command, unsurprisingly, agreed with his analysis. I would be permanently blacklisted from trying out for Sayeret Matkal. Beyond that, however, it would be my decision whether or not to lower my profile, as the army doctor who had initially evaluated me had cleared me for all combat units.

Before I had chosen to attend the Sayeret Matkal tryout, I was told that I had to choose between that tryout and the Paratrooper's tryout, since the two happened at the same time. Duvdevan, the unit that was the target of my aspirations from the start, operated as an elite unit within the Paratroopers. I was now facing the possibility that I'd lost the opportunity to try out not only for Sayeret Matkal, but Duvdevan as well. After placing a few phone calls on my behalf, one of the soldiers from Mador Sayerot, who had done her best to help me throughout the many setbacks I'd experienced, informed me that if I could somehow get my hands on a doctor's note that day, I would be able to attend the Paratrooper's tryout the following day.

As I walked away from the tryout and towards the bus stop, I felt defeated in a way that I never had before. I had fought many times with the bureaucracy of the IDF, and on the basis of relentless pleading and polite insistence, I had consistently persevered. I fought my way out of the army's language course that should have prevented me from attending the special forces tryout, which I passed despite my sub-par Hebrew. In each case, it was not on wits or strength, but on persistence that I had succeeded. It was the barrage of letters I wrote to high-ranking officers and the Hebrew I struggled day and night to learn. My then-11-year-old sister, Tara, had told me the night before the tryout that, "the amount of your desire determines the amount of your success." But as I walked towards that bus stop, emotionally exhausted from the morning's battles, for the first time in my life, that wasn't true. There was nothing I could have done. No extra miles I could have run or weights I could have lifted would have changed that doctor's mind. For the first time, persistence was not enough.

Despite the disheartening experience of the morning, I tried to stay positive and focus on what remained to be done. I knew that if I excelled in the Paratroopers tryout, I would still have a chance at making it into Duvdevan. I still needed a medical form to be eligible for the tryout. When Ayala picked me up from the bus station, she marched me into the closest doctor's office and demanded that he sign off on my form as my primary care doctor. He pushed back, rightfully noting that he was not my primary care doctor. She pushed back harder and louder. Within five minutes she had explained my predicament loudly enough that she'd gotten the entire waiting room on her side and, collectively, they bullied him into signing my medical form. It was but one of many "only in Israel" moments I would experience during my time in the IDF. I went to sleep that night exhausted but determined. The next day's tryouts would be my last chance at the special forces, and I did not intend to fail, no matter what it took.

CHAPTER 13: PARATROOPER SELECTION

The next morning, not wanting to take any more chances with my luck, I arrived at the tryouts several hours before the scheduled start time. As the morning progressed, candidates began to stream into the base and join those of us already sitting on bleachers that had been set up under a giant tent, which shielded us from the brutal Middle Eastern sun. By 10:30 a.m., the bleachers that had been nearly empty when I arrived were almost completely full. We were told that no more than 15 of the 100 lone soldiers present at the tryout would be accepted and that only about half of those would come from Garin Tzabar, though we were forty-four strong at the start of the tryout. Shortly before the tryout began, we were addressed by Tzvika Levi, widely considered the father of Israel's lone soldiers. His pep talk was short and to the point: "They only take a few people—only the best. If you want to be chosen, be the best."

Before the physical portion of the tryout began, all the lone soldiers were given a comprehensive questionnaire to fill out asking us about our interests, our education, and our family in and out of Israel. A few hours after lunch, we completed our two-kilometer timed runs, as is the standard start of every tryout.

For the remainder of the day, we were under the command of active-duty Paratrooper commanders, who led us around, forced us to drink ridiculous amounts of water, and got us our uniforms for the tryout. After we had changed into our fatigues, we stood facing our commander and awaited further instructions. As his eyes traced the group, they fell upon me. Amusedly, he asked me what was on my arm in a tone that suggested he already knew the answer. As I looked down at my right sleeve, I noticed three blue stripes with a small design that overlaid them and deduced that they were indicative of a rank I had not yet attained. Today I recognize those stripes as the mark of a first sergeant and a commander. After reprimanding me, he ordered me to change my shirt, chuckling with the other commanders as he called after me, "Maybe one day."

"I hope," I thought to myself. After dinner, we were brought back to our tents and told to be outside in a *chet*, or a U-formation open to the commander, at 3:15 a.m. with our uniforms on. After a dismal night's sleep rife with nerves and anticipation, my third in a row, 3:00 a.m. rolled around, and the first alarm went off in our tent. I savored a final few minutes of warmth in my sleeping bag before climbing out of my cot to get dressed. We waited in uncomfortable silence for our commander for what felt like an hour as we stood outside insufficiently protected against the pre-dawn chill. Finally, he emerged from the commander's tent with a list of names and separated us into groups.

While most of my friends were placed in a group consisting entirely of Garin Tzabar candidates, in my group of thirty-five, I was the only lone soldier. After several forced bouts of water consumption, we met the man who would be our drill sergeant for the tryout, a large, imposing figure who looked completely comfortable wearing only a T-shirt in the chilly winter morning. Those charged with running the actual tryout, including our drill sergeant, were all reservists in their late thirties or early forties, whose reserve duty each year was the implementation of the tryouts for the Paratroopers. Upon gauging the size of our group, I suspected that the first order of business would be to weed people out. As it turned out, I was correct.

After a light run to warm us up, we were lined up and told to sprint around a sandbag about 100 feet away and then back to the starting line. The commanders informed us they would record only the names of the first three candidates to complete each sprint. The road was too narrow for thirty-five people to line up evenly, and the path around the sandbag was too narrow for everyone to go around fairly. If they caught you blatantly pushing other people out of the way for position, they would mark you down, which would diminish your chances of acceptance. But given the lack of space, if you were not aggressive enough, no matter how fast you ran, you could not possibly be among the first three finishers. Throughout the exercise, our commander repeatedly told us in a friendly tone, "Anyone who wants can have a drink of water. You can stop running and just relax. All you have to do is say, 'I quit.'" More than a few people took him up on his offer. Many aspects of the tryout were similar to Yom Sayarot. After each sprint, as soon as the last person had crossed the finish line, our commander would ask the person he had designated as the timekeeper how long it had taken us, shake his head at the answer, and send us off again. Eventually, we were given a break to drink water and fill up sandbags. When the break time elapsed, we did the same drill again, but this time, when we crossed the finish line after completing the sprint, we were told to pick up the sandbags we had filled and hold them over our heads while keeping our arms straight. While this would have been uncomfortable under any circumstances, it was particularly difficult as we struggled to catch our breath after sprinting. The commanders recorded the names of those who were first to finish, as well as those who quit in the middle. Almost all the candidates who lowered the sandbags before being told to do so failed to make the final cuts for the Paratroopers.

Next, we loaded twelve sandbags onto two stretchers and began a fast-paced march with intermittent sprints. I did my best to make sure I was under the stretcher as much as possible. Those that weren't carrying the stretcher carried sandbags or jerrycans filled with twenty liters of water.

Interspersed throughout the day were group conversations in which the commanders assessed our ability to contribute meaningful insights within a group environment, as well as our leadership tendencies. Who took control of the conversation? Who was always talking, and who spoke selectively? I did my best to contribute each time a question was posed to the group. The other candidates were extremely patient with me, and while they spoke quickly and forcefully, often cutting each other off, they allowed me to stumble through my attempts to express myself in Hebrew without interrupting me. The conversations ranged in topic from government intervention in the economy to the pros and cons of doing business with hostile Arab nations.

In addition to group conversations, there were various group exercises. The goal of one such exercise was to get everyone in the group to the top of a wooden bar which was suspended six feet above a large pit of sand, equipped only with a garbage can and a fifteen-foot tree trunk. If anyone touched the sand, everyone had to do twenty push-ups and begin the exercise again from the start. The idea here was not necessarily to succeed in the time allotted, which would have been nearly impossible, but rather to give our commanders another opportunity to evaluate our personalities and our leadership capabilities. Our integrity was also being tested: if someone stepped in the sand, would they admit the infraction or carry on as though nothing had happened?

The last activity of the day was a ten-kilometer stretcher march. Stretcher marches are not like the movies, where four well-built men of equal height walk with ease at a steady pace. Much more frequently, four people of varying heights and body types must walk at a brisk pace and sometimes run to catch up with the commanders. They are forced to contort their bodies in awkward positions to account for height discrepancies while keeping two hundred pounds in the air.

The commanders ordered six sandbags to be placed on each stretcher and told us to replace one another under the stretchers as we got tired. It had been rumored that this was the most important part of the tryout, and I was determined to use it as an opportunity to leave no doubt in my commanders' minds that I belonged in the Paratroopers—if only because nobody wanted it more. I started and finished under the same stretcher, never leaving it once. We speed-walked, jogged, and then sprinted up hills and back down them. Each of us wore a number on our backs to identify us to the commanders, and every so often they would stop us and record the numbers of those under the stretchers. That day I had been given number three, and at a certain point, they simply started referring to the stretcher I was under as "number 3's stretcher." At times, the pain in my back and shoulders was searing, but I had worked too hard to arrive at the tryout to allow for the possibility of failure. In my mind, it simply was not an option.

Finally, we reached the road where we had done our original two-kilometer run. We all felt a rush of adrenaline as we realized that we had reached the final segment of the tryout. We were given the command to start and began to run in the direction of the base. With about 1,200 feet to go, our commander, who was in front of the group, accelerated his run and ultimately began to sprint. At that point, my stretcher was a few dozen feet behind the second stretcher. I glanced over at the guy next to me under our stretcher. As we made eye contact, an unspoken understanding passed between us, and we simultaneously broke into a sprint, dragging the two guys in the back of the stretcher with us in our quest for first place. With 300 feet to go, we passed the second stretcher and crossed the finish line alone, exhausted but victorious. Our commander, observing this, couldn't help but crack a grin. It was the first time we had seen him smile all day. With that, the physical segment of the tryout was concluded, and we were given time to drink water and stretch.

I had been under a stretcher for nearly two hours. As we began stretching, the adrenaline that had helped sustain my previous efforts wore off. My body made its displeasure known to me. Spasms of increasing intensity began shooting up and down my back. I tried to walk it off, but quickly found myself unable to stand. After several minutes of agonizing pain, the spasms began to subside. They were replaced by nausea, and I spent the next ten minutes hunching over my knees dry heaving. Eventually I was able to straighten my back and rejoin the group for stretches. The tryout had left me in excruciating physical pain; I had given every ounce of my strength in pursuit of acceptance into the Paratroopers. Win or lose, I knew I would never look back and wonder if I could have tried harder. Now, the outcome was out of my hands.

We were given an hour to shower, eat a light breakfast, and report to the center of the base for post-tryout interviews. When my name was called, I showed up with notes prepared and asked for permission to say a few things before the interview began. My interviewers, slightly taken aback but seemingly impressed, allowed me to proceed. I told them about my motivations for coming to Israel, and why I wanted so badly to serve in Duvdevan. I told them about my training regimen, and the five hours I spent each day in an intensive Hebrew language course in conjunction with two-hour private Hebrew lessons each afternoon. When I finished, they had a few questions of their own:

"Why do you think you will get along with 18-year-olds when you are already 22?"

"Do you have any leadership experience? Would you consider being an officer?"

"What are your greatest strengths and greatest weaknesses?"

After an hour of difficult questions the interview, and with it the tryout, finally came to an end. I left feeling confident that I had succeeded in conveying to those interviewing me the intensity of my desire to serve in Duvdevan; the rest was up to fate. With that, I packed up my things and headed to Tel Aviv to get a real lunch. After a morning like the one I'd just had, white bread and cheese was not going to cut it.

****

A week later, the results from the tryouts were released, and childhood dreams were achieved or shattered with a single word: yes or no. By noon, everyone on my kibbutz knew where they stood—everyone, that is, except me. A week before the tryout, I had been granted an opportunity to retake the army's Hebrew test with some help from Garin Tzabar.* Nissan, the coordinator for Garin Tzabar on my kibbutz, stressed to the office in charge of army ulpan that without a clean slate in the language department, my chances for acceptance into the top units of the IDF would be severely limited. Thanks in part to his pleading, about seven of us from Garin Tzabar were given the chance to retake the test, and we all passed, exempting us from army ulpan. This was no surprise given the intensive Hebrew programs we had all done on our respective kibbutzim. Still, the Paratroopers had not yet received my results, which meant that they could not yet make a decision about my acceptance.

I spent the day in an emotional limbo, desperately hoping that all I had fought so hard for would not be undermined by the inefficiencies of the army's internal communication system. Finally, at five o'clock, in an act so informal that, given what was at stake, it could only occur in the IDF, Nissan received a text informing him that I had been accepted into the Paratroopers. That night, for the first time in months, Eitan and I relaxed and had a few too many drinks, content with the knowledge that while much was still uncertain, in less than a month we would be entering the training regimen of the storied IDF Paratroopers.

---

*Our test was scored out of 9, and only those who received above a 5 were allowed a second opportunity to take the test. If you do Garin Tzabar, since the test is only a few weeks after you arrive in Israel, you must arrive with a solid grasp of Hebrew if you have any hope of placing out of the army language course.

CHAPTER 14: DRAFT DAY

"That was a memorable day to me, for it made great changes in me. But it is the same with any life. Imagine one selected day struck out of it, and think how different its course would have been. Pause you who read this, and think for a moment of the long chain of iron or gold, of thorns or flowers, that would never have bound you, but for the formation of the first link on one memorable day."
—*Charles Dickens, Great Expectations*

On November 3rd, 2010, I was drafted into the IDF. The period that began on that day would be the hardest of my life and would change me profoundly. That morning, Eitan and I made the drive from Tel Aviv to Tel HaShomer, the base to which we had been ordered to report, along with hundreds of other soldiers being drafted into the Givati and Paratroopers Brigades. We were chaperoned by Eitan's father, Shimon, a native-born Israeli who had come all the way from America to see his son off.

After presenting our IDs and proof of our draft date, we were ushered into the base and a scene of utter chaos. Soon-to-be-soldiers stood on top of benches, blowing vuvuzelas and alternating between screaming out the words to popular soccer chants and disparaging rival brigades. Their mothers alternated between snapping photos and crying. My merely basic grasp of the language left me confused about much of what was happening, but I was filled with pride. The day I had looked forward to for years had finally come. As reporters got word of the abnormally large presence of foreign soldiers being drafted into the Paratroopers, they began to assemble around us. A picture was snapped of a group of us by a reporter from Israel's largest newspaper, Yediot Aharonot. Days later, that photo would appear on the front page in an article about lone soldiers. The parallels between summer camp and the army on that morning were abundant. My memories drifted back to the Macy's parking lot where I had waited as a kid to board the buses to Camp Echo Lake.

I remembered emotional parents saying goodbye to their kids as calm counselors with big smiles on their faces ushered us onto our respective buses. That morning, a large board, rather than a megaphone, communicated the names and bus numbers of the newly drafted soldiers. Those who loaded us onto the buses, though the same age as the camp counselors, were now in uniforms and wore rifles over their shoulders. Few of them were smiling. I remember thinking to myself as I looked around that it was sad that teenagers in Israel become military commanders at nineteen instead of camp counselors. Yoni Netanyahu, the late brother of Prime Minister Benjamin Netanyahu, and the former commander of Sayeret Matkal, captured the sadness of the seemingly endless conflict in a letter he wrote when he was only 22 years old:

That harmony that characterizes a young man's world is not part of me anymore. Although I am still young, still strong and confident of myself and my ability, I can't ignore the fact that a sense of old age has taken hold of me... When I try to understand why this is so, and why this feeling has grown within me, I reach the conclusion that not only the war, the killing, the deaths, the wounds, and disabilities are to blame-these can be overcome. Their imprint may perhaps be dulled by time. The real cause is the sense of helplessness in the face of a war that has no end...It continues with every mine and killing and murder, with every explosion in Jerusalem and every shot in the north or the south. This is the "quiet" before the next storm. I've no doubt that war will come. Nor do I doubt that we will win. But for how long? Until when?... Hence the sadness I referred to earlier, the sadness of young men destined for endless war.

Later, when I was an active-duty combat soldier, I frequently found myself on the receiving end of deep hatred from people I had never met. In those moments, when I wondered how there could ever be peace in the face of such hatred, I began to grasp the sadness Yoni referred to in his letter. As I sat there on the morning of my draft, lost in my own thoughts, I was brought back to reality by the sight of the number I had been given earlier flashing on the screen, informing me that my bus had pulled up to the loading dock.

A short ride brought us to a new base where we were issued our gear and sent to a large room to try on our new uniforms and boots. Like high school students in the dressing room before a play, we struggled with uniforms that were either way too small or way too large. As we traded with each other and pulled uniforms from boxes trying to find ones that fit, I caught a glimpse of myself in the mirror. Israelis looked at me strangely as I stared at myself in wonder for entirely too long in my entirely-too-small-uniform. But at that moment, I couldn't have cared less what anyone thought. I was finally a uniformed soldier in the IDF.

After procuring a properly fitting uniform (Apparently, "tall, lanky Jew" is not a standard size in the IDF.) and the various pieces of equipment we were told we needed to sign for, we reconvened outside. We were organized into teams that would remain together for the next two weeks. Thereafter, we would have the final tryouts for the special forces. The next day was Friday, and we were released for the weekend. As would become a routine on our weekends off, Eitan and I ate too much, drank too much, slept too little, and tried in vain to find ourselves Israeli girlfriends. When, far too quickly, Sunday morning arrived, we boarded the train in Tel Aviv and settled in for the hour-and-a-half journey down south, arriving as ordered at the Kiryat Gat bus station late on Sunday morning. From there, a military bus took us an hour to the southwest, and shortly before noon, we rolled through the gates of the Paratroopers base that would be our home for the next eight months.

All the soldiers on our newly formed team were perplexed by Eitan and me. We were almost 23 years old, five years older than most of them, and two years older than our commander. They had dozens of questions for us: Why would you ever volunteer to join the army? Where will you stay on weekends? Is American college really like the movies?

In the middle of the first week, as we stood in formation awaiting the arrival of our commander, one of the guys on our team spontaneously began to clap for us, yelling out his praise for our decision to move to Israel and join the IDF. The rest of the group quickly joined in. Our commander arrived seconds later with a look of confusion on his face, told them to shut their mouths and asked them what the hell all the commotion was about. When they explained to him why they were cheering, his grimace turned to a smile and he encouraged them to continue, even clapping along with them.

Throughout the week, whenever I had problems understanding what was going on, the guys on my team practically tripped over one another to help me. Every night during our hour of free time, they ran to my bed and forcibly shared their food with me, and even insisted on helping me shine my shoes. I received multiple uncomfortably tight hugs before bed each night, and again could not help but laugh at the similarities between my days as a camper and my first week as a soldier. I will always remember the warmth and kindness shown to me by the young men on my team during that first week. In true Israeli fashion, they ensured that while I was a lone soldier, I did not feel alone.

CHAPTER 15: THE FINAL TRYOUT

Within every brigade of the Israeli Army (Givati, Golani, Nahal, Paratroopers, Kfir, Shiryon, etc.) there are special units you can only try out for once you've been drafted into that brigade. All Paratroopers are technically eligible to try out for the three Special Forces units within the brigade: Maglan, Duvdevan, and the reconnaissance company consisting of Palsar, Orev, and Palchan. In reality, however, one must be pre-selected to try out for Duvdevan. Of the fifteen groups of soldiers trying out, only four were watched by Duvdevan commanders, and thus only candidates in those groups had a chance of being selected.

A few days into basic training, my commander, who knew how badly I wanted to serve in Duvdevan, pulled me aside. Solemnly, he informed me that though his sources told him I had been a top performer during the Paratroopers tryout, I was not on the list for the Duvdevan tryouts. He believed the contributing factors were concerns about language, being a new immigrant to the country, and my status as a lone soldier, which would necessitate the unit paying me a higher salary and giving me more days off.

As he spoke, I was overcome by feelings of fear and frustration; it appeared that despite all the hard work I had put in to reach that point, my imagined future was slipping through my fingers. That night, when we had permission to use our phones, I called everyone I could think of who might have potential connections in the army. After several disappointing conversations, I reached out to a tour guide I had met on a trip to Israel four years earlier, who I remembered had served as a sniper in an elite unit. As luck would have it, he was connected to a high-ranking officer in Duvdevan, and he made a call on my behalf. He asked his friend, as I insisted he do, that I not be given anything more than what was given to native-born Israelis who excelled in the Paratroopers tryout: the chance to prove myself in the tryout for Duvdevan. As the date of the tryout approached, my anxiety mounted. A day before the tryout none of my commanders knew if my name was on the list.

Shortly before lights out the evening before the tryout, my commander called my name from the staff barracks in an agitated voice. I jumped out of bed and rushed out of the room to find him standing across the company compound with his hands on his hips and a stern look on his face. Both his tone and his facial expression indicated that I had done something seriously wrong. I ran across the barracks to where he was standing and snapped to attention, awaiting what I was sure would be a harsh scolding. The army punishes you so often during basic training that your immediate reaction to anyone's anger is to assume that you have done something wrong. I've heard it's great preparation for marriage. But this time, as it turned out, I hadn't done anything wrong. In fact, I had done something right. As soon as my hands hit my sides, my commander's face relaxed into a big grin. "I don't know how you did it, you son of a bitch," he said happily, "but your name is on the list for the Duvdevan tryout."

Over the two weeks leading up until that moment, I had lived in a perpetual state of frustration and despondence. Despite all my battles with the IDF's bureaucracy, until he uttered those words, twelve hours before the tryouts began, it looked like it had all been for nothing. But in that instant, with a single sentence, all of that pressure was released, and frustration turned to euphoria. Before I even realized what I was doing, I had embraced my commander in a bear hug as both of us laughed hysterically. Within seconds, we came to our senses and quickly looked around to make sure nobody had seen us. Though as of the next morning he would no longer be my commander, the army is the army after all. Sheepishly, I thanked him for the good news, floated back to my room, and climbed into bed to catch a few hours of sleep. From all that I had been told by friends who'd been through the tryouts, the coming days would push my physical limits in ways I had never done before. They were right.

The first day of the tryout was my twenty-third birthday. I reflected throughout that day, and the ones that followed, on the contrast between my life just one year earlier and my life as a soldier. I celebrated my twenty-second birthday at Oscar's Tavern in Philadelphia, drinking good beer with good friends. My twenty-third birthday was spent in a desert in Southern Israel, sleep-deprived, hungry, and crawling over rocks until blood had soaked through my uniform. The tryout tested every fiber of my determination. Much of the details are hazy, and when I think back on those three days now, the different sections of the tryout blend together like parts of a nightmare.

At around 3:30 on the morning of the tryout, we were gathered outside the barracks with the gear we had collected the previous day (tents, sleeping bags, water bottles, shovels, and blankets). We were taken to the basketball courts, where we were split into fifteen groups. Of the 550 or so people that made the Paratroopers, 450 began the tryouts that morning for the three elite units within them. In groups of thirty, we met our *mefakdeem* (commanders). As our group stood there, silently but obviously sizing one another up, my commander from the previous week approached the group and called me over. I ran up to him and stood at attention. He leaned closer and whispered in English in my ear: "If you don't make it into Duvdevan, I will personally kick your ass. And then I will work my connections to get you into my battalion," he said with a wink. I smiled, shook his hand, and rejoined my group.

At 4:00 a.m., the tryout officially began. We wore backpacks that appeared to be from the era of the United States' Civil War, most of which didn't tighten and had no padding. Each contained knee pads, elbow pads, two canteens of water, and a twenty-pound sandbag. In addition to each soldier's personal gear, we had, as a group, three folded stretchers, and two jerrycans weighing a little over thirty-five pounds each. With a command of "*acharay*" (after me), we began the first march of the tryout. As we walked through the barren desert, we left behind the comfort of the base and the fantasy world of our first weeks in the army, during which our commanders were forbidden from punishing us.

As we walked in silence, the first traces of daylight began to streak across the morning sky, illuminating the ominous landscape, and uncovering for the first time the dark clouds looming in the distance. After a half-hour of brisk walking, weighed down by backpacks, army boots, and gear, we reached our destination—a flat stretch of rocky desert terrain. The first segment of any tryout is designed to weed out the candidates who don't want it badly enough, and this tryout was no different. We were ordered to put on our knee and elbow pads, a clear sign that we would be crawling. Wearing protective pads had become mandatory after a candidate who was trying out for the unit had died two years earlier. A wound he had sustained while crawling had become infected. Theoretically, this was a great preventative solution. In practice, the pads were completely useless and slid off after the first two feet of crawling. As Eitan's father, Shimon, told me the day we drafted, the reason the army puts soldiers on guard duty outside of bases is to make sure reason doesn't enter through their gates. Sadly, throughout my service, many other examples would confirm his theory.

The tryouts were run by reservists who had served in the unit when there were very few (enforced) laws protecting soldiers in training. While we cut ourselves crawling over rocks, they sat in lounge chairs, smoked cigarettes, snacked, and listened to music. Their orders were cold and emotionless right from the start; they almost seemed to resent us. The first drill of the tryout was a race in which we crawled back and forth across a sixty-foot field covered in rocks. After about five feet of crawling, the simultaneous commotion of thirty soldiers crawling practically on top of one another kicked up so much sand that both breathing comfortably and seeing more than a foot in any direction became impossible. While crawling in such close quarters, one constantly needed to keep his head on a swivel to avoid the fatal kick of a military boot from the soldier in front of or alongside him.

After about forty-five minutes, we were given a ten-minute water break. Though we were only a few hours into the multiple-day tryout, one person from our group had already voluntarily withdrawn from the tryout. As I sat there breathing heavily, sipping water, and looking around, I couldn't help but laugh at the ridiculous sight of thirty-two soldiers with brown teeth. It was clear at this juncture that hygiene would play a very small role, if any, in the week's activities.

The physical challenges mounted in their intensity in the hours that followed. The throbbing pain in my knees grew worse as they swelled from their impact against the rocks. In moments when my resolve wavered, I thought of the resistance fighters of World War II, who fought against the Nazis—outnumbered, under-armed, and under-clothed in the harsh Polish winter. If they could face those conditions for the greater good, I could push through my discomfort to better serve the Jewish people in the IDF. After the crawling races came sprinting races, and eventually stretcher races which entailed running back and forth from the start line while every four candidates held up 200-pound stretchers.

Having endured hours of alternating between those three drills, we were given a fifteen-minute lunch break to eat our field rations, which consisted of four loaves of bread, six cans of tuna, four small packets of jelly, and four small packets of chocolate. Food was eaten nearly as quickly as it could be opened. Utensils were communal and hands were as good as forks. As I forced down a hastily crafted sandwich of tuna and white bread, I noticed that blood from a cut I had sustained on my right knee while crawling had begun to seep through my uniform. "Happy Birthday," I thought to myself.

Throughout our lunch, a reservist with a notepad observed us. Who ate first? Who opened cans and passed them to other people before taking food for himself? Who dominated the conversation? Commanders were always present, and always watching silently.

After the break, we loaded up our gear and set off again for unknown destinations as we alternated between speed walking and jogging to keep the pace of our commanders. An hour later, we had reached our destination. The ground in front of us was completely covered in small and medium-sized rocks for as far as the eye could see. We were given ten minutes to clear the rocks from the area in front of us before the crawling races began, which was the equivalent of trying to remove grains of sand from a beach.

Eventually, sprinting races once again replaced the crawling races. Around midday, one of the cadets in our group collapsed and began hyperventilating, presumably from heat-stroke. He was doused with an entire jerrycan by the medical staff, who were present throughout the tryouts due to the high potential for serious injury. He came to while being carried off in a stretcher to the waiting ambulance and began vehemently protesting his removal from the tryout. Unfortunately for him, his request fell on deaf ears, and he failed in his attempt to lift himself off the stretcher, which he was already strapped into. The temperature was well over 90 degrees Fahrenheit, and in response to this incident, our commander begrudgingly sent us off on a ten-minute water break. We had been crawling, sprinting, and hiking for about nine hours, and a feeling of desperation set in with the recognition that this was only the first day.

At every turn, our commanders played mind games with us. Throughout the drills, they would tell us every so often that the next lap was "optional" to see who would take the opportunity to rest. They did their best to trick us into thinking that the worst was still to come, and much more of it.

In addition to the physical component of the tryout, we were given group exercises and tests, typically during the hottest hours of the day. To test our navigation abilities, we were given maps to memorize and then asked for directions to various locations. On several occasions, we were asked to speak about topics ranging from what animal best symbolized us to an interesting experience that we had prior to drafting into the army. The speeches were difficult for me given my limited Hebrew, but I did my best to articulate my thoughts. One of the hardest parts of the army for me was recognizing how little my insights mattered if I couldn't express them in Hebrew.

After assembling our tents that evening, we marched to a rocky plain where the sprints and crawling continued. When the sunlight began to wane, we were given twenty minutes to dig an individual hole and to contribute to a group hole. Each of us was then asked to explain why we chose to position our hole where we did (i.e. good view of the enemy, good cover from grenades, etc.) and why we divided the time between the individual effort and the group effort as we had. We were sent to bed around 9:00 p.m. that night.

Sleep was difficult despite my exhaustion. After a day spent crawling on rocks, every move was painful. Each time I moved even slightly, I was jolted awake by the sharp pain radiating from cuts and bruises all over my body. Subjecting the body to immense physical hardship takes its toll on the mind as well, and even the few hours that I managed to sleep were plagued by horrible nightmares.

When we woke up with the sun the next morning, we were immediately brought back to the fields of rocks, where we crawled for hours, reopening all the scabs that had begun to heal over the previous day's wounds. Eventually, crawling was replaced by sprinting, and when it got too hot for the sprints, we were given a new drill. Each candidate was given a twenty-five-pound sandbag, directed to a point on the side of a nearby mountain, and told to do as many laps around that point as possible while keeping track of how many he had done. The goal of this exercise was not only to see who could do the most laps but, as in the Paratroopers tryout, to see who would report their number honestly. While they asked each of us for our number, I sensed that they were recording our laps by themselves as well.

At around 7:00 p.m. on the second night, having crawled and sprinted in the dark for over two hours, we were given dinner and told that the physical segment of the tryout had concluded. We breathed a collective sigh of relief but remained guarded, as there were rumors of a six-kilometer march at sunrise. After a brief celebratory feast that consisted of the usual white bread, tuna, and jelly, we were taken to the basketball courts where we had begun our tryout several days earlier. There we completed a form ranking our teammates on their performance and personalities. Shortly after we handed back our forms, a giant menorah was rolled onto the courts and the head rabbi of the base lit a candle for the first night of Hanukkah.

As I stood there at attention, I was mesmerized by the sight before me: 200 boys, down from the 450 that had started the tryout, far from being soldiers, and even further from being men, stood shoulder to shoulder and welcomed in the holiday. Our eyes were sunken and darkened from lack of sleep, and our faces were streaked with dirt. Our uniforms, most caked with spots of blood and mud, bore testament to the hellish few days we had suffered through together. Though we came from many different religious backgrounds, and represented twelve different countries, we all sang the Chanukah songs together in Hebrew, our (now) common language.

A few hours later, as I stood in line to exchange my sleeping bag, I was practically dragged up the stairs by ten overly excited teenagers in uniforms who had been part of my team during the weeks before the tryout. When we reached the top of the stairs, I saw that a menorah sat perched upon a small table. They insisted that I be the one to light the candles and begin the singing of the prayers. Everyone quickly joined in, and before long we were all in a big circle, arm over shoulder, screaming out the words to festive songs, dancing and laughing. It was such a powerful moment that the burning sensation from the deep cuts in my knees and elbows temporarily subsided, and I was reminded in the most special of ways that I was now a soldier in the world's only Jewish army.

The next day interviews were conducted, which we were told were just as important as the physical tryouts. On the four-member interview board sat a psychologist, a reserve commander, and two soldiers presently serving in the unit. As a lone soldier, I was asked about my family, my motivations for coming to Israel, and why I wanted to be in Duvdevan. As in the first interviews, I answered the questions as well as I could and hoped for the best. After we returned the gear that we had signed out three days earlier, we were told we would be free until dinner to rest and see the doctor if needed. We used our free time to send messages to our parents, shower for the first time in three days, and clean and dress our wounds. Looking around the base, it was very easy to see who had just been in the tryouts; all of us were limping.

On Monday morning, we assembled in the gymnasium, where we sat impatiently and waited for the lists of accepted candidates to be read aloud. Nervous chatter filled the air, and the occasional exaggerated laugh betrayed an edginess that we all shared to varying degrees. After what felt like hours, an officer stepped up to the podium. A deafening silence fell over the gymnasium. He opened his remarks with a few words about how good soldiers are needed in every unit, and how those who weren't accepted into the special units had nothing to hang their heads about. As true as his words might have been, they were neither reassuring nor comforting to those who had trained for years preparing for the previous week's tryouts. As he continued to prematurely comfort those whose names would not be read that morning, my thoughts drifted to the Friday morning training sessions on the Tel Aviv port with Tsevet Lohamim. I thought of the Hebrew classes I had taken in university, and the ulpan I had completed on the kibbutz. I was jolted from my daydreams and back to reality as I registered the sound of the first name being read from the list. Two teams of soldiers were to be accepted into Duvdevan in this draft, and when he read the list of names for the first team and my name was not on it, my heart sank. As the first team gathered their bags and headed outside, he began reading the list of names for the second team. My throat dried up, my chest tightened, and I found myself physically unable to breathe as I listened intently, praying to hear my name. Ten names into the second team's list, he called the name "Kogey Feltman." Never in my life had I been so happy to hear my name mispronounced.

I was overcome by a mixture of euphoria and shock, unable to fully process that everything I had worked so hard for was coming to fruition. I stood up in a daze and made my way towards the group of soldiers that had gathered around the podium where the names were being read. Friends shouted out my name from across the gym, patted me on the back, and even strangers congratulated me as I descended the stairs. I found myself unable to respond to them, still unsure if I was awake or dreaming. As I looked across the room, my commander from the previous week caught my gaze and gave me an enthusiastic nod of approval.

When I reached the floor after descending from the back row of the bleachers, my senses came back to me. I was hit suddenly and powerfully by a wave of stimulation; the dull roar of the auditorium, the bright lights above my head, the faint breeze running through the open doors of the otherwise stuffy gym. Nearly a year and a half of paperwork, training, studying, let-ter-writing to high-level officials, language-testing, disappointment, relief, and anticipation had finally culminated in my acceptance to the training program of one of the world's most elite counter-terror units.

When all the names for our team had been called, we were quickly lined up and rushed outside, where it began to rain, suddenly and heavily. We each had three large bags that held all our belongings. After the results of the tryouts were made public, everyone in our draft class was assigned to new teams. As a newly formed team, our first task was to remove all our gear from our bags within 45 seconds and place it neatly on the wet pavement. Just as quickly, we were ordered to pack it all up again and run after our commanders to our rooms on the other side of the base. This was not an easy task while balancing three heavy, awkwardly shaped bags.

We spent the day in interviews with the commanders who would be carrying out our training over the next year. They had each made it through the unit's notoriously grueling 14-month training period, and all of them were committed to holding us to the highest of standards of discipline. When they re-entered the teams after their assignment ended, their life could literally depend on our competency.

That night, as I crawled into bed, exhausted from the emotional intensity of the day, I took a few moments to reflect. While the future was uncertain, I now had some confirmation that the work I had put in so far had amounted to something. I knew that the road that lay before me would be long, hard and filled with many obstacles, but at the very least, I was finally on it.

PART FOUR:
TRAINING BEGINS

CHAPTER 16: BASIC TRAINING

Pat Tillman, the late NFL free safety turned U.S. Army Ranger, wrote the following in his diary upon his decision to turn down a 3.6 million-dollar contract and join the military instead:

Somewhere inside, we hear a voice, and intuitively know the answer to any problem or situation we encounter. Our voice leads us in the direction of the person we wish to become, but it is up to us whether or not to follow. More times than not we are pointed in a predictable, straightforward, and seemingly positive direction. However, occasionally we are directed down a different path entirely. Not necessarily a bad path, but a more difficult one. In my case, a path that many will disagree with, and more significantly, one that may cause a great deal of inconvenience to those I love.

My inner voice, like the late Pat Tillman's, led me down a path that strained my relationships with the people I loved most. My decision to become a soldier caused me to lose touch with close friends as our paths diverged, and distance tugged at the bonds that had once seemed so tight as to be inseparable. But despite the emotional and physical challenges of the military, in my heart I felt that the path of service in the IDF was a calling that I could not ignore. During a typical day in training, I experienced more emotional swings than I experienced in a week of civilian life. My passion for Israel's defense is what led me to enlist, and that same passion kept me going during the hard times, of which there were many during basic training.

One of the many challenges I faced during that period was reconciling the dramatic shift in my relationship with time. In my old life, as a university student, I had weeks and sometimes months to meet deadlines for papers and tests. As soldiers in basic training, dozens of times each day, we succeeded or failed by milliseconds on a stopwatch. Each morning, our commanders woke us up by throwing a training grenade into the barracks. From the moment it hit the ground, we had only a few precious seconds to jump out of bed, sprint out of the room, and seek cover from the imaginary explosion. We then had five minutes to change into our uniforms and stand at attention. If we didn't succeed in those five minutes, we did it again, and again, and again, until we got it right. One day we changed into and out of our uniforms seven times in the span of forty minutes. Each day we were given dozens of tasks to complete in seemingly impossible periods of time to teach us to report on time, even if the assigned task wasn't completed.

Basic training also gave me a new appreciation for what it meant to work a full day. During my first real week in the army, I experienced exhaustion unlike any I had felt before in my life. In addition to the strain of being awake and physically active for eighteen hours, I was mentally exhausted from trying to communicate in a foreign language. One day, I was so tired that I fell asleep in the shooting range, ten feet from bullets exploding out of gun barrels. In lectures, everyone struggled to keep their eyes open. At times, I had to physically hold my eyelids open to avoid falling asleep. Our commanders ordered those of us who fell asleep to dip our heads in buckets of ice water they had prepared outside the classroom door. Slowly but surely, we began to adjust to the length and the difficulty of the days, while they simultaneously became harder and longer.

CHAPTER 17: I CAN'T BELIEVE THEY ARE GIVING US GUNS

Shortly after the start of basic training, we received our M-16s. From that day forward, our guns became, as our sergeant put it, like our clingy girlfriends: "If you go anywhere without them, you are in serious shit." We ran with our guns, ate with them, showered with them, and slept with them. One night, Shahar, one of the soldiers on my team, went to sleep curled up around his gun after a long day of training. In the morning, he awoke to discover that he was cradling only the strap and the butt of the gun—the rest of the gun had been disassembled and stolen by our sergeant while he slept. When we lined up for roll call later that morning, our sergeant feigned genuine confusion as to why Shahar was missing half of his gun, even though we all knew it was he who had taken it. For two hours that morning, cries of anguish rang from the supply closet where our sergeant and Shahar remained hidden from view behind the locked door. Though Shahar never told us exactly what happened, we all learned an important lesson: letting down our guard, even while we slept, would result in painful consequences.

The next week, we began shooting—first to get comfortable with the act of shooting, and eventually, to tune our guns so that the sights were in the right place, much like tuning a guitar. Eventually, we got scopes for our guns, which made them much more accurate and, of course, made us feel much cooler. A refractive red dot projected by the scope could be placed on the target, making for improved marksmanship. This also required adjusting, which took another set of trial shots. Finally, when our guns were "tuned," we began target shooting. The furthest distance between our shots in each round of firing was recorded to mark our progress; the smaller the number, the better our aim.

Interspersed between the shooting and our physical training were classroom lessons. We learned in great detail about the parts of the M-16, the physics of firing a weapon, the trajectory of a bullet, and the proper form for shooting, the latter of which took place outside the classroom. We practiced shooting during the day and at night, standing and crouching, and then dropping from the standing position to the ground and firing off multiple rounds. I was shocked by the power that could be generated by only six pounds of metal. It felt surreal to hold such incredible power in my hands, and I reflected on the responsibility that came with such power.

At times when we were shooting, I cleared my magazine before my friends. During those moments, I would watch the barrels of their guns as they fired. When I concentrated intently enough, I could make out the red-orange glow of the explosion that accompanied the thrust of the bullet as it left the barrel in its deadly spiraling flight towards the target. I felt the burst of pressure created by the force of the 5.70 mm round squeezing through a 5.56 mm barrel, exiting at a staggering 3,000 feet per second. At first, the sound of the bullet piercing the air jolts your entire body—it forces an involuntary twitch that consumes you for a split second as it passes through you like a train through a tunnel. But after a while, like everything else done repeatedly, shooting became routine. By the end of the first week of shooting, the whole team was firing at once, and the sound of other guns firing next to me no longer became distracting. It was simply background music set against my own furious symphony of metal, gunpowder, and smoke.

****

Throughout basic training, the drag of the seemingly senseless labor would weigh my spirits down. I missed my friends and family, whom I hadn't seen in nearly six months. My thoughts drifted often to the freedom and uninhibited indulgence that defined my old life. The end of my service, even of basic training, seemed incomprehensibly far away. It was hard to fathom that my tortured existence was not a fleeting moment in time, but my present and future reality. During breaks in our training, I stared often into the grey clouds that peppered the vast and uninhabited desert landscape of the Paratroopers training base and dreamed of better days. While I had expected the army to be physically challenging, I had not considered the emotional toll that training would take on me.

At times I felt despondent; at others, I marveled at the fact that I was actually living out a fantasy that began on my first trip to Israel. On one occasion, a few months into training, we were at the shooting range. I was standing on the firing line, my M-16 in hand, a magazine secured in the gun, waiting for the command to fire. As I lifted my eyes to the setting sun, I watched it hang for a few beautiful seconds like a picture on the wall of a gallery, suspended in its partial descent over the towering mountains of Southern Israel. With the evening settling in, I felt a shiver down my spine that I realized was more than just the breeze. I became awestruck by the realization that I was training to defend the Jewish people in the land of Israel. Having grown up on stories of the Holocaust, I was acutely aware that six million of my people had been wiped out because the army I had joined a few weeks earlier did not exist then to protect them. The pride I felt during moments like these transcends words.

As basic training progressed, we began what are known in the U.S. Military as ruck-marches or, in Israel, *masaote*. These marches are hikes done at the pace of a slow jog wearing a vest with six full magazines, two full water bottles, and our M-16s. All of the masaote ultimately led up to the 70-kilometer (~43-mile) march that we would complete to earn our red berets at the end of advanced training. Our first march was only five miles, and as with all our marches during training, it was carried out in silence. After the first hour, we took a break for water. As the allotted rest time drew to a close, our commander ordered us to our feet, cleared his throat, and began to speak. After over an hour of hearing only the soft whisper of the wind and the shifting of gear, accompanied by the occasional grunt, the sound of a human voice forming words seemed almost unnatural. He described our surroundings: the mountains, the houses of a nearby village, the trees. "This," he declared solemnly, "is our homeland; the land we fight to protect." He was quiet for several seconds after he spoke, and as I internalized his words, I felt deeply proud of my decision to draft. But there was little time for contentment; as quickly as our rest had begun, it ended. Two beeps rang out in quick succession from our commander's stopwatch, and with a single word, "*acharay*" (follow me), he began to march. In silence, we followed behind him.

CHAPTER 18: BEING A LONE SOLDIER

While my idealism was unquestionable, my Hebrew was unremarkable. Throughout basic training and beyond, my struggles with Hebrew got me into trouble. Often, I did not understand the commands and would be a few seconds late whenever the team began a task, as someone first had to explain to me what needed to be done. Twice during basic training, I lost my weekend privileges as a result of misunderstandings related to language. In the army's twisted application of language, this punishment is referred to as being "given Shabbat." In fact, Shabbat, designated by G-d as a day of rest, was being taken, not given. My officer was angered by what he interpreted to be my lack of commitment. In reality, I tried to show my commitment at every opportunity. Throughout training, I kept a small notepad with me in which I wrote down words that I heard throughout the day that I didn't understand. In our limited free time during meals and at night before bed, I would study those words to improve my Hebrew. I always returned to base on time on Sunday mornings, and once, when I received a five-day medical leave, I refused it and instead returned to base to resume training with my team. Aside from these occasional miscommunications, throughout basic training my commanders were incredibly understanding and helpful. In every classroom lesson, they made sure I had a translator who sat with me and helped me to understand the subject matter. When I had issues that needed attention, such as faulty phone bills or issues with my bank account, they helped me address them, and when they couldn't, directed me to someone who could help.

While all four of our commanders were significantly younger than I, all were incredibly qualified to train us, and served as great models for the soldiers we were striving to become. Despite their feigned heartlessness, time and again they showed their true colors by putting our needs before their own. Once, after spending twenty-eight straight days on base, my commander overheard me saying to a fellow soldier that I had no clean clothes left. Later that day, he pulled me aside, and without offering further explanation, told me to leave my dirty clothes outside the room that evening before we went to bed. The next day after breakfast, I came back to the barracks to find all my clothes sitting on my bed, washed and neatly folded. I would later find out that my commander, in an act of complete selflessness, had stayed up after his last meeting, cutting into his own sleep time, to wash and fold my clothing for me. It was one thing for our commanders to tell us to put our friends first: to take extra shifts under the stretcher and not wake them up for guard duty when they were especially tired. But what really drove home their message was that they didn't just talk; at every opportunity, they led by example.

Were language my only struggle, the transition to army life might have been easier. Unfortunately, there was also an undeniable gap that existed between my perspective and that of most of my teammates. The majority were 18 years old, and fresh out of high school. Some were 19 or 20, having completed a year of national service before drafting. All were used to following someone else's schedule and rules, either as high school students in their parents' homes or within the National Service Program. In contrast, I had spent the previous four years living away from home while attending university. While there, I had been encouraged to question assumptions and become independent. As a result, I had much more trouble than my fellow soldiers did adjusting to the harsh reality of army life, in which nearly every decision is made for you.

Making matters more difficult, while basic training is physically and mentally tough in every unit of the IDF, it was particularly hard for our company. In 2010, soldiers accepted into nearly every top unit of the military did their basic training embedded within infantry units. As soldiers in Duvdevan and Maglan, however, we did our basic training in a separate company from the Paratroopers infantry cadets. After basic and advanced infantry training, which are required of all combat soldiers, we would no longer be associated with the Paratroopers. As such, we were more like visitors than residents on the Paratroopers base; the rules of the base surrounding how much food we had to be given, how many hours we had to sleep, and most notably, what constituted acceptable punishments, were treated more like suggestions.

And so, four months after moving to Israel, and six months after spending nearly every night of the week drinking with my friends, I found myself in one of the most difficult, unforgiving basic training regiments in the IDF. I spent many nights during those first few months in the field flattening thorn bushes with my body, crawling up the sides of mountains, shivering through cold nights with insufficient clothing. All the while, I struggled to understand a language and a culture that I did not yet not fully grasp, making it difficult to connect with my teammates and commanders. Fortunately, my lone-soldier friends Rafi and Rudy from my pre-army training were in my company, and the three of us turned to each other throughout training for strength and support.

CHAPTER 19: FRAGS AND FAMILY

In our second month of basic training, we threw grenades for the first time, which are affectionately called frags in the U.S. Army. When you shoot a gun, provided you know what you are doing, you feel some degree of control over the chaos your bullets cause. That feeling of control is notably absent when you throw a grenade. If you are smart, the only thing you feel when you throw a grenade for the first time is fear.

After donning our defensive vests and helmets, our commanders instructed us to read aloud stories of various mishaps that had happened in the past while soldiers were learning to throw grenades. After they had succeeded in scaring the shit out of us, we were sent to a concrete bunker on the top of a nearby hill. There, we were met by our officer with a grin on his face and a grenade in his hand. We were given three practice throws to get familiar with the motion. Then, we counted to three, pulled the pin, and threw the grenade out of the bunker. It rolled down the hill, exploding four seconds later with a popping noise that seemed entirely too short and too quiet for the destruction we knew it could cause. A grenade has a kill radius of sixteen feet. Anyone within that range when the grenade detonates, that is not hiding behind a solid structure, will likely be dead. Anyone within a fifty-foot radius will sustain injuries. Yet, by the time we lifted our heads after the grenade had exploded, a small cloud of black smoke was the only evidence that anything was awry.

Shortly after I threw my grenade, I was pulled away from my team to check my gun into the armory for the week. My mother's parents had graciously flown the entire family to Israel in celebration of my grandfather's eightieth birthday, and my officer had equally as graciously given me a week off to see them.

After checking my gun into the armory, I returned to the field with my commander. At that point in our training, we were rarely left alone. I noticed a number of people halfway up a nearby mountain, moving slowly higher. I deduced that this was my team. "How did they get up there," I asked my commander. His response, "Guess," and the grin on his face were both solid hints that I would be spending the duration of the afternoon crawling up the side of that mountain. A mixture of sprinting and crawling, dictated by the whims of my commander, brought me to the top of that mountain an hour and a half later, where I rejoined my team.

At the top of the mountain, to give us a few minutes' rest, our commanders instructed our medics to give us a quick demonstration of how to stop the bleeding from a bullet wound. After the short respite, we were all brought back down to the base of the mountain so that we could once again crawl to the top. In my unit, as our commanders often told us, thorn bushes are not well-liked. Our instructions, as we crawled, were to crush all the thorn bushes in our way. Actually, not just the ones in our way. We were instructed to actively seek out thorn bushes for destruction. At one point, my commander told me to stand up, approach a thorn bush, and dive into it to make up for the first ascent, which I had missed. I approached the bush as though it was the edge of a diving board, clasped my hands together, and after letting loose a war cry, I completed a perfect swan dive into the bush. My team and my commanders, though the latter tried to hide it, both laughed at the ridiculousness of the situation. The adrenaline was surging, which meant that the stinging pain from the thorns that were now firmly entrenched in my hands, forearms and legs didn't hit me until I stood up at the top of the mountain. At that point, I reconsidered whether the optional swan dive I had performed was really a good judgment call.

By the time we got back to base that night, I was in significant pain from the dozens of thorns I had been unsuccessful in removing from my body. Rather than try to finish the job before bed, I spent my free hour packing my bag, full of anticipation for my departure the following morning for a one-week leave with my family. With little to do but daydream during long days and nights spent on base, I had meticulously played out the clip of my family's arrival at the airport during the previous weeks, and my greeting them there in uniform.

The next morning, I arrived at Ben Gurion airport several hours before their flight was scheduled to land. As I waited in the arrivals hall, I thought about all that I had experienced since I'd last seen my family—six months had felt like several years. People exited the security point in waves as their flights arrived. I saw dozens of happy reunions, running hugs and smiles, as I waited impatiently for my impending reunion with my own family. Finally, I recognized the towering figure of my younger brother, and a few short seconds later I found myself locked tightly in the arms of my mother and my two younger sisters who, upon seeing me, shrieked, abandoned their luggage, and ran towards me at a sprint.

As we stood there embracing, time seemed to stand still. All around us, new immigrants to Israel were entering the country for the first time as Israeli citizens. They were greeted by Nefesh B'Nefesh volunteers, who had come to meet them at the airport to welcome them home to Israel, as they had done for me six months earlier. Dressed in full uniform, hugging my mother, and with a sister hanging off each arm, I was overcome with pride and joy. It was the first time my family had seen me in person in my uniform, and the life I had been living since I drafted finally became real to them. No longer was my existence as a soldier just words on an internet blog and pictures on a computer screen. My uniform was real, and the cuts and thorns in my arms and legs were a tangible testament to the life I was living as a soldier in training for an elite combat unit. After everyone had gathered their luggage, eighteen of us boarded a minibus bound for Jerusalem.

Whether or not one is religious, there is no denying that there is a special feeling in the air of Jerusalem. It is palpable as one traverses 2,000-year-old streets and imagines what life might have been like at various periods throughout history in the very place that he or she is standing. For me, that magical feeling was intensified by the presence of my family. Sitting at the dinner table on that breezy Wednesday night in Jerusalem surrounded by my family, I was as happy as I had been since my arrival in Israel. Over the prior six months, 6,000 miles from everyone I loved, I realized, in a way I had never fully appreciated, just how special my family is.

The week with my family was full of incredible memories, and the quintessential beauty of Israel blended into each one. That first Friday night, we danced at the Western Wall with dozens of IDF soldiers to welcome in Shabbat. Later that week, we climbed Mount Masada, where we learned about the difficult choices made by Jews during the Roman revolt, whose two alternatives were enslavement or suicide. We floated in the Dead Sea (it's so salty you can't sink) and covered ourselves in mud. Then, as a family, we took the obligatory "covered-in-Dead Sea- mud-from-head-to-toe" photo. We ate delicious Israeli breakfasts in the hotel each morning, which I would later dream about in the army. I took my sisters, then 11 and 13, for ice cream each afternoon in what became our daily vacation ritual; I was amazed at how grown up they had become in six short months. My cousins, of or around the legal drinking age, and I spent a night out in Jerusalem. As the drinks flowed, we jokingly recounted old memories and made some new ones. My cousin Hillary and I had a nightly "thorn-removal ritual," in which she attempted with tweezers to remove the dozens of thorns still embedded in my arms and legs from the prior week. Hillary, now a pediatrician, to this day maintains that I am the first "child" she ever treated. We went on a moving tour of the Holocaust memorial that served as a powerful reminder to me of how important the IDF is in the protection of the Jewish people. We traveled to Ammunition Hill, where the Paratroopers suffered heavy losses in a fierce battle against Jordanian aggressors before ultimately liberating Jerusalem in the 1967 six-day war. My mother read aloud the plaque memorializing the story of Michael Levin, the Philadelphia-born IDF paratrooper who was killed in the 2006 Lebanon war. Michael's heroism inspired a generation of lone soldiers, myself included. Today, a resource and support center for lone soldiers bears his name.

At the end of the week, I brought my parents and brother to meet my commanders—connecting my real family and my army family. In one of the many incredible traditions of the IDF, the commanders of IDF combat soldiers pay house visits to every soldier under their command to introduce themselves to the soldier's parents. Since this would have been impossible for them to do for me with my parents living abroad, I decided to bring my parents to them. During hard times in the army, I thought back often to the incredible memories from that week with my family.

CHAPTER 20: THE MAKING OF A SOLDIER

The week I spent with my family was the best I'd had in six months. The one that followed was one of the most miserable of my service. *Shavua Sedauote* (The First Field Week) is one that every combat soldier, regardless of the unit in which he or she serves, remembers forever. It's the week during which you truly go from civilian to soldier. You learn what it means to be hungry, to be tired, and to be cold. During that week, my previously conceived notions of discomfort, including those from previous tryouts, were shattered.

I've come to learn that the IDF is guided by three core values: the defense of Israel and Jews worldwide, a strong sense of morality, and thriftiness. The condition of our bags was a testament to that third value. Most of them had busted hip straps, and the padding on the shoulder straps was nearly non-existent. We spent hours double-checking our gear to make sure everything was secure. This included tying every piece of equipment to our bags. On a real mission, anything we lost could betray our location to the enemy.

After we had put the final touches on our equipment, we assembled shortly before 9:00 a.m. for morning line up. We were given some brief words of motivation by our company commander, after which the flag was raised as we sang *"Hatikva,"* ("The Hope") Israel's national anthem. Though I'd sang Hatikva dozens if not hundreds of times before, I felt a surge of emotion as I sang the words for one of the first times while wearing an IDF uniform. I made note of the pride and the sense of commitment that I felt so strongly in that moment. I knew from friends who had drafted before me that the week to come would test every fiber of both.

In addition to our personal gear, we had hundreds of pounds of team gear to divide amongst us. Our journey began on Monday morning, just as the desert sun began to intensify. Each of us wore a helmet and a twenty-pound ammunition vest under our larger bags. The weight of the bag on my shoulders was staggering, and I wondered how I would make it through a day, let alone four days. After an hour of drilling, drenched in sweat from maneuvering in the morning sun, we exited the gates of the base and made our way into the field. We marched at a brisk pace, and shortly after noon, we reached the area where we would be building the company field headquarters later that evening. Once there, we were able to drop off the large bags we had been carrying until that point.

We were given twenty-five minutes to eat our lunch of field rations. In that time, we had to open all of our canned food using one semi-functional can opener, eat, and clean up after ourselves so not a trace was left. At all times, half the team guarded those eating in a 360-degree perimeter. For the rest of the week, before every meal, our field rations were placed on a hill above us. We were made to crawl as far as 800 feet uphill to reach our food, while still meeting the allotted time requirement. Those ranged from fifteen minutes to as few as seven. On the second night, unable to locate our dinner rations in the darkness in the time allotted, we ate what we had - three slices of white bread per person. This, of course, put only a tiny dent in the hunger that had amassed in the eight hours of drilling since we had last eaten.

Throughout that week, we remained in our ammunition vests with our guns over our shoulders at all times, even while sleeping. We were told of a group of soldiers who, eight years earlier in 2002, had done their first field week and had not been required to sleep in their gear. Two terrorists infiltrated the camp, shot the soldier on watch, and wounded many more soldiers before they were stopped. In Israel, unlike in other countries, the enemy is not across an ocean or even, in many cases, across a border. As a result, soldiers only a month into basic training must be trusted to guard their friends and commanders with loaded weapons as the last line of defense. As a point of perspective, an American Marine goes through three months of basic training, four months of infantry school, and six months of pre-deployment training before they are put into combat situations. Israeli soldiers, as a consequence of the size of the military and their proximity to danger, do not have that luxury.

Between guard duty and the staggering cold that woke us up intermittently, sleep that week was difficult, despite our exhaustion. Each night, we were given twenty-five minutes to dig foxholes in which to sleep. After the allotted time had passed, just when we expected we would be going to sleep, we would inevitably be told to put on our backpacks and assemble in formation behind our commanders. As we marched in silence through the cold desert night, the weight of the bag was initially preoccupying. Gradually my arms would grow numb as the straps choked off my circulation, which was a welcomed sensation given the severity of the initial pain.

Intermittently during these hikes, our commander would give the signal for "360 degrees." This required us to set up a defensive perimeter with each soldier lying down facing outward, thereby simulating the protection of an injured soldier awaiting aerial extraction. At one point during that week, I unknowingly dropped down directly on top of a red ant colony. One of the bites ultimately became infected, and to this day I have a scar that was left by an overly excited doctor who removed it with a scalpel. As we lay there, forbidden to sleep and consumed by our hunger and the cold, at times for as long as an hour, my thoughts drifted to my old life. To Friday night dinners with my family. To my days at Tel Aviv University. To Tuesday nights at Smokey Joes' and fraternity and sorority formals. To summer camp and old romances. I thought about how much I missed little things that I had taken for granted, like riding my bike to work in center city Philadelphia with the cool spring breeze blowing against my face. The simple ability to choose my own schedule was gone. To go to the gym if I wanted. To walk to the art museum. To grab a burger with a friend. The realization of just how little control I had over my life unsettled me. I thought about my family and my friends, and what they might be doing at exactly that moment. They felt incredibly far away as I lay there, the weight of the poorly constructed bag on my back distributed solely on my right shoulder. Despite the immense discomfort, I was too exhausted to do anything about it. Throughout that week, I reached states of mental and physical exhaustion that I never imagined I could endure.

Interspersed between the drills and the crawling were lessons. We learned basic navigation techniques, patrol formations and how to determine which direction was north using only a shadow and the time. One of the most difficult challenges of the week was climbing Hill 402, a Paratrooper tradition. At 7:00 p.m. on Tuesday evening, our sergeant ordered us to arrange ourselves in a straight line facing the giant hill before us, whose incline was so severe we had to strain our necks to see the top. He asked us nonchalantly if we loved each other, to which we all responded with the obligatory, "Yes, Sergeant". Having expended his small budget of humor for the day, he got down to business. "Good. Assume the crawling position and follow me," he barked. The first two minutes were fun. The adrenaline was surging, and we all crawled and sang together. And then the enormity of our task set in, as each man summoned the strength he needed to get himself up the mountain. The cold compounded the difficulty of our task. Those who have experienced it will swear that the cold of a desert night is a living, breathing thing. It chipped away at my strength and confidence and began to plant dangerous seeds of self-doubt: with a full year until the end of our training, was the pain worth it? Did I have what it took to make it to the end?

As we ascended, the rocks and thorns began to tear at our flesh. The mood was somber. But for the sound of sliding rocks, and the occasional grunt, the night was silent; each man was lost in his thoughts, searching for the motivation to push himself forward; in basic training, the end is too far away to be comforting – you survive drill to drill, hour to hour, minute to minute.

I sustained a knee injury during basic training, which had worsened severely during that week. While it would be easy to say that my knee injury was the reason I arrived five minutes after everyone else, after an hour of crawling up the rocky mountain face, it wasn't. The real reason was that after an hour of crawling up a hill that seemed endless, I felt defeated. I had barely slept or eaten in several days. Thirty-six hours earlier I was enjoying the love of my family, and a luxurious vacation lifestyle. I had not yet flipped the mental switch back to the reality of cold, emotionless army life.

Fifteen feet from the top of the hill, our sergeant ordered everyone on the team to join me for the last strip. When I reached the peak, he walked backward another ten feet and ordered me to crawl to him. And so the game went on. Each time I approached where he was standing, he would move further back. At that point, my frustration, the cold and the pain shooting through my knee all came together, and I felt a single teardrop run down my face. It might have been from pain or from bewilderment, but most likely, it was from frustration. I rarely displayed emotion in public, and until that point had never shed a tear in the army.

When I close my eyes today, years later, I can still remember how I felt at the top of that hill. I've been asked many times if I ever thought about quitting during training. The truth is that I did not. Being accepted into the special forces took rigorous training, years of studying Hebrew and overcoming bureaucratic hurdles. I never allowed myself to entertain the idea of quitting simply because the training was hard. At times, I doubted my ability to succeed in the unit. At points, I felt sad, despondent, and angry, but quitting was never an option. The only remaining choice was to persevere. At the top of that mountain, neither Zionism nor a sense of purpose was fueling me. I was cold, bruised and frustrated. The only thing driving me at that moment was my desire to complete the drill. I surged forward with all my strength to the spot where my sergeant was standing, and quickly rose to my feet before he could continue moving backward. At long last, the hill had been conquered, and it was dinnertime.

As a reward for our efforts, we were given a generous thirty minutes to eat our field rations. Shortly thereafter we began a navigational exercise. An hour into the exercise, our commander announced a new drill that would begin immediately; an I.E.D. had exploded and two soldiers from our team had been wounded. Since we were only carrying one stretcher, I picked up the second wounded soldier and put him on my back. After carrying him for a few minutes, it was clear that I would not be able to move fast enough to keep up with the pace that our commander was setting. With the help of two others, we put him in the "jeep" position, in which the injured soldier is suspended by three of his fellow soldiers somewhat resembling the shape of a jeep. With one "injured" soldier on the stretcher and the other in the jeep position, our commander led us up and down an incredibly steep hill, which was covered in rocks that made gaining traction impossible. Our pace was not fast enough, and we spoke in frustrated whispers to one another against orders. As punishment, we were made to ascend and descend the hill again and again. We rotated under the stretcher and under the jeep, but given the growing number of soldiers on the team who were forbidden from carrying weights due to injuries, the respites were few and far between. After each step, I wondered where I would find the strength to take the next one. The weight of the stretcher was crushing, and my shoulders were throbbing. Despite the physical pain it was causing, that drill struck a chord with me. Soldiers get injured in combat, and instant evacuation is not always an option. I motivated myself with the fantasy that my friend on that stretcher really was injured, and I pushed forward through the discomfort and the pain. We dropped the stretcher several times, and it was by sheer luck that we made it through the drill without causing any serious injuries.

The winter of 2010 in Israel was unseasonably cold, and the temperature in the Negev desert routinely dropped down into the forties Fahrenheit at night. On Wednesday night, I took the team's twenty-liter jerrycan in my bag. The cold desert wind whipped against our exposed skin and through the buttons of our insufficiently insulated uniforms. As we walked, our bags pulled against our shoulders, packed to the brim with gear, food, and water. As soon as we fell to the ground, as we did every so often to set up a perimeter around an imaginary injured soldier, within a few short minutes our heart rates fell, and our wet bodies became conductors for the cold breeze that sings its chilling tune through the seemingly endless desert nights.

Not long after we began that night's march, the jerrycan I was carrying began to leak. Each time we dropped to the ground, water would soak my legs and back. When I served, IDF uniforms were 100 percent cotton. As every outdoor enthusiast will tell you, cotton is completely useless as an insulator once it becomes wet.

Each time our pace slowed, my muscles began to tense, and before long my entire body was shaking. I grew increasingly tired, as we marched on in silence, and the line between reality and imagination began to blur. Gradually, I became unsure of whether I was awake or asleep, trapped in an inescapable nightmare. As we approached the hill where we had dug our holes hours earlier, our sergeant spun on his heels, halting our progress, and hurled a green stick light into the air. I still remember the way it glided through the pitch-black desert night. It reminded me of a planet rotating through space; a small glowing light suspended in a sea of blackness. I remember thinking in my state of delirium that we, too, were small bits of warmth and light, surrounded completely by blackness.

Before I could process what was happening, my legs were moving, and I was running with my team towards the place where the stick light had fallen. As soon as we arrived, we attempted to organize all our gear on blankets and arrange ourselves in groups of three. Not surprisingly, we failed at finishing in the unreasonably short amount of time we had been given.

Each time we failed to complete the task to standard in the allotted time, our sergeant shook his head angrily, retrieved the stick light, and hurled it again into the darkness. Our hearts sank with the dim green light as it fell towards the ground. When it landed, he would yell a single word that pierced the silent desert night like a dagger: "Again". By the fourth or fifth time, I was still shaking and beginning to feel confused about where I was. In my state of quasi-dementia, I believed that to ask for help would be a sign of weakness. Fortunately, one of my teammates noticed that something was off and told our commander, who forced me to run sprints to raise my body temperature. When my confusion faded sufficiently and I exhibited signs of increased cognition, indicating to him that I was no longer in immediate danger of hypothermia, he sent me to rejoin the team.

We continued to chase the green stick light across the desert until our sergeant, either out of boredom or malice, ordered every other person to fall injured. Those who were not selected were told to lift their friends onto their backs and to carry them up the hill that lay in front of us. The terrain was so unstable and the slope so steep that I would not have walked up it alone during the day, let alone with a friend slung over my shoulders at night— that is, if I had any choice in the matter. Many of us slipped and fell as our sergeant continued his ascent up the hill, urging us to quicken our pace and reach him. At the top, he told us that we hadn't moved quickly enough. As punishment, we had to repeat the exercise. After the second trip up and back down the hill, we were finally brought back to where we had dug our holes and given the order to go to sleep. It was 3:30 in the morning. We had been awake and drilling for twenty-six hours.

Less than an hour later, I was jolted awake by a stabbing pain in my right shoulder. As I struggled to find a position that would mitigate the pain, I began to shake uncontrollably from the cold. My teammate Liron, with whom I was sharing a foxhole, immediately removed his own blanket and placed it over mine as an added layer of warmth. As time passed and my shaking did not subside, Liron woke friends sleeping in nearby foxholes, who put blanket after blanket on top of me while attempting to summon our officer over the forty-year-old radio. For the first half-hour, they did not succeed in reaching anyone. Only weeks into training, with no concept of where we were, and surrounded by unforgiving desert, I began to think that I might die in that foxhole. Finally, forty-five minutes after Liron had first called for help over the radio, and fifteen minutes after he had contacted our commanders, our officer arrived at our location, accompanied by a medic who whisked me to the medics' tent. The prognosis was mild hypothermia. When I awoke the next morning, I tried to rejoin my team. After several hours of drilling, the heat picked up, my pace slowed down, and my head began to throb. Eventually, it became clear that remaining with my team was ill-advised. Joined by several other soldiers with varying ailments and injuries, I was taken back to base to be seen by the doctor. A few hours later, I was sent home to Tel Aviv with a fever that ran well over a hundred degrees. Before I left base, I caught a glimpse of myself in a bathroom window and was stunned by the sight of the figure staring back at me—it was the first time I'd seen myself since the week began. My eyes were sunken and darkened, and I had the look on my face of a man who had seen a ghost. Of the soldiers on my team who began that field week on Sunday, more than half were pulled out early due to injuries, sickness, and minor cases of frostbite and hypothermia.

CHAPTER 21: TEAR GAS

Weeks turned to months and basic training progressed. To the extent it was possible, we began to adjust to the rhythm of army life. To reach our final combat-ready profile of 07 at the conclusion of advanced training, there were several boxes we had to tick along the way. One of those was the infamous experience of being tear-gassed.

My training in the IDF brought many first time experiences. Some of those experiences were positive, but many more were not. Getting tear-gassed undoubtedly fell into the latter category. Similar to the requirement that police officers in the U.S. be tasered during training as preparation for being allowed to use a taser, so too are IDF infantry soldiers required to be tear-gassed before they are cleared to use it.

The day began like any other day in basic training. We were awakened by the sound of a training grenade rattling across the barrack floor, at which point we had five seconds to get out of our beds, sprint out of the barracks, and throw ourselves to the ground. After several uneventful hours, we were brought into the classroom for a lesson about non-conventional weapons. A murmur rose in the room as the lesson progressed; we all began to wonder silently, and then out loud if today would be the infamous day. When the lesson ended, our sergeant looked at us, smiled an evil smile, and barked the words we had feared but expected for some time: "Two minutes. Downstairs... with gas masks on."

I had mixed feelings. On the one hand, it is cool to tell people that you have been tear-gassed. On the other hand, I firmly believed before, and even more so after, that actually getting tear-gassed sucks—a lot. As soon as we reported to our sergeant with our gas masks strapped onto our faces, the suffering began. Without any added stress, wearing a gas mask is itself a very uncomfortable experience; the straps must be pulled extremely tight for the mask to do its job. Breathing through it is akin to the experience of trying to breathe through a straw. If one is standing still, it is not a big problem. Unfortunately for us, as soldiers in basic training, we were never at rest.

After everyone had secured their gas mask, our commanders began running us back and forth. They eventually brought us to a nearby field where we continued sprinting as well as changing between various shooting positions in rapid succession. As anyone who has ever gotten knocked down by a wave knows, the feeling of needing air and not being able to get it is terrifying. What began with shortness of breath gradually turned into dizziness. When I started swerving, my commander ordered me to remove my mask. Though I hadn't been nauseous, the return of oxygen into my lungs was quickly accompanied by dry heaving and, ultimately, the departure of my breakfast. As I looked around, I took solace in the fact that I was not alone. When our commanders were satisfied that we had suffered sufficiently, we lined up to hear an officer speak about exactly what we would be expected to do while inside the tear gas tent. After giving her instructions to the group, she pulled aside those of us with beards and told us that we couldn't participate, as the mask wouldn't grip our faces well enough to prevent the gas from entering. We begged her to reconsider, not wanting to be left out of this horrible but memorable experience, and ultimately, she allowed us to perform a test to check the effectiveness of the mask. The idea was simple: After putting on the mask, you rub banana-scented oil on your neck. If you can smell the oil, the mask is not working. I failed this test, as did everyone else with a beard, but we decided we were going anyway. While our commanders couldn't say it outright, it was clear to all of us that we were expected to participate, whether our masks would protect us from the gas or not.

On the signal of the officer who had addressed us earlier, three soldiers would enter the tent at once with their masks already secured on their faces. Inside the tent were two commanders wearing full unconventional weapons suits standing beside a canister dispensing a steady stream of tear gas, accompanied by a sinister hissing sound. All three soldiers were ordered to begin performing aerobic exercises. After twenty to thirty seconds, the commanders gave the first soldier in line the signal to remove his mask while the other two soldiers continued to exercise. They demanded various tasks from the immediately shocked and un-coordinated soldier, ranging from giving his army ID number forwards and backwards to singing a song. Prior to removing the mask, assuming the mask is working properly, one is not meant to experience the effects of the gas; only the exhaustion of exercising while wearing a gas mask.

I entered the tent second in line. Within a few seconds of entering, I started to feel the effects of the gas because the mask, as predicted, did not work. We all began to do jumping jacks, which I was able to do for about ten or fifteen seconds, at which point I started to hyperventilate. Each time I inhaled I was breathing in tear gas and my body was both surprised and upset. Soon I was forced to stop exercising altogether and focus all my energy on staying on my feet. I had to wait another fifteen seconds until my friend, who was first in line, finished his exercises and then another twenty seconds until he finished his song, at which point I was given the signal to remove my mask. For most people, the removal of the mask was the beginning of their exposure to the tear gas. In my case, the removal of the mask simply exacerbated an already painful situation. Forty seconds in, all I could focus on was the blaring pain in my chest, the stinging in my eyes, and my seeming inability to draw oxygen into my lungs despite my heavy breathing. I still remember the terrifying feeling of taking a breath and feeling more out of breath than I was before I inhaled.

My commander demanded that I sing a song, so I sang the first thing that came to mind: the national anthem of the country whose army I had elected to join—by whom I was now voluntarily being tear-gassed. I made it through four words before falling to my knees. I drew a breath for the next verse but found the substance I was inhaling impossible to utilize for purposes of breathing. As panic overcame me, though my mind shut off, my body sprang into action. Apparently, I somehow crawled out of the tent. When I eventually came to my senses, I found myself curled up in the fetal position around one of the tent posts. I tried to regain my breath well enough to stand up. With the help of a friend, I rose to my feet, incredibly grateful to be breathing in normal air.

We left the experience acutely aware of the pain that tear gas can cause and, therefore I believe, much more qualified to use it. While I didn't know it then, tear gas would one day save me from severe injury, if not death.

CHAPTER 22: THE PARATROOPER'S OATH

Another (far more enjoyable) rite of passage during Paratrooper basic training was being sworn in at the Western Wall. After weeks of drilling and watching our commanders and officers get yelled at by the base's sergeant major—a nice change of pace from them yelling at us—the day of the ceremony finally arrived. As we completed our final practice run that morning, a videographer went around and asked each of us to say a few words. Those clips would be played later that day on a massive screen as the thousands of friends and family members who would be coming to see us streamed into the Western Wall plaza. Everyone rambled off quick sentences in Hebrew. When the camera turned to me, I said the first thing that came to mind: "Hi, Mom!"

The ride to Jerusalem would take a little under three hours. Though it was only 8:30 when we pulled out of the gates of our base that morning, we had already been awake for several hours cleaning our living quarters, as we did before every weekend leave. In a rare display of mercy, our commanders allowed us to catch up on some much-needed sleep during the ride.

We arrived in Jerusalem several hours before the ceremony began, so our officer took the opportunity to walk us around the Old City, explaining the religious and political significance of the city from a viewpoint east of the Western Wall. We walked the route taken by the Paratroopers to the Western Wall during the 1967 war, which they traversed under heavy fire from the Jordanians. As we walked the final stretch of the route they had taken in mandatory silence, I tried to imagine what it would have been like to be part of that moment: the fear, the sense of purpose that must have surged through those soldiers as they fought to take back the most important site in Judaism. At one point during that silent journey, we listened to one of the most riveting recordings in modern Israeli history: that of the IDF military frequency during the battle of Jerusalem. We listened in awe to the sounds of gunfire and the shouting of officers giving commands under extreme duress. Most notably, we heard the radio transmission of Colonel Motta Gur, commander of the 55th Paratrooper brigade, who would ultimately liberate the Old City and the Western Wall: "All company commanders, we're sitting right now on the ridge and we're seeing the Old City. Shortly we're going to go into the Old City of Jerusalem, that all generations have dreamed about. We will be the first to enter the Old City. Eitan's tanks will advance on the left and will enter the Lion's Gate. The final rendezvous will be on the open square above." Finally, after a lot of shouting and gunshots, we heard Gur's famous words: "The Temple Mount is in our hands! I repeat, the Temple Mount is in our hands!"

The power of his words, made even more awe-inspiring by the sounds of gunfire in the background, moved all of us, religious and secular alike. I imagined how I might have felt hearing those words over the radio during a battle that had such incredible significance for Israel and the Jewish people.

Finally, we arrived at the Western Wall tunnel and began to line up for the ceremony. Our company would be the last to march out of the tunnel onto the promenade, which meant that we were in the back of the line, affording us a great view of the madness unfolding before us. While Paratroopers are renowned for being the first into battle, conjuring up images of professionalism and composure, you would not have known that from the scene that unfolded in the tunnels in the hours before the ceremony. Soldiers put one another up on their shoulders as they formed spontaneous dance circles, shouted the words to popular soccer chants, and unleashed general mayhem, all while their commanders looked on with subdued smiles. Everyone was filled with joy, excited to have reached this milestone and for the impending weekend off base.

This outward showing of joy was, of course, completely absent from our company. Before we had even arrived at the tunnel, our commanders threatened that if we sang so much as a single lyric, we would live to regret it. "We are the Special Forces," they explained matter-of-factly. "We hold ourselves to the highest standards." So while our friends danced, we stood at attention. Our sergeant eventually entertained himself by forcing us to practice the maneuvers that we would be carrying out during the ceremony with our guns, except that our guns were already in place on the promenade, so we pretended to be holding guns. And then, to the hilarity of the other commanders, we got reprimanded when the occasional imaginary gun strap touched the ground, which was obviously impossible, and completely at our sergeant's discretion.

A few hours later, before the ceremony began, an intimate reception was held in English for lone soldiers and their families. As I sat next to my mother, who had come from America for the long weekend to watch me be sworn in, we were addressed by a lieutenant colonel in the Paratroopers. He commended us on our commitment to Israel's defense and the sacrifice we had made in leaving our home countries to serve in the IDF. We were also addressed by Tzvika Levi, affectionately known as the father of Israel's lone soldiers due to his tremendous work in raising awareness and money for those without family in the country who serve in the IDF.

The Paratrooper's motto is "After me!" and more than one of our high-ranking speakers that night reminded us that when Israel found itself in trouble in the past, it was the Paratroopers that led the charge into battle. They reminded us of our duty to carry on that legacy with honor. In a ceremonious fashion, we received our guns from our officer, rendered salutes, and fell back into formation. A high-ranking officer read aloud the pledge that every IDF combat soldier must swear to uphold. Six hundred soldiers' voices rang out as one, and the words "*Ani neeshbah*" (I swear) echoed through the walls of the Old City. With that, the ceremony was concluded, and we left with our families for a long weekend, this time—and for the first time in our service—with our guns.

Before going off to search for my mother, my friend Rafi and I fought through the crowd to the promenade immediately in front of the Western Wall. Though we had both been to the Western Wall dozens of times, it felt different after being sworn in as Paratroopers. We approached it with awe, as if for the first time. As we stood with our faces and hands pressed against the cold stone of one of the holiest sites in Judaism, berets upon our heads and guns at our sides, I was overwhelmed by emotion. Since my first trip to Israel when I was sixteen, I was enthralled by the sight of Paratroopers at the Western Wall, where they fought the historic battle to retake Jerusalem. To become a part of that history was not only a tremendous honor but the fulfillment of a teenage dream. That night my Mom and I celebrated the milestone with delicious food and a few bottles of wine, which marked the start of an amazing weekend spent enjoying each other's company.

When I returned to base on Sunday, training picked up right where it had left off. The celebrations of the previous week were quickly forgotten as our misery resumed. When we weren't on kitchen duty or drilling, our time was occupied by other things, most notably by punishments, which were often harder than the planned workouts. In one instance, we were given 90 seconds to run from our barracks up a hill to a distant wall and back. We began at 6:00 a.m. and didn't succeed until 7:30 a.m. The cause of these punishing sprints was a single, seemingly tiny, mistake: we were 1.8 seconds late for our commander during morning formation. In a highly specialized counter-terror unit, timing is essential. The terrorist will not wait the extra two seconds for soldiers to arrive before he bolts out the back door. It was not a punishment devoid of reason. But the legitimacy of the punishment did not decrease the strain on our legs and our lungs.

CHAPTER 23: JUMP SCHOOL

One of the most exciting experiences in basic training was attending the IDF's Airborne School, widely known as Jump School. Special forces units within the Paratroopers attend Jump School a mere three months into basic training, a recognition by the army and our commanders of our (supposed) maturity. During the first week, we were taught how to jump out of planes, and, more importantly, how to land. During the second week, we put theory to practice with our lives quite literally hanging in the balance. When we started Jump School, my fears were mostly centered around jumping out of a plane. By the end of the week, after learning about all the potential problems that can arise and the speed at which you hit the ground, I was significantly more afraid of the landing.

The lessons themselves were relatively fun, which by basic training standards meant any activity that was not pure suffering. We spent the first day with Ofik, our 20-year-old instructor, in a giant sandpit. There, he taught us the first lesson of the course: how to roll after hitting the ground at fifteen feet per second to avoid breaking one's bones. Though the importance of what we were learning was obvious to us, that session marked the first time in our service that we found ourselves away from the watchful eyes of our commanders. Instead of rising to the occasion, we took the opportunity to lower our disciplinary standards. Understandably, this did not make Ofik very happy. Though Ofik's intentions were good, and his frustration with our behavior legitimate, we were agitated by his attempts to discipline us. Each night as we walked to our tents, we passed Ofik's living quarters. The music and laughter we heard coming from the coed parties we could see as we walked by served as a reminder of the irritating contrast between our lives and his. Despite this tension, we were there to learn how to jump out of airplanes, and Ofik was there to teach us, so occasionally we listened to him. We practiced our rolls for hours on end. We started from the ground, but ultimately moved to a three-foot and eventually five-foot platform, the latter of which was quite unpleasant. Even more unpleasant was the next progression in our training, the zip line. This exercise requires an ill-fated participant to climb up to a twelve-foot platform and descend towards the ground on a bar suspended from a zip line. On the instructor's command, admittedly to the delight of those watching, the unlucky participant releases the bar and attempts, almost always unsuccessfully, to execute a proper roll. Each time Ofik gave the command to drop, the anticipatory silence would be abruptly shattered by the crack of the bar snapping back up to the cable and the grunt of a teammate as he collided ungracefully with the ground. Inevitably, he would lie on the ground in a disheveled heap for several seconds before climbing painfully back to his feet.

In the final station meant to prepare us for our jumps, we hiked up a sixty-foot tower, strapped into harnesses, and one after the other jumped out of a mock plane door. After fifteen feet of free fall, the bungee we were harnessed into snapped us back up. Momentum then carried us down the length of the 150-foot zip line leading to a patch of sand on which we were meant to execute a landing roll. When I first looked out the door, I told myself that it would be just like a ride at Disney World, which is how I got myself to jump. Unfortunately, this mentality led me to act as though I was indeed on a ride at Disney World. The prescribed course of action was to jump out the door, count to three, check the imaginary primary chute, drop the kit bag holding one's gear and gun, and pull the release on the secondary parachute to simulate a main-chute malfunction. Instead, I jumped out the door, yelled "Oh, shit!" and let out a string of woo-hoos as I soared toward the patch of sand that was designated as the landing strip. This did not go over very well with the head instructor who called me over on the megaphone and told me, ironically, that I was not at Disney World.

The following week, which in Israel begins on Sunday, we arrived at Jump School full of anticipation. Our first jump was scheduled for Monday, and we were a healthy mixture of excited and scared. After lunch on the day of our first jump, we were called to attention by our commanders and told we had thirty minutes to talk on the phone, which was unusual at that point in our training. For me, it solidified the danger of what we were about to do.

After speaking to our loved ones, we met Ofik, who took us to pick up the bags containing our main and reserve parachutes. I held each with the delicacy of a newborn baby. I was terrified that I might do something to unravel the parachute that would be my lifeline as I jumped out of a moving airplane 1,200 feet above the ground. When we arrived at the airfield, we were arranged into two rows according to the side of the plane from which we would be jumping. Ofik provided a final review of what to do in the face of the various mishaps that might occur. This included tangles in the straps, the main parachute failing to deploy, becoming tangled with another paratrooper mid-air, holes in the parachute, or a partial deployment of the main chute. We then fastened our harnesses, attached our reserve parachutes, secured our helmets, and stood to be checked by an instructor. When everything had been verified, we were seated on the tarmac where we awaited the arrival of the Hercules flight that would be our means of transport into the sky.

You hear it long before you see it. The roar of the four-engine turboprop military transport C-130 aircraft is unmistakable. It shakes the ground and sends shockwaves through the air. Despite our earplugs, the sound was deafening. When the plane finally screeched to a halt in front of us with the engines still running, one of the instructors motioned for us to fall into two lines and begin boarding. As instructed during training, from this point forward we kept a hand on our reserve parachute at all times to ensure it didn't become tangled or in any way compromised; it was truly our last resort. Sixty Paratroopers were crammed into each aircraft, thirty on each side. With all sixty soldiers on board and seated, the plane began its loud, laborious, and terrifying journey towards the runway.

We completed five jumps. Each time, as the plane took off, someone spontaneously began reciting the words of the traveler's prayer, practically screaming over the roar of the engines in order to be heard. Each time, at the prayer's conclusion, the voices of all sixty paratroopers, religious and secular alike, sounded in unison as all shouted "amen." It was a very powerful reminder that although most soldiers in the IDF are not religious, as the famous quote goes, there are no atheists in hospitals or foxholes. They should add C-130's to that list.

When we reached an altitude of 600 feet, we removed our seatbelts. As practiced, thirty paratroopers rose from their seats and stood in line, fifteen beside each door, awaiting the go signal, which would be a green light directly over the door. When the green light went on over the jump zone at 1,200 feet, (for context, that is approximately the height of the old World Trade Center) the instructors quite literally threw us out of the plane at a rate of about one paratrooper per second. As we were standing in line before the light came on, I attempted to distract myself from what I was about to do. Since distraction proved impossible, I sang *Hatikva* in my head, Israel's national anthem, to remind myself of why I was about to do it.

After all the preparation, anticipation and fear, suddenly it happens.

The soldier in front of you jumps, and before you can blink you are falling towards the earth. The first few seconds of that first jump were among the most spectacular of my life; I felt removed from my body, as though I was watching myself from above in a silent film. The deafening roar of the C-130s engines was erased, immediately replaced by a heavy silence. The complete disappearance of sound combined with the weightless sensation of freefalling seemed to halt time. The trees that dotted the coastal strip below me looked like toy Legos, and the entirely foreign sensation of the sky being both above and below me left me breathless as I squinted into the waning rays of the setting sun.

And then, as suddenly as the world had seemed to stand still, it once again began to move as I was jolted back to reality by the sensation of my parachute deploying, which halted my free fall and slowed my speed to fifteen feet per second. The world once again had sound, and I was back inside my body, checking the straps and making sure all was in order. The entire experience felt surreal until I was 100 feet from the ground, which was approximately when I remembered that I was about to make a hard landing. Instantly, the bewilderment and excitement of the first half of the jump were replaced by anxiety. I tightened my legs together, bent my knees, clenched my elbows to my helmet, and prayed like hell for an easy landing. After landing safely, I remained motionless right where I had landed, staring up at the evening sky as I internalized the fact that I had just jumped out of a perfectly good airplane. I probably lay there for a bit too long, as a concerned medic approached me and asked if I was okay. I remained there, sprawled out like a snow angel, and told him that I was fine—just happy to be alive. He chuckled and walked away to search for soldiers with real injuries.

We did our final three jumps that week with our ammunition vests and guns, which were secured in a bag that was tied to each Paratrooper's leg. Jumping out of an airplane with gear is significantly more stressful; if you don't drop your bag in time, you are nearly certain to break one or more bones when you hit the ground. While I would not describe any of my landings as "soft," I successfully graduated Jump School without a concussion or any broken bones, which as far as I was concerned was a victory. The bruises would heal.

The week ended with a ceremony during which we received our Jump Wings. When it was over, with Friday morning only a few hours away, I finally allowed myself to get excited about our impending weekend liberty. I had spent the prior two weeks planning, in every free second, what I would do with my 48-hour leave. Unfortunately for me, my weekend liberty was not to be. That evening, I was called into a dark room and found myself sitting across the table from my solemn commander. He informed me that, as a punishment for several small infractions, including failing to proactively report one evening that I hadn't brushed my teeth, I would be "given Shabbat." That meant I would be spending the weekend on base. Anyone who has experienced this can attest to the fact that it's very much like showing up to the airport in December to depart on a vacation to a tropical location, only to be told the flight has been canceled and will not be rescheduled. It was nothing short of devastating.

Shortly after I got the news, we boarded buses and departed Jump School bound for our base. The bus was abuzz with talk of weekend plans, dates, and gatherings with friends. As I sat there quietly looking out the window, I was brought back in time to a moment six months earlier. I had been sitting on a similar bus looking out a similar window at Israel's breathtaking landscapes, wondering what it would be like to look out those windows as a soldier. That bus had brought me from Tel Aviv to the kibbutz where I spent the months before my service preparing for the military. I thought back to all I had experienced in the past four months and how dramatically my sense of time and my way of thinking had been altered by the military. I thought, too, of how much of my service was still in front of me, and more immediately, how much longer I would now be on base before a weekend leave. As a soldier in basic training who had been taught to count milliseconds on a stopwatch, the idea of spending another twelve days on base without going home was unimaginably difficult.

Closing Shabbat is not difficult because of what you have to do on base. It's not about the mandatory three meals a day you have to attend when you'd rather be sleeping, or the fact that you have to wear your uniform for most of the weekend. It's what you can't do because you're on base. It's the laughs you don't get to share with friends. It's the home-cooked meal you don't get to eat. It's the girl who will be dancing with someone else on Saturday night. It's the freedom to forget, even if only for forty-eight hours, that you belong to the army; that your life is centered around preparing for war. The freedom to remember what it once felt like to be in control of your own life. To sleep in a bed instead of in the barracks or on the ground. To be able to speak freely with your family and friends without wondering who is listening to your conversation. When I hung up my uniform on weekends and took apart my gun, for forty-eight hours I could forget about the army and dream. I could dream of my old life, of the comforts of home and my family, of the freedom to make my own schedule and my own choices. But on base, there was no forgetting.

During the hard times, of which there were many, I did my best to stay focused by searching for inspiration wherever I could find it. I learned to capture beauty in a few fleeting moments and use it to sustain me for minutes, hours, and sometimes days. The sight of the F-16 streaking across the sky as the flag of Israel waved in the foreground during a hard week of field training. The pink hue of the evening sky as the sun retreated over the desert landscape on its way towards the Mediterranean. A simple "thank you" from a stranger returning from temple as I stood on guard duty in Hebron on a six-hour shift, wearing a heavy bulletproof vest on a hot Saturday morning. During those moments, my spirits soared, despite the weight of army life threatening to hold them down. As the days got longer and harder, I continued to hold on to moments like those to get me through training.

Tsevet Avi after a 27 KM march

Getting ready for a weekend off base during basic training

The Feldman family at the Western Wall, Winter 2011

With my mom at my
swearing-in ceremony

Guarding a closet during
basic training

Taken after Yevesheem with gas masks,
my all-time least favorite activity

On our way back to base
during basic training

Rafi and me "enjoying" a meal on base

Getting ready for our third jump at the IDF's
Parachuting school

Rudy and me after the Duvdevan tryouts

CHAPTER 24: A BEAUTIFUL PRISON

As I entered my fourth month of basic training, several important changes began to occur. Most notably, the soldiers in my squadron who had started as acquaintances turned into friends as we learned increasingly more about each other. The IDF is the fabric that weaves together the diverse, multilingual, multicultural Israeli society. The twenty-five soldiers I began training with came from varied socioeconomic backgrounds and hailed from cities, moshavs*, and kibbutzim all over Israel. Some were religious, others were secular. Some were the sons of immigrants, and some were themselves born outside of Israel—and yet, all were Israeli. All had made a choice to serve their country, not just in a combat unit but in one of the more difficult combat units in the army. I was proud to serve alongside them.

As our team grew closer and more cohesive, we functioned more efficiently as a unit. While at first, the army felt more like a summer camp turned horribly wrong, as we became more capable, we were increasingly given greater responsibility. We were treated more and more like soldiers rather than fraternity pledges whose only purpose was to endure suffering. And yet, as the initial thrill and excitement of army life faded with the passage of time, so too did a quiet sadness begin to set in. The rapid milestones of the beginning of basic training, like receiving our guns, getting our unit tag, being sworn in at the Western Wall, and earning our Jump Wings, were all behind us now. It would be many more months of grueling work before the next milestone.

One afternoon, on a coveted five-minute break from one of our classroom lessons, I took a second to lean out the window of the room and take in the view. My face was instantly enveloped by the warmth of the sunny March afternoon. My eyes were drawn to a well-manicured grass lawn directly under the window, many of which dot the Paratrooper's training base. Towering above the lawns were palm trees, swaying in the cool spring breeze, and to my right were several well-kept basketball courts, which were used more for Krav Maga lessons than anything else. Such beautiful surroundings should have invoked feelings of tranquility and civility, yet both were notably absent from our training. A commander slammed his fist against the door of the

*A cooperative settlement of small, individual farms.

classroom, signifying the end of our break. The abruptness and volume of the sound shattered my fleeting moment of serenity. As I turned away from the window, it occurred to me: I was trapped in a beautiful prison.

I made my way back towards my seat and, out of the corner of my eye, I caught a glimpse of a newspaper that had been left open to a page advertising flights to vacation destinations. At various points throughout my army service, I longed to book one of those flights and fly far away from Israel and the army to a place where I could spend my days on a beach rather than a shooting range. Where I could wake up to soft music rather than the loud prattle of a training grenade hitting the floor of the barracks. The irony of those longings lay in the fact that I was kept there only by my own desire to serve Israel. I was quite literally a prisoner of my own resolve. At times, during the coldest nights and the longest days, I did wish I could fly away. Yet I knew that a day spent lying on a warm beach or any other luxurious escape my mind could imagine would feel underserved if I did not complete my three years of combat service as I had committed to doing.

Later that evening before bed, in a moment of quiet contemplation, I reflected on basic training and the link between suffering and appreciation. Deep pain, as the renowned journalist David Brooks wrote, smashes through a floor that you previously believed was the bottom of your soul, revealing a cavity below. In basic training, the physical and psychological hardships I experienced uncovered deep layers of sadness and pain that I was not previously aware existed, and in so doing increased the range of my emotions. The daily suffering during basic training taught me a greater appreciation for life's joys. The taste of food in a restaurant was never as good as it was after eating field rations for a week. Normal things, like sipping a freshly ground cup of coffee in a lively café, induced deep feelings of satisfaction. Seeing my family after half a year apart, I appreciated them more than ever before. One of the greatest gifts the army gave me was the ability to find pleasure in every moment of unscheduled time, and gratitude for things I had previously taken for granted. As we transitioned from basic to advanced training, the rigor of the physical challenges we faced increased, and with them came an emotional intensity that would test our limits and commitment.

PART FIVE: ADVANCED TRAINING

CHAPTER 25: SUNDAY MORNINGS

The hardest part of the army isn't the crawling. It isn't carrying people up hills wearing a gas mask or jumping into thorn bushes. It's Sunday mornings.

It's watching tour groups start their day, and seeing children running through the park as you ride the city bus to the central station, preparing to return to base. It's saying goodbye to her, confident that words will prove ineffective in describing your life as a soldier; the daily tortures of training, the lack of sleep, the long cold nights and the blazing hot days. It's watching civilians on a leisurely bike ride, and store owners opening their doors for business. And then there's you. Dressed in your uniform, a gun slung across your shoulder, and certain in the knowledge that of all those you pass, none would trade jobs with you for an hour, let alone a day or a week. No matter how much they hate their jobs. Where you are going is a place where normal civil boundaries and the lines between possible and impossible are blurred. The hardest part is flipping that switch from civilian to soldier. From watching the sunset from a resto-bar on a beautiful beach in Tel Aviv to watching the sunrise in the desert, holding the push-up position in a thorn bush. By Monday, you've been in the army for twenty-four hours and have already flipped that switch, but on that Sunday morning bus ride, Saturday night for your friends back home, you live in the middle of two worlds.

You look out the window, every tree bringing you closer to that place you both love and hate. The place where you're fulfilling a dream, fighting for your beliefs, but also fighting to stay awake, to stay motivated, and to keep focused on the horizon, to the end of training. Then you'll finally be an operational soldier and start doing what you came here to do.

Your friends complain about their hours at work, upcoming tests, and unfair bosses. And you try to empathize because it's hard for them in ways you can't imagine. You've never been a teacher or a law school student or an investment banker. But they can quit. They can tell friends and family it was a bad fit and move on. You can't do that. You are bound to the IDF and to the State of Israel.

Your friends own their time and their lives. In the army, you belong to something greater than yourself, but you nonetheless belong to something. You signed up for this. It was your choice, and you knew what you were in for, or so you thought. But it doesn't make Sunday mornings easier.

5/1/2010—Paratroopers Advanced Training Base. Be'er Sheva Region

CHAPTER 26: GUARD DUTY

After closing twenty-eight days on base in the wake of my punishment, though my team spent the weekend on base, I was released on weekend leave as an act of mercy. At that time, I was seeing a girl named Ally, who was studying abroad at Tel Aviv University. During basic training, I only had two to four days off base each month and a single hour of free time each evening during which I was permitted to use my cellphone. Despite those limitations, we spoke or texted whenever possible and spent every weekend that I was off base together.

That weekend, I surprised Ally in Eilat, where she was celebrating her birthday. With the help of her friend, I found her on the beach, snuck up behind her lounge chair, and interjected myself into the conversation she was having. The look of shock on her face when she spun around and saw me made the four-hour drive south worth it. I spent the weekend with her and her friends drinking far too much, eating everything in sight, and reliving my college glory while hanging out with college students. Unfortunately, unlike the students I was with, Sunday would not spell the start of classes for me but rather the start of the week's training. Far too quickly I found myself on a bus heading north towards base. I didn't feel ready to return to base after such a brief respite. As I would learn many times throughout my service, however, the army cares very little about what you do and do not feel like doing.

As we progressed from basic training to advanced training, we went from cadets to soldiers. And as we became increasingly more professional, the responsibilities and demands of the army grew proportionately larger.

One Thursday afternoon, the day before we were meant to be released on weekend leave, we were told we would be closing the weekend in Judea and Samaria. We were being sent to Hebron, where we would be manning roadblocks and guarding Jewish settlers on their route to prayer.

Hebron is the second holiest site in Judaism, and the site of the oldest Jewish community in the world, dating back to biblical times. It was in Hebron that King David was anointed the king of Israel. A thousand years later, the city was the site of extensive fighting during the Jewish revolt against the Romans, and according to Jewish tradition, the Patriarchs, Abraham, Isaac, and Jacob, as well as the Matriarchs, Sarah, Rebecca, and Leah, are all buried in Hebron.[7] Today Hebron's Arab population numbers close to 200,000. The 1929 Hebron Massacre ended the continuity of Jewish life in Hebron with the murder of sixty-seven Jews, and the relocation of the surviving population to Jerusalem. Today, less than a thousand Jews remain of what was once a vibrant Jewish population.[8]

Hebron, or Al-Khalil in Arabic, is the fourth holiest city in Islam, partially as a result of its association with Ibrahim (or Abraham), who Islamic tradition holds as the founder of monotheism and the precursor of Muhammad. Al-Khalil is also believed by some Muslims to have been a stopping point on Muhammad's night journey to Jerusalem, and it has thus become a significant site of Islamic pilgrimage.[9]

Tensions have always existed between the Jews and the Arabs living there, both of whom see the other as encroaching on land that belongs to them. In recent years, dozens of fatal shootings and stabbings have taken place in Hebron, several of which occurred in the months prior to our weekend of guard duty. It was into this precarious environment that we were thrust on that Friday afternoon.

Shortly after we arrived at our base of operations, we were briefed by the ranking officer of the Givati Brigade, whose soldiers we would be replacing for the weekend. Over the previous months, there had been several stabbing and stoning attacks by Arabs against Jews on their way to prayer. Our charge was to guard the Jews as they made their way to synagogues over Shabbat. Palestinians living in Hebron, who are not Israeli citizens, are subject to military law, while the Jews living by their side are subject to civilian law. At times, the Palestinians are mistreated and even attacked by settlers. But we were not there to play judge and jury. We were there to guard.

With our orders clear, we donned bulletproof vests under our ammunition belts and boarded heavily fortified armored vehicles. We drove in a convoy toward the center of the city and were dropped off in pairs along the way at the stations we would be guarding.

Driving armored vehicles through the streets of a city is, of course, not a normal nor ideal situation, and it evokes images of occupiers in a foreign land. Indeed, Hebron is home to many Muslims whose families have lived there for centuries. However, as the second holiest site in Judaism, mentioned eighty-seven times in the Bible, Jews have also consistently called Hebron home since it was founded in 1720 B.C.[10]* Since that time, for almost 4,000 years, Jews have had a steady presence in Hebron, but for a thirty-eight-year period during which Jews were forced to abandon the city due to Arab pogroms. Just as the Muslims that call Hebron their home have justification for doing so, so too do Jews. Over the past several decades, terror operatives with access to high-capacity explosives living among the local population have explicitly stated and proven their intention to kill IDF soldiers. As a result, armored transport vehicles are used to protect the lives of those who protect Hebron's Jewish population.

On Friday night, I was stationed in an Arab neighborhood along the route used by a handful of Jews to get to the temple. After the briefing from the Givati officer about the extent of the threats facing Jews and soldiers in our sector, I could not shake the feeling that I was a sitting target. Though I knew I was only a radio call away from support, and was guarding with another soldier, I felt very alone.

As the hours of my shift crawled by, the children of the neighborhood grew emboldened and ceased observing me from a distance. A group of four kids, seemingly between 7 and 14 years old, approached me cautiously. Using my basic Arabic, I asked how they were doing, and they responded warmly, happy that I had initiated the conversation. We attempted to communicate using the ten or so words of English, Hebrew, and Arabic that were common to all of us. It was clear that they were as fascinated by me as I was by them. After about thirty minutes of communicating, using mostly hand gestures, the 14-year-old, the oldest and bravest of the group, leaned in to try to see through the scope of my gun, which I was gripping tightly despite my friendly demeanor. Moments later, a group of soldiers from another brigade on vehicular patrol rounded the corner, and in a split second the kids scattered in different directions. They did not return, and I was once again left alone with my thoughts. I thought about the symbolism of a Palestinian boy looking through the scope of an IDF soldier's gun, and the conflict that is created when two people looking through the same lens see vastly different pictures.

Shortly thereafter, the muezzins of dozens of Mosques throughout the city rang out the call to prayer in a cacophonic harmony. It was my first time hearing the call to prayer in a predominantly Muslim city, and while hanging out with the neighborhood kids had left me more relaxed than I'd been after our earlier briefing, the sound of the muezzins brought me back to reality. I was immediately reminded that I was standing guard over hundreds of Jews in a city of 200,000 Arabs, many of whom were not pleased by the presence of the IDF. Suffice to say, I wasn't in Kansas anymore.

During Jewish prayer times, Arabs were forbidden from walking on the main street that Jews used to access the synagogue and instead had to take the smaller path on the side of the street. In the wake of several terror attacks that had occurred in the prior months and the visible animosity I witnessed in the eyes of more than a few Jews and Arabs as they passed one another, this was deemed to be the easiest way to prevent further incidents. During my shift of guard duty one morning, a 6-year-old Arab girl and her mother, seemingly oblivious to the standing order, began to make their way down the middle of the street. I was stricken by how cute and innocent the little girl looked, and called over the radio to ask my officer if I could escort them down the street. He asked me who would be manning my station if I did that, and in that moment, I realized that although my orders were not easy, they were in place for a reason. I was not there on a humanitarian mission; I was there to prevent violence between Arabs and Jews, which in consideration of recent incidents, seemingly necessitated that the two groups be separated.

I called out to the woman and her child as they approached and motioned them to move to the path on the side of the street. The mother tugged at her child's hand, and together they made her way towards the path that ran parallel to the road. As the little girl looked back at me through her inquisitive blue eyes, I could see that she was confused. She couldn't understand why she could not walk in the middle of the street, and her eyes seemed to be asking me, "Why not?" I felt her mother's stare upon me, and as I lifted my eyes to meet hers, my glance was met by her piercing brown eyes, which were full of anger and hatred. I wished she could see past my uniform and into my heart.

I thought in that moment of the dichotomy between the Israel her

Scholars say that 1720 B.C. is about the time when, according to the biblical narrative, Abraham would have arrived in the city, which was nearly 2,000 years before the birth of Mohammad and Islam.

founders dreamed she would be and the present-day reality. Seventy years after the creation of the state, it is tragic that armed soldiers must enforce a rule that Arabs in Hebron must walk on the side of the street during Jewish prayer times. It is tragic that social and economic disparities between Jews and Arabs living in Judea and Samaria are so severe. It is tragic that a Palestinian government could teach and incite hatred and violence so successfully and with so little pushback from the international community that it could promote an armed uprising. That uprising, known as the "intifada," led to the murder of nearly 1,000 Israeli civilians in suicide bombs and other acts of terror, as well as over 2,000 Palestinians, among whom were nearly 800 Palestinian civilians.[11] Between 2000 and 2003, seventy-three suicide bombings originating from Judea and Samaria killed hundreds of Israelis. Heightened security measures were taken to prevent further terror. These included targeted killings of terrorist leaders, a ground operation to root out terror operatives, and the creation of a 435-mile-long security fence separating Judea and Samaria from the rest of Israel. Between 2003 and 2006, afterthese measures were taken and the fence was completed, there were twelve suicide attacks, an 83% decrease.[12] I believe at the time the Israeli government was right to take extreme measures to address extreme threats to the safety of its citizens. I also acknowledge that the fence and other security measures, in the words of former head of the Shin Bet, Carmi Gillon, are "making the lives of millions unbearable."[13]

Many Palestinians in Judea and Samaria neither commit nor sanction violence. Under the present systems of checkpoints, all Palestinians suffer, the innocent along with the guilty, and that is not fair. But neither is it fair that Israeli civilians should live in fear of terror. Israel, like any nation, has the right and responsibility to take measures to keep her citizens safe. Sadly, there are very few mainstream voices in the Palestinian community calling for peace, or taking a public stance against violence. Until that happens, a less intrusive way of keeping Israel's civilian population safe can be implemented, or a true partner for peace emerges with whom Israel can negotiate, it is unlikely that things will change. In both 2000 and 2008, Israel offered to cede control of nearly 95 percent of Judea and Samaria to the Palestinian Authority. In 2008, Olmert also offered to withdraw from the Arab neighborhoods of East Jerusalem, and to place the Old City, home to Jerusalem's holiest Jewish sites, under international control. The offer was rejected.

****

The next weekend, shortly before the start of Shabbat, four soldiers from the team and I were taken to a settlement outside the city limits to assist in guarding its perimeter, which had become necessary in the wake of increased terror activity in the area. The settlement was located high in the hills of Judea and Samaria, and from the front gate we could see thirty miles across the country to Ashkelon and the Mediterranean coast. The sunsets I watched from that post were among the most beautiful I'd ever witnessed.

I spent that Friday night at the home of a family who had volunteered to take in soldiers for the Sabbath meal. They had two small children, which was perfect for me, as my level of Hebrew at that time seemed to be fairly close to that of a young child. Seven hours later and 7,000 miles away, I knew that my own family would be sitting down at their table for Shabbat dinner. Though the language at their table would be English, the blessings and the atmosphere would be very much the same.

One of the most beautiful aspects of Judaism is its traditions. Across oceans, borders, cultures, and millennia, these traditions have remained intact and, for the most part, unchanged. The comfort of their consistency was something that I particularly appreciated during my service when almost nothing else about my life was consistent. Sitting at the Shabbat dinner table with my gun resting between my legs, I realized how much I had taken for granted growing up in the comfort of a safe neighborhood in the United States. There was no fence around my house, nor a gate on my street. The army did not patrol my neighborhood, and we did not live in fear that armed terrorists might burst through our front door and begin shooting at us simply because we were Jewish. Unfortunately, in Israel, terror has become a reality. I took a moment to appreciate how difficult it must be to raise a family in such a precarious environment. Soldiers love to complain, and when you complain enough, even if only out of habit, you start to believe that you are the victim of a system that is out to get you. But sitting at dinner with that family, I realized that though my previous week had felt like a nonstop shift of guard duty, with heavy gear and little sleep, I was the lucky one at that table.

CHAPTER 27: TRAINING CONTINUES

Throughout training and my active service, I learned to become comfortable with uncertainty. Marches and training sessions were never announced in advance; forced bouts of water consumption and the telltale taking of our pulses by the company's medic were usually our indication that a ruck march was imminent. We were rarely told if we would be off for the weekend until a day or two beforehand. At times, weekend leaves were canceled at a moment's notice due to rioting or other unforeseen factors. During the difficult times, I tried to remind myself why I had enlisted.

One scorching hot day, we drank nearly 8 liters of water each (over 16 pounds) to make up for fluids we had lost drilling in the punishing heat. It was so hot that day that live-fire exercises had been banned for reasons of safety. That evening, a medic lined us up and took our pulses. We knew what was coming.

As we waited for the march to begin, our medics gave us a lesson on treating gunshot wounds. I was so tired from the heat, the physical exertion, and lack of sleep that I began to hallucinate. As we sat in a circle, practicing the application of tourniquets, I looked over at my friends. A dozen of them slowly morphed into a giant cow, which turned its head and began to stare at me. I pondered what a cow might be doing sitting in on our medic's lesson, and concluded that it was not actually there. In fact, cows as large as the one I was looking at did not exist anywhere. Curiously, these realizations were not enough to dispel the image of the cow from my brain, and the image reappeared intermittently over the next hour. At around eleven p.m., we were given a snack of bread, fake chocolate spread, and meat, which we devoured. Finally, at midnight, the march began.

A white night in the army, unlike a white Christmas, is not something that you look forward to or sing about joyously. A white night in the army is when a day of drills turns into an all-night march, culminating in several kilometers under heavy stretchers. I had often heard stories from friends who had drafted into the army before me about being so tired that they fell asleep while they were walking. Until that march, I couldn't imagine what that felt like. By two in the morning, I understood. At points, I would wake up mid-stride, unsure of what had kept my legs moving while my mind had shut down. I looked to my side and noted that I was not alone; a friend to my right stumbled repeatedly as he fell asleep between his steps, waking up just in time to catch his footing before he fell. A few of us took turns hitting him in the face every few seconds to keep him awake until he got his second wind.

"*Negevists*," or those who carry the Negev light machine gun, suffer more than most on marches. Their gun weighs close to sixteen pounds (ten pounds more than an unloaded M-16), and their vests weigh twice as much as everyone else's due to the added ammunition they carry. Shar, our team's Negevist, was also a lone soldier, which meant that, like me, he had no immediate family in Israel. Shar had moved to Israel from Canada right after high school, and at 17 years old, he was the youngest candidate to make it through the Duvdevan selection. Shar and I were, respectively, the youngest and the oldest candidates in the training class. We were also two of the only native English speakers on the team, and as training progressed, we became close friends. When you are forced to spend as much time with another human being as we spent together, without technology as a distraction (phones were forbidden while on guard duty), you learn everything about them. We spent dozens of hours together on guard duty. We shared stories about our families and friends and laughed about drunken weekends from the days before we drafted. As our friendship developed, we shared our longings for the budding romances we had left behind, which at times led us to question our decision to enlist. We grew so close that a single word exchanged between us was often enough to convey an entire thought, or remind the other of a funny story that would send us both into hysterical laughter.

But laughter and the past lives about which we loved to reminisce seemed far away as we marched that night, more asleep than awake. Though Shar would never ask for help, I could see that he was struggling with the Negev, so I offered to carry it for several miles. After an hour of walking under the weight of Shar's gun, I had a new appreciation for just how difficult it was to carry the Negev for the entirety of every ruck march. When we crossed the fourteen-mile mark, we opened two stretchers and fastened six sandbags to each of them. At the same time that we were given the command to lift the stretchers and resume marching, the sun crossed the horizon, signifying the start of a new day. It was the second time I had watched the sunrise since the last time I had slept. During special forces training, it felt at times that we were trapped in an endless cycle of suffering. The sunrise brought with it a reminder that no matter how cold and dark the night, it is always followed by the dawn. Every difficult act ultimately came to an end.

The last mile of that march was the hardest. By that time, most of us were limping, and the responsibility to replace friends who were under the stretcher was one of the last things pushing me forward. That, and the thought of breakfast and a few hours of sleep, both of which I was certain would be awaiting us when we arrived at our base. Our commanders told several people who had spoken against orders that, as a punishment, they could no longer help the team carry equipment. Every training exercise in the army is meant to prepare you for the real thing. During combat or a mission, speaking could give away our position and put all of us in jeopardy of enemy fire. In theory, those who spoke would be shot first, and unable to help carry the team gear. In practice, their punishment meant more time under the stretchers for the rest of us, and more weight on our backs. As always, with a few hundred feet left, we upped our pace from a fast walk to a sprint and willed ourselves across the finish line. When we reached our company quarters, though I was panting heavily and my feet and shoulders were throbbing, I felt a tremendous sense of pride and accomplishment. While the marches were by no means enjoyable, I loved the sense of camaraderie that emerged during these acts of incredible physical demand. They brought us closer together and reminded us that we could push ourselves harder and longer than we ever imagined.

After fifteen minutes of painful stretching, we were given ten minutes to shower. The sight of 120 soldiers, naked except for ammunition vests, limping to the showers, is one I will never forget. It was then eight a.m., and we hadn't slept in twenty-seven hours. During that time, including the drills and all-night march, we had covered over thirty miles. We were certain that we would now finally be going to sleep. We were mistaken. After breakfast, we were informed that we would have a surprise inspection of our gear that evening and would have the day to prepare. Throughout the day, our commanders and sergeants appeared unannounced to check the rooms for sleeping soldiers. Fear of punishment alone kept us from stealing a few minutes of shut-eye, despite the immense temptation.

At one point I watched my friend, who was rewriting his gear list, repeatedly fall asleep as he was writing. Each time he did, the sound of the notebook hitting the floor snapped him back to consciousness, and he would pick up the book and continue where he had left off. I fell asleep several times while refastening my knee pads. I was so exhausted that I didn't wake up until I was actually falling off the bench. Fortunately, the scissors I was using fell to the ground, which saved me from stabbing myself. After what felt like an eternity, our officer completed his inspection and sent us to bed. We had been awake for thirty-nine straight hours. The mental struggle of staying awake for 12 hours after thirty miles of marching far eclipsed the difficulty of the march itself. Within seconds of crawling into my shitty, metal-framed army bunk bed, I was fast asleep.

****

The following week was Yom HaZikaron (Independence Day). Our company was charged with guarding the annual ceremony at the Western Wall Plaza in Jerusalem. This was a huge honor and responsibility given the significance of the ceremony. When we arrived in the Old City, we were briefed by a high-ranking police officer about potential threats and our responsibilities. We stood there, a group of fifty (mostly) 18-year-old soldiers on one side, and a group of fifty (mostly) 25 to 35-year-old policemen on the other. Standing in the middle of the two groups was the ranking police officer. He called the name of one of his police officers, pointed at one of us, and the two would be sent together to a position. As we waited, my eyes scanned the group of police officers and fell upon a strikingly beautiful policewoman. I noted her name, which was prominently displayed on her uniform: Rotem. As I began to dream about our future together, a plan formulated in my mind. I knew that what I wanted to do might get me stuck on base that weekend while all my friends went home. Despite the risk, I decided I was not going to leave my next eight hours to chance. When I heard her name called, thankful that I had not yet been assigned a partner, I immediately shot my hand up. My enthusiastic volunteering drew heavy laughter from those present, including my commanders. The commanding police officer smirked, looked at my officer for approval, and on receiving a nod, sent me over to join Rotem for eight hours of guard duty. While she rejected my premise that 23 was the new 29, she told me that she would set me up with her younger sister as a consolation. As the hours passed, thousands of people streamed through the gates of the Old City into the plaza. The ceremony began at 8:00 p.m. with the annual Memorial Day siren.

Every year at exactly 8:00 p.m. on Yom HaZikaron, a siren sounds throughout the state of Israel on every public loudspeaker, radio, and television in the country. At that moment, in an event that is without equal in any other country in the world, an entire nation stops completely in its tracks to pay homage to those who have made the ultimate sacrifice. For those sixty seconds, the country screeches to a halt: chefs, waiters, and patrons at restaurants stop cooking, serving, and eating, and rise to their feet. Buses pull over on highways and trains stop in their tracks. For a full minute, civilians and soldiers stop what they are doing and stand at attention to honor Israel's fallen. As the ceremony progressed, we heard stories of those who had given their lives while defending the country. Many of those in attendance had lost someone, and I was proud that our presence allowed them to pay their respects in safety.

CHAPTER 28: DUVDEVAN

After eight months of basic and advanced training on the Paratroopers base, we prepared to move to the unit's base, where we would undergo six more months of training before becoming operational. The final week of Paratrooper's training is officially called War Week. Those who have experienced it more accurately refer to it as Hell Week. Weeks in the field are notoriously miserable. One of the few comforts a combat soldier is given during such weeks are the sweets packed into each box of field rations. Before War Week began, all of the coveted treats were ceremoniously removed from our field rations. When someone asked our company commander why he had ordered them to be taken out, he replied matter-of-factly, "Because war isn't sweet".

We endured five scorching days and frigid nights, alternating between long marches with heavy weights and intense drills executed on steep, thorn-ridden hills. Water was often short and thus rationed. Although this was of questionable legality in a training exercise, it accurately simulated potential wartime challenges. Our commander intermittently signaled us to drop to the ground, where we would lie in wait for an imaginary enemy's ambush. After consecutive nights of a maximum of four hours of sleep, lying down without drifting off was as challenging as the physical drills. The week culminated in a long stretcher march to the kitchen of the Paratrooper's base, where a feast awaited us. That night, for the first time in our military service since being accepted into the unit, we were permitted as much sleep as we wanted. The following day, a few soldiers in our company, known for their sense of humor, were chosen and given time to prepare for that evening's ceremony at which they would roast our commanders. The rest of us spent the day nursing our wounds from the previous week and cleaning and organizing our gear.

After dinner, we filed into the auditorium to hear our company commander's final address. He summarized our eight months under his command and spoke of the obstacles we had overcome and all that we had achieved. After heartfelt applause, ten of our fellow soldiers moseyed up to the stage and spent the next 45 minutes mocking various commanders and officers in our company. After eight months of having to raise our hand every time we needed to pee, making fun of those in charge of us right to their faces was not only terrifying (we were sure we would all be punished for their insubordination) but also hilarious. We erupted in fits of laughter at various inside jokes and mockeries. By the end of the show, I was laughing so hard I was crying.

At the forty-five-minute mark, the show ended abruptly, and after loud applause, it was back to reality. Our commanders took control once again and sent us back to our living quarters. The moment we arrived they ordered us to assume the push-up position on our knuckles on the stone floor and began berating us for insulting them. We were sure that this was the moment they would "break distance" with us, or close the emotional distance that exists between commanders and soldiers in training. Traditionally, this is done when commanders return to their units after advanced training is complete. As a result of our suspicions, their stern scolding was met with more than a few smirks and giggles. Unamused by this, they ordered us to begin doing knuckle push-ups. A few minutes later, we were wearing full rain gear and gas masks as we did continuous burpees in the crowded barracks on our sergeant's command. Finally, as we were all gasping for air and wondering if we had actually crossed a line, the moment we had looked forward to for eight months finally arrived. The voice of our officer rose above our pants and pained grunts: "Five minutes...the whole team in room 1...with all of your candy". We immediately understood that this was the transition to the long-awaited "breaking distance" during which our commanders would dissolve the walls of formality that had defined our relationship. Screams of joy pierced the walls of the barracks as we jumped up and down like school children and congratulated each other. For the last eight months, we had tried desperately, and almost always unsuccessfully, to earn the praise of our commanders. Now, we were finally welcomed behind their curtain. For the next three hours, a few dozen soldiers and our three commanders sat in a big circle and spoke as friends. We joked with them about all of the things (we thought) we had snuck by them. Eventually, our officer ended the festivities, and sent us to bed. We were exhausted from hours of laughing, but jittery from all the chocolate and sugar we had just eaten, so we lay in bed for another hour joking around before finally drifting off to sleep.

****

Duvdevan is clouded in secrecy. It was formed in 1987, drawing into its ranks soldiers from the Navy Seals and the Paratroopers, both of which are reflected in its crest. In the early days of the unit, groups of four or five soldiers dressed as Arabs were deployed undercover into Judea and Samaria with disguises, pistols, and orders. If anything went wrong, it was up to them to figure it out. Since that time, the unit has grown and developed. The teams are often larger with individual roles more specifically defined and missions more precisely planned, but the legacy of its badass heritage has remained.

Before moving up to the unit, we had one final march to complete. It would bring us forty-five miles through the hills of Judea and Samaria to the front gates of the storied unit. Due to an injury I had sustained to my right meniscus, the doctor had forbidden me from participating in the march. Fortunately for me, the doctor was riding in the first-responder vehicle that accompanied the team throughout the night. In response to my relentless begging, he eventually allowed me to join my team for the final five miles. In the eleven hours prior, my team had covered nearly forty miles. Walking at four miles an hour is a reasonable pace for a healthy person out for an hour of exercise on the local high school track, or through the streets of a suburban neighborhood. Holding this pace for eleven hours over rough terrain with changing elevations, full gear, and the additional weight of the stretchers is an entirely different experience. By the time I joined them, my friends looked more like zombies than people. I tried several times to join them under the stretchers but was reprimanded by my officer and the doctor for contradicting orders. Eventually, resigned to my fate, I contented myself to walk alongside my teammates and offer them words of encouragement. Long after the sun had risen, and after what for my teammates likely felt more like days than hours, we reached the gates of the unit. A scene of utter madness awaited us, one that felt more like a movie set from *Seal Team Six* than reality. If you're hoping for details...enlist.

In the late afternoon we were sent to bed and allowed to sleep until early the following morning. In the days that followed, we began to settle into our new home. The rumors quickly began to spread about the infamous first session of Krav Maga that every new team in Duvdevan experiences.

Krav Maga is a self-defense system known for its practicality and efficiency, and the brutality of its counter attacks. It was derived from street-fighting skills developed by a Jewish, Eastern European boxing and wrestling champion named Imi Lichtenfeld. In Czechoslovakia in the mid-1930s, Lichtenfeld organized and trained young Jewish men to defend their neighborhoods against anti-semitic attacks. In the late 1940s, following his move to Israel, Lichtenfeld began to provide combat training to the forces that would ultimately become the IDF. To this day, IDF soldiers are taught Krav Maga as a method of practical self-defense. Before one learns the techniques, however, the army teaches its soldiers the most important self-defense tactic of all—the ability to flip the switch from calm to rage, and channel one's aggression toward an enemy attacker.

After a week and a half at the unit, we finally heard the dreaded four words that we had been anticipating and fearing for months: "Four minutes: Krav Maga." Four minutes to change from your uniform into shorts and a T-shirt with your name in big, bold letters on the back, and arrive outside the Krav Maga room with the necessary gear. Four minutes to transform into a fierce, aggressive, special forces operative. At the unit, Krav Maga has a legendary status. It's what turns boys into men, men into soldiers, and soldiers in training into fighters. Quite simply, it is where special forces candidates learn to flip the switch.

After what felt like hours of standing in silence outside the Krav Maga training room, we were startled by a loud bang that sounded like a gunshot. The door of the Krav Maga room flew open, propelled by a push kick from Kfir, a six-foot-five, well built, incredibly serious-looking individual. The first words out of his mouth were: "From now on, nobody looks me in the eyes."

We were all happy to oblige him. He added, as if to dissuade anyone who might have thought he was joking, "The next time someone looks me in the eyes, in or out of training, you will very much regret it." We all believed him. With those words, our training began.

On Kfir's command, we sprinted around the room and punched a designated spot in the corner of the room where the foam that lined the rest of the wall had been cleared away. More simple instructions followed but, inevitably, one of us would manage to do something wrong. This landed us in the push-up position on our knuckles. From there, push-ups would follow each time someone glanced anywhere but straight ahead. Whenever someone lowered a knee or committed some other act that was akin to lowering standards, we would be punished. In the middle of one such punishment, in a deep, bellowing voice, our instructor told us that every one of our commanders had passed through the same thing, and that every fighter in the unit had at one point been in the very same position we were now in. Those of us still capable of listening drew motivation from his words. The session carried on for nearly three hours. When we were given a water break an hour and a half into the training, I had to use the closed knuckles of my left hand to pry open the fingers of my right hand in order to grip the water bottle. We had spent so much time in the push-up position on our knuckles that my fingers had locked shut.

Shortly after that first Krav Maga session, and two weeks after our arrival at the unit, I was told by my officer that five other soldiers on my team and I would have our training status reviewed by the head of the unit. I knew that a large contributing factor for my review would be the training I had missed as a result of my knee injury, but what course of action would be taken remained a mystery. When the day of the review finally arrived, I shined my boots, straightened my pins, and entered the feared chambers of the one man who had the power to remove me from the unit's training with a flick of his pen. In the room alongside the head of the unit, were my officer, my sergeant and the head of the training school. Over fifteen minutes, the head of the unit reviewed my service record, including comments my commanders had made in my file, and scores I had received on various graded exercises. Everything had been recorded down to the smallest detail. He told me that based on the recommendations of my officer, despite the training I had missed, he would not be dropping me from training. However, he would be sending me back to the Paratroopers training base to complete an important week of training

I had missed due to my knee injury. With the verdict given, the meeting was adjourned. I rose to my feet, saluted, and left the room. Given the alternative, I was more excited than anyone has probably ever been by the prospect of repeating a week of field training.

The following week, I arrived as ordered on Sunday morning at the Paratroopers training base with more than a little déjà vu. While physically the week was incredibly challenging, the commanders refused to let me join under the stretcher during marches and generally treated me very well. That week highlighted for me that the hardest part of our training was not the physical acts but rather the discipline, scrutiny, and constant judgment of our commanders. That week carried with it the same physical demands as other hard weeks I had experienced before, including long, sleepless nights, constant drilling, frigid cold, and general discomfort. And yet, it felt much easier than any week of field training I'd had before that point because of the way I was treated by the commanders.

When I returned to the unit the following week, it was business as usual. We were sent to the field to execute an infantry exercise, as we would do many times throughout our training. One of the most fundamental skills of any combat soldier is the ability to participate in a team exercise to conquer an objective, be that a house, a hill, or in many cases, a series of hills. We set out from our base in the late afternoon in a tight formation behind our officer. After forty minutes of walking through the scorching desert sun, our officer raised his fist into the air, signaling that we were approaching our objective. As the commanders gathered around him, the rest of us lowered to one knee in the shade of a group of boulders a thousand feet south of the hill where the enemy was reportedly lying in wait for an ambush. After we were briefed on the plan of attack, we crawled to our position on the high ground east of the hill and waited for the other half of our forces to reach their starting point. When they arrived at their designated position, we received the order to open fire, and we poured ammunition over the targets checkered across the hillside. Though hard to make out in the evening twilight, the targets were clearly visible through the scope of our sharpshooter's gun, and he called out their locations to us. Our objective was to keep a steady flow of fire on the enemy so our comrades could advance up the hill.

On our officer's command, we ceased firing and broke towards the stream at the base of the hill. As my vest flapped and my chest pounded, I tried to concentrate only on my objective. All around me M-16 cartridges were exploding. The ear-splitting explosions seemed dangerously close, but I pushed my fear aside, trusted in the aim of my teammates, and focused on the task at hand. As I lay in wait for our final push to the summit, I panted like a dog and tried in vain to slow my breathing. My cotton uniform stuck to my body in the heat of the breezeless desert evening, and my helmet trapped a puddle of sweat against my brow.

To my left were my friends and to my right was my commanding officer. In that moment, nothing was important except my cover fire and my next sprint up the hill. As we came within ten feet of our targets, my officer ordered a grenade, which for the sake of the training exercise, was actually a rock. After it had been thrown, we counted out 5 seconds, then jumped to our feet and charged the targets with guns blazing. Fortunately, cardboard targets don't shoot back, and after everyone was accounted for, the exercise was declared complete.

We rose to our feet, cleared our weapons, removed our helmets, and took advantage of the brief respite from our training to enjoy the picturesque view spread out before us. The grey silhouettes of the buildings of Ma'ale Adumim, one of the largest predominantly Jewish cities in the West Bank, were contrasted against the pink hue of the post-sunset sky. A blanket of silence fell over the desert, and the ringing in our ears from the punishing sounds of exploding cartridges began to fade as our bodies acclimated to the post-drill calm. As I walked back to the base of the mountain, the enormity of the desert spread out before me gave me a feeling of humility as I realized just how small we are.

CHAPTER 29: NAVIGATION BEGINS

While learning how to fight in close quarters is critical for a special operations combat soldier, particularly one in Duvdevan, it's useless if he can't successfully arrive at the location where he will put those skills to use. As such, shortly after arriving at the unit, we began navigation training. During a typical week of navigation, rather than taking the bus back to base on Sunday, we would report to our commanders at the main bus stop in the area where we would be navigating that week. Often it was up north, in the more mountainous region of Israel.

To prepare, we would study maps and write down the steps that would take us from Point A to Point B. The stakes were high; failing to plot the correct route, or successfully memorize it, could spell hours of aimless wandering with weight on your back at the expense of much-needed sleep. Before each navigation, we had briefings with reservists, who would rank our knowledge of the path we intended to take and our understanding of the territory we were to traverse. Anyone rated below a seven on a scale of ten was required to redo the briefing.

At around 7:00 p.m., after another standard meal of tuna and bread, we would board the buses to the starting point. We would begin the night's navigation around 9:00 p.m. Navigation is done in pairs in the IDF. The navigator puts the radio, which weighs approximately twenty pounds, into his ammunition pack, bringing the total weight he is carrying to about fifty pounds. From there, with another soldier on his team as his silent escort, he endeavors to reach his four points. After reaching the fourth point, the roles are reversed and the exercise continues to the next four points. Each of the two navigators is meant to walk between six and eight miles on their individual navigations, bringing the total per pair to about fourteen miles. That is, if both partners navigate perfectly. Unfortunately, I rarely navigated perfectly, and on many nights, I walked as many as twenty miles. It was a rather unpleasant way to spend an evening.

By 5:00 a.m., the last of the pack had usually arrived. At that point, everyone who had arrived early enough to steal some extra sleep was awoken. We then completed a final check, ensuring that all the gear was accounted for, before boarding the buses to head back to the campsite. There we would eat a quick breakfast of tuna and attempt to catch six hours of sleep before being awakened to study and plan for the next evening's navigation. The frustration of our reality was multifaceted. Throughout the week, we were in constant physical pain from walking over a dozen miles the night before with weighted bags. Anyone who has been short on sleep can attest that every physical pain and emotional strain is magnified when one is sleep-deprived. The elements also took their toll on us; the heat and the flies made much-needed sleep elusive despite our exhaustion. There was also a third layer to our misery, one unique to the military—our supreme lack of control. The next day's hike would not be our choice any more than the previous day's hike was. When or if we managed to fall asleep had no impact on when we would be woken up. What we would eat was not what we had chosen to pack, but what we had been told to pack.

Every Wednesday morning, after all the groups had returned from their navigations and the company gear had been checked, we boarded buses, allegedly bound for base. Without fail, an hour or two after we departed the site of the navigation, we were awakened to the awful sound of the exhaust spitting its pollutants into the air in a quick burst, signifying that the bus had come to a stop. It's a sound that every former combat soldier in the IDF knows from training, and one that still haunts him on public buses long after his service. At that juncture, we would find ourselves face to face with a very large mountain. Seven minutes later we were outside the bus with our ammunition vests on, and stretchers opened with sandbags placed atop them.

The hike up the mountain under those stretchers was almost always the hardest part of each week. The pain and muscle fatigue from the lactic acid in our legs was exacerbated by the heat of the morning sun and our complete and utter exhaustion. Ultimately, like everything else in the army, the march would come to an end, and we would again board the buses and return to base.

While on occasion we were able to sleep three to four hours on the bus ride that brought us back from wherever we had been navigating, this was the exception rather than the rule. More typically, we were ordered to begin working on the team's gear to prepare it for inspection by our officer later that evening. Throughout the day and night after our return to base, we would have two training sessions, each of which lasted over two and a half hours. We were given only five minutes' notice to prepare for each session. This meant that to arrive on time, we needed to drop everything and sprint to gather the necessary gear and assemble it in the designated location. By the evening, having navigated all night, hiked up a mountain with stretchers, and completed two training sessions, we were approaching twenty-eight hours without sleep. At that point, we would enter a zombie-like state in which we were too tired to realize that we were tired. Confrontations would emerge over inconsequential things and dissipate just as quickly as the arguing parties forgot what it was they were arguing about. For sixteen weeks our lives followed this grueling, predictable routine, culminating in the infamously difficult navigation final.

Joined by my parents at the Paratroopers red beret ceremony

A (forbidden) run-in with friends
during a navigation exercise

Training under the stretchers

Drilling near the Kinneret

Preparing for a week of camouflage training

On top of Mt. Masada

R&R with the team on a break from training

CHAPTER 30: CONFRONTING A FAÇADE

Two weeks before our navigation final, I was given eight days of leave to fly home and see my family. The trip was a blur of family gatherings, nights out with friends, and quality time with the people who meant and mean the most to me. During my first weekend home, my parents and I drove to Washington D.C. to visit my brother at George Washington University. As fun as it was to be back on a college campus, as we moved from one fraternity party to another, I could not help but notice how much I had changed. In an environment that twelve months earlier had felt completely comfortable, after eight months as a soldier, it now felt foreign.

Seven short days after I had landed at JFK airport, I was back on a plane again, headed towards Ben Gurion airport. My orders were to return directly to base to begin preparations for our navigation final, which would take place the following week. In addition to the warmth and love I received from my family and friends, I took back to Israel with me something less expected as well: a reality check about the assumptions I had harbored about the life I was missing back at home.

When you examine a Monet from across the room, the painting is crystal clear; it is almost as if you are staring into a photograph. Leaves glisten, and the reflections of the trees from which they hang are mirrored back in the water so believably that the viewer can be transported to a different time and place. It is only as one gets closer to the painting that the brush strokes become apparent. As one approaches and ultimately stands alongside the painting, it looks nothing at all like it did from far away. All of the strokes, shadow-work, and imperfections become clear. Living 7,000 miles away from home, it was easy to look at the lives of my friends and family from afar, like a Monet, and declare them to be perfect.

I often fell into the trap of daydreaming about the lives I had conjured up for them; nice apartments in fun neighborhoods, cool jobs, and the freedom to do whatever they wanted every night after work. But just as the Monet hanging on the museum wall creates an illusion from a distance, so too was it an illusion that life for my family and friends back home was easy or perfect. Nobody wants to complain on the phone, especially not to a combat soldier, so I heard almost exclusively about the positive happenings in their lives. I heard far less, if at all, about the difficulties and disappointments. As a result, I used inaccurate details as I painted the picture of my friends' lives in my mind. When I visited home and approached the metaphorical paintings I had created since I moved to Israel, I saw the brush strokes. I saw the errors, the over-shaded areas, and the faults of my assumptions. Life in the big city was not idyllic; work was hard, free time was limited and, at the end of the day, my friends harbored many of the same fears and doubts about the future that I did. I saw past the façade I had created and realized that everyone was struggling in different ways. With a firmer grip on reality, I returned to Israel ready to face what would turn out to be one of the most challenging weeks of my life.

CHAPTER 31: THE NAVIGATION FINAL

Everything you learn during IDF training culminates in a test which is designed to evaluate not only your proficiency in the relevant subject matter but also your determination. Our navigation final stretched the limits of both.

Several days before the final began, we were each given a map and twenty points scattered over a 190-square-mile area. Over a period of four days, it would be our mission to walk a minimum of eighteen miles per night in search of those points. While most weekends on base in the army are spent eating, resting, and lounging, this Shabbat was different. Those of us who were not religious/Sabbath observers studied our routes. We looked at computers and Google maps on our iPhones, and did all that we could to make sure that we knew our routes as well as possible. We knew that every misstep would be paid for in spades. Straying from our route would leave us wandering through the Judean hills, without adequate food or sleep, while carrying thirty percent of our body weight.

Throughout the week, each navigational pair was given four cans of tuna and one loaf of bread per twenty-four-hour period. This was insufficiently filling under normal circumstances and even more so after ten hours of hiking with our gear. The pangs of hunger we felt at times were comparable to a full day's fast.

On the first night, we were sent off into the darkness in staggered groups to prevent collaboration, each of us nervous and excited for the challenge that lay ahead. My partner Maor and I had prepared very well for most of that night's navigation. Unfortunately, we neglected to pay sufficient attention to the middle point. For all intents and purposes, it is the same as any navigational point because it must also be found, like all points during the navigation, without the use of a map. This point, however, is also one at which everyone is required to check in and refill their water.

Our lack of attention to this detail cost us dearly. For three hours, during which we trekked nearly eight miles, we walked back and forth past Mini-Israel (a tourist attraction) from one end of the intersection to the other. Finally, with a little guidance from our officer over the radio, four hours after we had found our previous point, we reached the middle point. Our commander, who was manning the point, told us with a sarcastic grin that he had wondered if he was going to see us that night. We all had a laugh, filled up our water containers, and went on our way. Despite the three-hour delay, we ultimately collected all but one of our points that evening.

The final two-mile stretch of the navigation was alongside a major Jerusalem highway. Night had long since given way to dawn, and I guessed it to be around eight or nine in the morning as we trudged towards the endpoint of the navigation. I watched the cars go by, many no doubt carrying passengers on their way to work and marveled at how physically close I was to the people in those cars, and yet how remarkably different our lives were at that moment. After checking in with our officer, we were given a can of tuna each and sent off to bed. I was so physically drained by that point that I had to force my body to stay awake long enough to consume the first bit of food I had seen in fourteen hours, and which I knew my body desperately needed.

We slept in the shade of a field of olive trees about a thousand feet from the highway. The serenity of the morning breeze and gentle shade of the olive trees stood in contrast to the intensity of the challenge that lay before us. Later that afternoon, after everyone had received the minimum six hours of sleep required by army law, we were woken up and told to prepare for that night's navigation. .

To reach the starting point of the navigation, we had to crawl through a drainage pipe that ran under the highway. It took about four minutes, crawling on our hands and knees with bulky backpacks over rock-covered cement, to reach the other side. From there, with some damage to our spirits already inflicted, likely by design, we began the journey towards our first point.

Navigating from memory is incredibly difficult. When studying the map, every geographical marker seems distinct and unique. But when theory turns to practice, vaguely outlined shapes replace the clear contour lines, altitude markers, and distinct riverbeds that seemed so obvious on the map. After an hour of walking up the side of a mountain that we believed would lead us on the path to our first point, we agreed that we were lost. We began to descend the far side of the mountain in search of our path, but as we did, I became distracted for a split second and lost my footing. In the blink of an eye, I had tumbled more than twenty feet down the side of the dangerously steep decline. Luckily, I was able to stop my fall by grabbing onto the trunk of a tree. As the rocks and foliage I had uprooted with my fall cascaded down the side of the mountain, the cacophonic rustle of their movement was shortly replaced by silence. I took stock of my surroundings and gratefully noted that I had seemingly not broken any bones, nor torn any ligaments. As the ringing in my ears subsided, I realized that a previously unintelligible sound was my partner Maor, calling out my name, with a noticeable fear in his voice. I yelled back up to him that I was OK, dusted myself off and checked to ensure that I hadn't lost any of my gear during the fall. Together, we continued our descent towards the riverbed, this time concentrating intently on each and every step.

The frustration of having missed our first point, compounded by the exhaustion of having walked up and down such steep surfaces carrying heavy gear for so long, was beginning to wear on us. It was not the last time during that week that we would be overcome by feelings of hopelessness. During our journey through the riverbed, we would stop walking now and then to bend over and give our backs and shoulders a break from the weight of our bags. High in the hills of Jerusalem, a chilling wind whips through the mountains at night, and each time we paused, our sweat-soaked uniforms acted as conductors for the cold evening breeze.

Within a few minutes of stopping to rest, we would inevitably find ourselves shivering. As I write about that week from the comfort and warmth of a New York City café, I can still remember the heavy feeling of despair that overcame me as I walked through the riverbed that night. About halfway through the four-mile journey, neither of us had spoken in an hour. While absorbed in our own personal thoughts, we were both assured of our mutual unspoken misery. Suddenly and unexpectedly, we heard our officer over the radio. After speaking a few words of motivation, he played a song into the radio from his cellphone and, for three minutes, we walked silently to "The Star of the County Down," an upbeat Irish folk song (the Israeli version, of course). While it might seem trivial, that small act reinvigorated us. The music reminded us of our civilian lives and of a place beyond our suffering, which had seemed minutes earlier as though it was impossibly far away.

In order to reach our final point that night, we had to scale an absurdly steep mountain. It looked more like a rock-climbing wall one might find in a gym than something that could be scaled without ropes and 30 percent of our body weight on our backs. But as they say in the army, the difficult is done at once, and the impossible shortly thereafter.

As we climbed, the concentration required to search for footholds, handholds, and feasible routes fully occupied my mind. Not until I reached the top and looked back down at the terrain we had scaled did I realize the extent of my physical and mental exhaustion. Our elusive final point that evening was situated within the ruins of an ancient temple. When we finally reached it, we heard the sounds of a megaphone and the dreaded, unmistakable voice of our Krav Maga instructor in the distance. Normally we would be excited to reach our final point. Now, we were less than jubilant with the realization that tonight, the end wouldn't really be the end.

When Maor and I had both completed the Krav Maga drill, we were instructed to begin the next day's navigation. Having failed to consider the terrain when mapping our route, our path took us down and then up another steep mountain. We fought through tree branches and intense forestation, at times unable to see more than a foot in front of us. Finally, we reached the tent, marking what appeared to be the end of the evening's hardships (though it was now well after sunrise). As we limped towards our officer to check in, he began to unroll his map. On previous nights this had preceded his revealing a surprise navigation to be undertaken immediately. When he saw our eyes go wide, he chuckled and put the map away. As fear turned to relief, the three of us shared a laugh and Maor and I headed toward our tents.

After forcing myself to stay awake long enough to eat, I rolled over and attempted to fall asleep, which should have been an easy task given my utter exhaustion. However, due to the cuts on my sides and back, which were caused by my heavy gear, every slight movement sent razor-sharp pains up the side of my body. Wounds that had been small at the start of the week had grown progressively larger and more painful.

As usual, we were given the minimally required six hours of sleep before our commanders woke us up to prepare for that evening's navigation. We had walked for just a few hours when my knee started throbbing. I began dragging my right leg behind me in an effort to keep my knee straight as we ascended and descended the punishingly steep slopes of the route. In my old life, I would have called for a doctor on the spot, convinced that I was doing permanent damage, and that a person was not meant to fight through such severe pain. After a year in the army, I popped two pills of extra-strength Aleve, my third and fourth of the night, tightened the straps of the bag on my back that weighed around seventy pounds, and walked for another sixteen miles.

At 9:00 p.m. the following evening, we set off for what I thought, at the time, would be the last training navigation of my life. What began as a walk quickly became a limp as the sharp pain in my knee worsened. The weight of the gear and my injuries pushed me to my limits. Luckily, we had plotted our route well and arrived early enough to catch some much-needed additional sleep while the latecomers stumbled in.

When everyone had arrived, the head of the training program woke us up. He congratulated us on making it to the end of the week and told us that we had one more challenge that still lay before us. With broken bodies, wearing full equipment, we set out on a three-mile stretcher march that took us up the steep path to the top of Tel Azeka. Halfway into the march, I was dragging my leg as I struggled under the stretcher. One of my friends, noticing my pain and inefficiency, pulled me from the stretcher and insisted that I carry the radio rather than further injure myself. I begrudgingly agreed and discovered that simply walking with the additional weight of the radio in my pack was one of the greater challenges of the week.

When we finally arrived at the peak, spread out before us was the beautiful Ela Valley, the site of the famous battle between David and Goliath. The sun warmed our faces as we stood in formation with the stretchers still in the air, and our commander addressed us. I closed my eyes for a moment and felt the cool morning breeze blow across my body and the warm sun upon my face. Slowly I opened my eyes and ears and absorbed the words being spoken to us; words which recounted the story of the war that had occurred in the valley below us. A war in which a young shepherd named David had gone to battle against an impossibly larger and stronger opponent to successfully defend his home and his people.

I will never forget the satisfaction I felt as we finished that march and watched the sunrise over the valley. After we had taken some time to congratulate each other and enjoy the view, we trudged down the peak towards the feast that awaited us below. As the adrenaline wore off, the pain in my knee became crippling. My teammate Michael, noticing my pain, silently put his arm around me and helped me limp down the steep decline. Moments like those reminded me that it was our training that transformed us from acquaintances into brothers in arms.

When we arrived at our base later that day, we were told that there was still one final challenge that remained: the *"Bochen Lochem"* (Fighter's Test). The first part of the test was a timed obstacle course. Our officer took us around the base that night at a slow jog, showing us the exact path that we would be taking the following morning and explaining each of the obstacles we would need to complete. We wondered, silently at first and then out loud, how we would be able to complete the test in the allotted time. It would have been difficult even if we had been well-rested, and we were not. We had each hiked around eighty miles over the past week with thirty percent of our body weight on our backs.

Throughout the week, I had dug deep within myself to find the inner strength to persevere through the severe pain that shot up my leg each time I put pressure on my knee. When things got particularly bad, I comforted myself with the knowledge that if I kept moving forward, even if it took me longer to arrive, I could collect the necessary points and pass the navigation evolution. As we jogged the route that night, I fell behind the group dragging my leg behind me as I struggled to keep a pace that was not much faster than a brisk walk. Realizing that I would have to run the same route with full gear to pass the next day's test, it seemed I had finally reached a point where mental strength alone would not be sufficient to overcome my obvious physical impairment. In pain and frustrated, I approached my officer that night and told him I would be unable to run the next day. He told me it would be a shame for me to have to repeat the entire week with the next training class which, he explained, would be the required course of action if I chose not to run. His final words to me before leaving me to make my decision were a phrase every soldier in the IDF has heard before: "There is no I cannot. Only I don't want to." The next morning, I took a few more Aleve tablets when I woke up and enlisted a friend to run behind me. If the choice before me was twenty minutes of severe pain to avoid sixty hours of navigating, I would choose severe pain.

When we arrived at the starting point, we strapped on helmets, bulletproof vests loaded with magazines, and our guns. Somehow, with my friend's help and inner strength I didn't know I had, I pushed through the shooting pain in my knee and completed the obstacles and the run in the allotted time.

The next test evaluated our shooting skills. Some of the drills involved the M-4, others the Sig-Sauer pistol, others switching between the two guns. Everything was timed and evaluated.

When everyone had finished the obstacle course and the shooting tests, we were sent to the gym to complete our Krav Maga evaluation. There, we formed a circle, and one by one each soldier was called into the middle and matched against one of his peers in hand-to-hand combat. As soon as the opponent tired, he would be replaced by a fresh soldier to keep the heat on the soldier being tested. When my turn came, I was so frustrated and in so much pain that sheer anger powered me through the drill. In my half-conscious state, each and every person that stepped into that circle was not a friend but an arch enemy who stood between me and the temporal end of my excruciating knee pain.

When the drill finally ended, I was exhausted and trembling in pain. I limped slowly out of the gym and collapsed onto a bench where I sat for several minutes with my head down clutching my knee and struggled to slow my breathing. My officer, who had seen me from a distance, walked towards me and called out my name. I didn't rise to meet him as I normally would have, but lifted my eyes to meet his. He seemed to sense my pain and frustration. Cautiously, he approached me and sat down. Never long on words, he put his hand on my shoulder, looked me in the eyes, and uttered a brief sentence that carried with it much weight: "I'm very proud of you for this week. Good work." He held my stare for a few more seconds, and with his point made, stood up and walked away. It was among my proudest moments in the military.

CHAPTER 32: THE SCHOOL OF COUNTER-TERRORISM

A few weeks later, we began the most intensive counter-terror tactics week we would experience during training—the unit's in-house preparation for Lotar, Israel's world-renowned counter-terror school. Lotar is internationally recognized for dramatically increasing the close-quarters combat effectiveness of its attendees. The school is so well respected that Israel's allies send their elite troops from all over the world to train and collaborate with Lotar's world-class instructors. The week spent preparing for Lotar is reputedly among the hardest weeks a soldier in Duvdevan experiences during his training. Tremendous emphasis is placed on aggressiveness and on completing complicated tasks in very short periods of time. Duvduvan, as one of the top counter-terrorism units in the world, takes great pride in sending soldiers to Lotar already prepared for what they will experience. By nearly all accounts, the week of preparation for Lotar at the unit is harder and more intensive than the school itself.

One of the main goals of the week is to bring the team together. Each trip to the shooting range required the help of everyone to move targets, boxes of ammunition, coolers, tables, and more from the living quarters to the shooting range hundreds of feet away in very short periods of time. The standards were set to near perfection; the first time we attempted the act we were sent back to do it again because a single unmarked cooler wasn't facing in the proper direction. My team struggled through five attempts before ultimately succeeding. Outside of mealtimes, which averaged about twenty minutes, we spent every waking hour that week on the shooting range, in Krav Maga, or in *yevesheem* (an exercise in which we practiced the proper form for close-quarters shooting).

Our instructors maintained complete professionalism throughout the week and disciplined us only when we failed to meet their high but achievable standards. They accepted nothing less than our full effort in every exercise. More than once, when we didn't meet the given time for an exercise, one of the instructors would ask by a show of hands who *really* ran their absolute fastest. Few could say they had, which nearly always resulted in a forced display that allowed us to prove to ourselves that we could push ourselves harder, faster, and longer than we realized. In one such display, our instructors requested a volunteer to hang from the rafters (triangular metal bars with sharp edges) by his fingers for as long as he could. His time, fifty seconds, then became the minimum standard for the team.

For the next 30 minutes, we tried again and again unsuccessfully to stay airborne for fifty seconds as a team. Each time, inevitably, one of us would fall from the bar just seconds before we reached the fifty-second mark. By the end of the half-hour, nearly all of us were extremely frustrated and bleeding from our hands. Later that day, the instructors chose a number of soldiers who had been the first to drop to try to break fifty seconds in front of the rest of the team. They succeeded, proving the instructors' point yet again: we pushed ourselves harder when we were put on the spot, which meant that when we failed to reach our goal, it was because we were not giving our all for the sake of the team. The message was clear: there is no room for takers in an elite combat unit. Two days later, after repeatedly hanging from those rafters in thirty-, forty-, and forty-five-second increments, we finally achieved our team goal.

In the early days of the unit, no real rules governed the training, and that ethos was very evident whenever reservists trained us, as they did that week. One day during training, one of our reservist instructors threw one of my teammates into a wooden target, snapping it in half. The soldier's crime was that he had grinned during the drill. The type of shooting that we learned that week, close quarters, rapid-response shooting, required us to clench our abs as hard as possible. Several times throughout the week an instructor sent a soldier to the ground with an uppercut to the stomach when he felt the soldier wasn't clenching his abs hard enough. Here again, the standard was made clear: people who do not give their all 100 percent of the time, even when they think no one is watching, are not wanted in the unit.

At the start of the week, I could load an M-16, aim it, fire at a target forty-five feet away, drop to one knee, load a new magazine, and hit the same target in eight seconds. By the week's end, I could carry out the same act in five seconds, nearly 50 percent faster. Every millisecond counts in combat, and so we worked tirelessly to improve our firing speed and marksmanship.

Yevesheem was a prominent part of the week's training. The skills we sharpened during those drills would spell success or failure on the shooting range. Though I weighed nearly 200 pounds and was as strong as I'd ever been, we drilled so long and so hard that by the end of our training session on Wednesday night, I struggled to hold up the seven-pound gun with one hand. During the yevesheem sessions, we were instructed to put safety before everything. If you were given four seconds to get back to the firing line for the next drill, you were not allowed to move until you reset the firing pin and switched on the safety. You were simply expected to be safe and to run faster.

No dry shooting session began until all the guns were checked for ammo, doctored so they couldn't fire, and white ribbons were tied around their barrels so they could be identified as checked weapons. We drilled entering the shooting position over 2,000 times that week, part of which entailed slamming the stock of the gun into the skin directly under the collar bone above the pectoral muscle. Those training us checked us regularly for bruises and punished those who didn't have them.

During one of the drills, a reservist felt I wasn't slamming the barrel hard enough and asked me if I was saving myself for a modeling job on the weekends. Not really sure how to reply, I told him we didn't get out enough on weekends for me to model. He grinned but said nothing. Believing I had charmed my way out of disaster, I breathed a sigh of relief and rejoined the drilling with the team. Seconds later, he called me off to the side and proceeded to drill me individually for five minutes, squeezing the barrel into my shoulder each time he felt I hadn't slammed it hard enough. After our private session, my bruise, to his tremendous satisfaction, was much more apparent. He rewarded me with the semi-creepy shoulder massage he had come to be known for, telling me in English with a thick Russian accent, "That's bayter."

During these sessions, we were also taught how to take on a terrorist in a crowd. How to run holding the gun in one hand while moving people out of the way with the other. The proper way to enter the shooting position from a sprint. The proper way to neutralize a fallen terrorist. All of the training was extremely professional and based on real combat experiences. The targets we used featured cutouts of terrorists, some of whom were holding pistols to the heads of hostages. Even in the training sessions without ammunition, shooting before establishing perfect aim was strictly forbidden, and the cardboard cutouts featuring the faces of hostages were meant to reinforce that point. Anyone who violated a safety rule during the week was required to stand and address the entire team during one of our breaks and describe what he had done and why it was dangerous.

One exercise required us to set our M-16's to automatic, which was something we had very rarely done before; IDF soldiers shoot for accuracy, and therefore never utilize the automatic setting. We fired eight rounds, meant to simulate the rapid speed at which we'd be expected to shoot single rounds in rapid succession. This exercise was done early in the week, and nearly all of us found our barrels rising throughout the burst with the last few bullets hitting the top of the target or flying over it. As we perfected the shooting positions and learned to tighten our abdominal muscles and pull the guns into our bodies in the proper manner, we found that we could shoot rapidly on semi-automatic without experiencing the rising barrel effect.

The final component of the week was Krav Maga, which occupied a minimum of two and a half hours each day. During the sessions, focusing your eyes anywhere but on the spot on the wall directly across from you would earn you time in the "superman" position. This required the unfortunate offender to hold the top of the push-up position on his knuckles with his feet high up on the wall. At my size and strength relative to my 19 and 20-year-old teammates, Krav Maga was the area of training where I shined. Many of the drills were reminiscent of high school football practice. One common drill involved two soldiers going head to head with the objective of fighting the other back to the opposing wall. In another, one soldier sat atop his teammate, pounding him with shots to the chest and stomach. The victim fought to flip his attacker onto his back while absorbing as little punishment as possible. Strangely, I found my happy place in the Krav Maga room.

While strength is important in Krav Maga, speed is equally important, since the first-mover advantage is critical to success in an aggressive interaction. The most effective among us learned to channel our intensity into bursts of aggression that we could summon on a split second's notice. The most difficult drill we would perform that week came on Thursday evening and involved the following setup: First, the instructor would yell "next," at which point two to four soldiers who decided they wanted a turn would sprint to the predetermined spot in the corner of the room and fight for position. The soldier who dominated the combat, or who the instructor decided had expended the most effort, would be chosen to begin the drill. On command, the participant stood ready, facing a line of ten of his teammates standing shoulder to shoulder, whose job was to obstruct his exit from the corner where he began the exercise. After freeing himself from the corner, the participant faced a gauntlet of another ten soldiers. The object at this stage was to throw jabs and crosses at a pad being held by the instructor while the soldiers lining each side of the pad showered him with hooks, uppercuts, and crosses to the stomach, ribs, and back.

As I was completing the drill, though I felt I was giving every ounce of my strength, our instructor stopped moving backward as I hit the pad he was holding, and I struggled to straighten my body despite the punches I was absorbing. It wasn't long before my strength gave out, and before I knew what had happened, I had been swept by the crowd of punchers ordered by our instructor to attack me and drive me back to the opposing wall. I was knocked to the ground and faded out of consciousness for a few seconds as my body tried desperately to acquire air.

When my eyes came back into focus, the first thing I saw was our instructor's face hovering over me. He ordered me to my feet, and on his command, the drill picked up where it had left off. Again, I fought my way to the wall, only to be taken down again, this time by a misplaced shot that caught me on the chin. When the drill was completed, I stumbled back to the wall to rejoin the others, more than a little disoriented. The instructor shouted something at me in Hebrew several times, which in my state of oxygen-deprived delirium I could not understand. After a few attempts, he gave up on Hebrew, grabbed me by my headgear and said in broken English: "Don't pass out." Though to an outside observer these sessions might appear chaotic or even reckless, the degree of professionalism with which Kfir conducted them was remarkable. Whenever we were short of breath and energy, he challenged us to keep fighting, always taking us exactly to our edge, but never to the point of serious injury. Since leaving the military, Kfir has founded a Krav Maga Organization called Instinct, which now has locations all over the world.

On Sunday morning, after returning from a well-deserved weekend leave, we began making the final preparations for Lotar, Israel's counter-terror school. The five weeks we spent at Lotar were among the most challenging but enjoyable of my service. We perfected our close-quarters shooting techniques, trained in hostage rescue situations, and learned to work quickly and efficiently as a team. Each time we were bussed to the shooting range, we would have only a few short minutes to take out and organize all our gear, set up the shooting range, and stand in formation to await instructions. The instructors were incredibly professional and seemed to truly desire that we complete the required tasks in the given time rather than be punished for our failure to do so.

Lior, the non-commissioned officer in charge of our training, was a scary character. He was tall and wiry and had a slow and dramatic way of speaking. He, along with his team of instructors, significantly increased our level of professionalism as a team and as individual soldiers. One evening, we were commanded to assume the push-up position on our knuckles as we waited to enter the Krav Maga room as punishment for an infraction. Due to a combination of bad luck and bad planning, within seconds I realized that a small rock was trapped between my knuckle and the pavement. As my bodyweight pressed down on the rock, I felt it slowly entering my skin. Just as I was about to shift my position, one of the instructors shouted that if anybody moved so much as an inch, we would remain in that position for an extra three minutes after the three minutes we still had left. Unable to justify subjecting my team to another three minutes of misery, I resigned myself to my fate, and called upon the words of advice given to me several weeks earlier. During our preparation week for Israel's counter-terror school, as I was hanging from the sharp rafters of the shooting range experiencing a shooting pain so severe that I wasn't sure I could continue, one of the instructors sensed my weakening resolve. Just as I was about to let go, he walked in front of me, looked me in the eyes, and uttered a sentence I returned to many times throughout my training: "Your body has to be here, but your mind doesn't. Go somewhere else."

When I needed to retreat inward, and block out reality, as I did in that moment, I went back to 2006, to a bar near Echo Lake Summer camp where the staff gathered during our time off. If you drive down Main Street in Lake George, New York, on the opposite side of the street from the Price Chopper, next to the park where everyone watches the fireworks on Independence Day, there was a deck restaurant and bar called "Simple Simons." The world seemed to stand still during the lazy Thursday afternoons we spent on that deck, surrounded by friends, a breathtaking view, and the soothing sounds of Don Eddy's guitar. Don had played at Simple Simons for over twenty-four years, and he was as much a staple there as the wooden deck on which he performed. When I revisit Simple's, it's always a beautiful Adirondack summer afternoon, with blue skies above, Don Eddy on the guitar, and a cold beer in my glass. It's about 3:00 pm, late enough to have been there for a few hours, but not so late that the thought of leaving has crossed anyone's mind; we are completely consumed in the moment. Nigel, a large red-haired Irishman, is telling me about the Bushmills distillery twenty kilometers from the house in which he grew up. Darren, my partner in crime on our Montreal day-off adventures, sits to my right. He has smoked two full packs of cigarettes and drank several pitchers of beer. As usual, he is quicker and wittier when he's inebriated than most people are when they're sober. Kenny, the laid back, hard-drinking Newfoundland native, has a contemplative look on his face as he sips a White Russian, parts his long blonde hair and, as usual, says very little but notices everything. Bobba Wadda, the Hawaiian former college linebacker, is hiding last night's hangover behind a pair of dark sunglasses while washing down a burger with a Jack and Coke. I look up from Nigel's story and am not surprised to see my co-counselor and friend, Eric, dancing with a local woman in her seventies to the entertainment of all those watching.

As I reach for the pitcher to refill my glass, the words of our instructor shatter my daydream. "Stand up!" he commanded, and we all jumped to our feet. My attention was immediately drawn to the throbbing pain in my knuckle caused by the rock still embedded in my skin. I pulled it out quickly, diminishing a decent amount of the pain, but the scar it left remains to this day.

As Lotar ended, I reflected on all we had been through during the past year. Over the course of basic and advanced training, navigation training, the unit's preparation for Lotar, and now counter-terror school, we had achieved a sufficient level of proficiency in all the skills we would need to become operational. The final months of training would be used to build our cohesiveness as a team and to test our willpower. As we entered the weekend, I was in high spirits, tired from the grueling week we had completed but simultaneously excited that the end of training was finally in sight. Though I didn't realize it then, the following week would bring heartbreaking news.

CHAPTER 33: THE DEATH OF A DREAM

When we arrived at base on Sunday, our officer called us together and announced that five soldiers were to have their status reviewed to determine whether they would continue in the training program. Throughout the training period for elite units, soldiers are cut along the way for infractions of standards, as well as at the discretion of the officer leading the team. As we stood around nervously, in a voice devoid of emotion, our officer read out the five names as though he was running through a list of soldiers for kitchen duty. When I heard my name called among the five, I was in disbelief. My heartbeat quickened as I quickly played out the potential outcomes in my head, none of which ended well.

My status had previously been reviewed by the head of the unit due to training I'd missed as a result of injuries. It was widely understood in Duvdevan that, regardless of the cause, nobody has two status-review conversations with the head of the unit while they are in training and remains in the program. Becoming an operational soldier in the unit was everything that I had worked for over the previous two years. I spent the rest of the day in a fog, unable to fully comprehend that everything I had worked so hard for seemed to be crashing down around me.

The following day, after taking some time to calm my nerves, I approached my officer. I was disappointed and confused. I had received solid marks on our most recent evaluations and had even been complimented by my officer, who was not big on flattery, for my performance in my navigation training and fighter's test. I asked him if he could share with me what I had done wrong or in what areas I had fallen short, but no answers were given. My officer made his case to the commander of the training school, and the two of them proposed a review of my status to the head of the unit, which was then scheduled for two weeks later.

On the day of the meeting, I reviewed the speech I had practiced in my head a thousand times in preparation for this day. I knew the odds were stacked against me, but I also knew that I had been a good soldier. I had not been caught sleeping or on my phone during guard duty, nor had I under-performed in any major test. My marks were among the highest on my team in Krav Maga, and I had completed the navigation final with a passing score that placed me above the 50th percentile. I naively believed that my results, my commitment, my passion, and the support of my teammates would make me an exception.

When I arrived at the head commander's office, I was told to enter the room in which he, my officer, and several other commanders were already seated. My heart sank as I saw the solemn looks on the faces of all those present, and I immediately understood that this would not be a trial but a sentencing. After a few compliments about my work ethic, my Zionism, and my motivation, the head of the unit informed me that I would not be continuing my training in the unit. Having little to lose, I pressed him to explain what it was that they wanted from me that I had not given. I offered to drop a training class and return to advanced training if the issue was the training I had missed due to my injury. With a pained smile on his face and a gracious acknowledgment of my commitment, he informed me that this was the end of the line, and with that, the case was closed. Fifty-two weeks into training, during a ten-minute conversation, my dream of being a fighter in Duvdevan was shattered forever with just nine short weeks before I would have reached the end. I was told that I would be contacted by the army within a few weeks with my options for reassignment. As I walked back to the barracks, I felt nauseous. I looked around me at the base, abuzz with soldiers going to and from training sessions and missions. All were a part of the community I had wanted so badly to join, which would now be forever out of reach. My teammates, some of whom had become very close friends, would continue their training without me. The pain of losing the chance to be a fighter in Duvdevan was intensified by being separated from them.

For the first time in my life, I had wanted something—truly wanted something with every fiber of my being—and failed to achieve it. It wasn't that everything always went my way, though it would be naïve not to acknowledge that I had benefited tremendously from the stability of my upbringing. But my successes were not just luck; I had worked extremely hard to achieve the things people told me I could never do, and I made a habit of never taking no for an answer. Up until that point, determination and a strong work ethic had been enough.

As I've since learned, everyone experiences a heartbreaking failure at some point in their life—the utterly debilitating feeling of giving one's self completely to something or someone and falling short. The memory of facing that failure, learning from it, and turning it into something positive marked a milestone in my maturity. It was an experience that, while devastating at the time, ultimately made me a humbler, stronger, and more empathetic person. As Ernest Hemingway once wrote, "The world breaks everyone, and afterward, some are strong in the broken places."

I was given two choices. The first was reassignment to the Paratroopers, which although only reachable by tryouts, was a regular infantry unit. The second alternative was to transfer to the Givati Brigade, where I would have a chance to join their special operations company. I chose the latter. I had set out to serve Israel to the best of my ability, and I felt that a special operations team would give me the best chance to do that. With twelve months of counter-terror training under my belt, I was certain I would be assigned to Palsar, the unit within Givati that specializes in reconnaissance. I also expected that I would complete my training in two months with the team that had been drafted with me in November 2010. As it turned out, things would not go as smoothly as I'd planned.

CHAPTER 34: GIVATI: RECONNAISSANCE INFANTRY

Arik was intimidating. When he yelled from his office for me to come inside, I quickly pushed open the door, stood at attention, and saluted. His facial expression told me that he was somewhere between appreciative and amused by my gesture in an army notorious for informality, and he motioned for me to take the seat in front of him. At six-foot-one, he was pushing 200 pounds. He walked with a slight limp, the lingering remnant of a bullet he had taken in his left leg during the Lebanon war. He would later serve as the commander of the training school for guerilla warfare, though I didn't know that at the time. All I knew was that his assessment would determine my assignment over the next two years, which in the army, is an eternity.

Some people have a demeanor that is at once both calming and intimidating. When Arik looked at you, he seemed to immediately know everything you were and were not. As such, I felt resigned to the idea that he already knew everything I had to say, and quickly became quite comfortable with him. After exchanging pleasantries, we dove right into the purpose of our meeting—my assignment. Arik looked me straight in the eye and asked me point-blank why I was reassigned out of Duvdevan. He assured me that he knew my commanders, their commanders, and the commanders of those commanders—the point being I had best be honest. So I was. I told him that I had asked several times for a reason. I was hoping at least for some closure, and at best for constructive feedback to take with me to wherever was next. I was given nothing.

Arik looked at me after I had finished speaking, just a few seconds longer than you might expect, and exclaimed without a trace of joking, "That is such bullshit." Reading the expression on his face and the look in his eyes, I knew he was not doubting the validity of my explanation but rather expressing his empathy for the situation in which I found myself. As a major in a special forces combat unit, a man accustomed to making lightning-quick, momentously important decisions, I was humbled by the few seconds he took to gather his thoughts before he launched into his analysis and prognosis.

Arik complimented me on my resolve and my commitment to Israel. He noted that with a degree from a good university, I could have stayed in America and had a far easier life. He added that though our current positions would not allow for it, he hoped that we would one day be friends.

Fortunately, Arik shared my view that my training put me in a strong position to join the particular unit within the company known as Palsar. However, he feared that because I was coming from a similar unit, it would invite comparisons that would imply that where I came from was better than the unit in which I ended up, a sentiment with which he did not agree and did not want any hand in perpetuating. As such, he decided he would place me in the anti-tank unit within the company which, he noted, had won every single company competition since they had drafted.

Quite suddenly, Arik rose to his feet, and I did the same, startled by the speed of his movements. He shot out his hand, looked me in the eye, and said, "I am proud to welcome you into the Orev Givati family." In the same breath, he informed me that though I had completed a year of training and would theoretically need only two more months to be operational, in practice he could not allow that to happen. "The men you go through training with become your brothers in arms," he said matter-of-factly. As such, he insisted that I complete training with the soldiers that had drafted in March 2011 rather than November 2010. His plan would mean a 6-month extension of my training. With that, he whisked me out the door. My head was spinning from everything Arik had said. Once outside, I found myself face to face with his second-in-command, Kfir, who began rattling off all the things I needed to do, where I had to report, and when.

Orev, Palsar, and Palchan are the three specialized units within each infantry brigade of the IDF. Orev is charged with long-range reconnaissance and is trained in the use of several special missiles that can be deployed against enemy tanks or positions. Palsar is the reconnaissance company, charged with leading the brigade into combat in wartime and going door to door to clear houses of terrorists. Palchan specializes in explosives and will often deploy with the Palsar to create custom charges as dictated by the situation. In practice, during wartime, all three units lead the brigade into battle and are charged with clearing houses of enemy combatants to allow the brigade to advance before executing their more specialized missions. During times of peace, the entire company, in addition to shouldering their share of guard duty, carries out arrests of suspected terrorists. In Givati, as I came to learn, there was no discernable distinction in the quality of the candidates among those selected for the three special operations units within the company.

I had arrived on base that morning expecting to be told that I would have the opportunity to join the Palsar unit of the Givati Brigade and finish training in two months. Instead, I was told I would have to repeat five months of training and would be joining a different unit altogether within the company. I had a lot to wrap my head around. I asked Kfir if I might have a little time to reflect before diving in. He told me to take the next few days and come back to him on Thursday with an answer.

Returning to my apartment that night, I stopped and bought myself a nice bottle of scotch. When I got home, I put my phone in a drawer, and spent some time alone with my thoughts. My body was in great shape; my military training to that point had been some of the best in the world. The only thing that stood between me and excelling in my new unit was my ego. My new unit was not as sexy or storied as Duvdevan. There would be no high profile arrests or going undercover. What there would be was hard work, long shifts of guard duty and lookouts through the scope of our missile camera at potential terror positions. There would also be patrols, arrests, riot control, and the high probability that we would be the first boots on the ground in the event of a Gaza operation.

Late Thursday morning, after taking those few days to come to terms with my decision, I packed a bag with enough clothes for a few weeks and hopped on a bus. I was bound for Mishmar HaNegev, a base thirty minutes outside of Be'er Sheva, that would serve as my home for the next year. When I arrived, the team was still in the field. By chance, the one soldier who was left behind to guard the team's equipment while the team trained was Noah, the only other American on my team. Noah had grown up in South Central L.A. Unlike most of us, he had held a gun long before he ever wore an IDF uniform. In his neighborhood everyone had guns, and if you didn't, you hung out with people who did. Noah gave me the rundown on the guys, the training, and pretty much everything I wanted to know about the unit that would be my new home. It was extremely comforting to know that I would be serving with another American. After Noah had answered all my questions, we switched to more comfortable subjects—America, girls, and weekend stories. From the start, it was clear to me that even though two Jewish Americans could not have come from more different backgrounds, we would get along very well.

I was restless that first night, nervous for the next day when I would meet the guys I would be serving with for the next two years. The team returned from the field around three o'clock and arrived at the company compound. I answered the question "Who are you?" at least twenty times before my new officer, Bashari, finally caught wind that his team would have a new member. Comically, and tellingly, he found out about it not from his commanding officer but from one of his own soldiers, who mentioned it to him in passing. A few hours later, Bashari and I sat down together next to the volleyball court at the edge of our company's living quarters and got to know one another. I could tell that Bashari was inherently skeptical. Trust in a serious combat unit was not given for free—it had to be earned.

Many military officers advance because they don't upset their superiors and because they dutifully check the boxes required to reach the next rank. That was not Bashari. Bashari became an officer because the people who knew him well were so fiercely loyal to him that the idea of him not being a leader was unfathomable. Bashari grew up outside of Arad, a small city on the edge of the Negev desert. He'd spent twelve years in a yeshiva, and though he'd gone through a rough streak during his teenage years, he found himself in the army. Bashari was not long on words, but the few words he chose to speak were uttered with complete confidence and could not be misinterpreted as suggestions. You took those orders as gospel, not for fear of punishment but for fear that you would disappoint him. Throughout my service, though we did not always see eye to eye, we always respected each other. He respected my commitment to Israel, and I respected his leadership, quick-thinking, and fierce loyalty to his soldiers. Where other officers handed down orders from their superiors without a second thought, Bashari fought tooth and nail to get us the best of everything.

In Duvdevan, having finished counter-terror school, a twelve-week navigation course, and 85 percent of the training we would undergo before becoming operational, we were treated well. The lack of all basic freedoms that defined the first eleven months of training had gradually been replaced by increased freedom and responsibility. We had earned the right to use our phones at various points throughout the day instead of just an hour before bed, and we referred to our officer by his first name. When I joined Orev Givati, however, I was quickly reminded that soldiers eight months into their service are treated much differently than those who have passed the one-year mark. In the first few weeks with my new team, we were disciplined frequently for minor infractions, such as violating the grooming and cleanliness standards, and we spent hours each day in the push-up position.

The man responsible for carrying out most of that discipline was my new sergeant, Togeba. Togeba was not immediately intimidating like my sergeant from Duvdevan. He was smaller and more soft-spoken. Like Bashari, though, Togeba was confident, quick-thinking, and pragmatic, all of which made him an effective leader. Both Bashari and Togeba were street-smart. They demonstrated a practical leadership that can't be learned in a classroom or read in a book. Though I would eventually develop great respect for Togeba, our relationship had strained beginnings.

CHAPTER 35: NEW BEGINNINGS

My first full week with my new team was spent in the field. December is the heart of the rainy season in Israel, and it poured for most of the week. It was so cold and wet that whenever a military jeep approached our campsite, we sprinted to wherever the car had stopped to capture a few seconds of heat from the hood. Shortly after we arrived in the field, one of my new teammates discovered that he had forgotten to bring a sleeping bag. Eager to fit into my new squadron, I offered to share mine with him. I unzipped the bag, and the two of us slept beneath it. The result was that both of us were freezing as the temperature dropped into the upper thirties, but we survived. The next morning, my new friend decided to air out the sleeping bag, which he thought would be the considerate thing to do after sharing it. Unfortunately, this decision preempted the settling of the morning dew, which is one of the many problems with waking up before 5:00 a.m. When he went to return it to our tent shortly after lunch, he found it was soaking wet. As they say, the road to hell is paved with good intentions. Fortunately, Bashari managed to find us a new sleeping bag, which we continued to share for the rest of the week.

When I completed my navigation final in Duvdevan, it was one of the happiest moments of my training, as I was sure that I would never again have to complete another navigational exercise. Unfortunately for me, when I joined Orev Givati, my team had not yet begun their navigation training, and in the ten weeks that followed, to my despair, we repeated many of the same navigations I had completed during my training in Duvdevan. In recognition of this, I was left behind on base for a disproportionate number of these navigations to guard the equipment and man our team's post on the edge of the base.

The post, known simply as "the bunker," was for all intents and purposes located at the end of the earth. It was both a curse and a blessing to be stationed there. It was a curse because it was over half a mile away from our living quarters. At night, and particularly in the rain, the walk was extremely unpleasant since it led through trees and ditches that flooded in the winter. But it was also a blessing. As a soldier in training, you are almost never alone. You are constantly surrounded by your fellow soldiers while eating, showering, sleeping, and everything in between. Doing guard duty was the only time you could be alone while on base. Our commanders had held the post as soldiers and were well aware of the temptation to steal a few extra minutes of sleep while guarding there. As a result, they asked that the vehicular patrol that circled the base check on us to be sure that there was someone standing upright in the tower.

Out of fear of punishment, as well as my desire to utilize every minute of respite from the cacophony of life on base, I never slept on guard duty. I did, however, take advantage of the time in ways that were not exactly in line with the army's prescribed method of guarding an empty landscape. Since Israel is seven hours ahead of New York and my shifts were often in the middle of the night, I made good use of my bluetooth, which nobody would be able to see from the road, to speak to friends and family at home. My friends recounted weekend getaways, crazy nights out, and exciting experiences. Though I knew that I was exactly where I belonged, at times I felt like I was getting left behind as those closest to me moved forward with their lives. Despite the strength of my conviction, life as a soldier was hard physically and, especially, mentally.

CHAPTER 36: THE LIFE OF A SOLDIER

There is a restaurant in Tel Aviv called Benedict, which is Israel's slightly more upscale version of IHOP. On long weeks in the field, I would dream about their breakfast, and as a result, it was almost always my first stop when I was given weekend leave. As I sat with whatever friends happened to be off base that weekend, ordering all the food I had dreamed about, I consumed more calories in a meal than most people consume in a day. In the afternoons, I liked to sit at my favorite café on the corner of Ben Yehuda and Nordau, sip on a cold beer, and write about the army. Whenever I was given the chance to get away from the responsibilities and unrelenting scrutiny of army life, even for a short while, I felt it was important to take some time to reflect. When possible, I tried to share those reflections with friends and family in blog posts that ultimately became the inspiration for this book.

After particularly tough weeks, I would skip the café and retreat to my room, where I would ice my latest ailment as I wrote and drank scotch to kill the pain. Often, it was not only physical pain I sought to escape but also loneliness. Despite a good network of friends, I missed my family and the stable support system they provided to turn to when times were hard.

For any soldier who has sought escape in the form of a few too many stiff drinks, the routine is a familiar one. It starts with a cold beer. That first sip, that first moment the cold beer washes across your palette, is simultaneously refreshing and relaxing. As the alcohol sets in, a sip becomes a bottle, and one bottle becomes three. Gradually, your reality begins to drift to a state beyond stress, beyond the shouting of your sergeant, the sleepless nights in the field, and the other tortures of army life. With each sip and each finished bottle, the reality of your existence slips further and further from your consciousness.

The high that you seek is not one of inebriation but rather freedom from commitment, order, and accountability—your three masters for at least twenty-four days each month. As you laugh, drink, and swap stories with friends, inevitably weekend trips, post-army travels, and lunch plans for the following afternoon are all promised, all with the best of intentions. But these promises made over strong drinks are washed away with the first rays of the dawn and replaced by a dull throbbing as the morning brings with it the harsh reality of your existence: your life is not your own.

At that time, nearly five months after the girl I had been seeing had returned to the United States, I had started seeing another girl to whom I had been introduced by a mutual friend. I met her on a Friday, took her out that Saturday, and quickly found myself very interested in her—a dangerous thing for a combat soldier courting a girl visiting from abroad. After hanging out that weekend, I went back to base, and we texted back and forth for several hours each day. As the weeks went by, however, the strain of army life began to take a toll. Our lives were dramatically different: she was living in Tel Aviv on a gap year from graduate school, and I was training for the special forces. After a few cycles of two weeks on base and one weekend off, our texting grew strained, and it was clear that distance was wedging a gap between us. During one such cycle, we set plans for the following weekend when I was scheduled to be off base. As that weekend approached, and our excitement grew with the anticipation of seeing each other again, our conversations grew more frequent.

I was confident things were back on track, and on the Friday morning of our intended departure from base, I was as high spirited as one can be while still on a military base. I happily mopped the floor of our room in preparation for inspection, showered, trimmed my beard, and prepared for my highly anticipated reentrance into civilian life for the weekend. At 8:00 a.m. the rumors began, which by 10:00 a.m. were confirmed: rioting in Judea and Samaria had canceled our weekend leave, and we would be spending the weekend on guard duty.

With a heavy heart, I texted her the news, promising that we would hang out the next weekend I was off, but I knew even as I typed the words that this final army-induced hiccup would lead to the end of our budding romance. Her responses to my texts became increasingly shorter in length and slower as the week progressed, and the next time I was off base, she told me she had friends in town and wouldn't be able to hang out.

While I have adopted most of what I wrote in my blog for inclusion in this book, there are certain things I wrote which I feel so accurately captured my emotions when I wrote them that to change them would be to betray their raw honesty. This blog entry I wrote shortly after our canceled weekend leave was one such post:

3/31/2012

When you look forward to something enough, you set yourself up to be disappointed. And yet, hours of guarding an empty landscape forces a soldier to dream. He must do so, if only to stay sane. And so he dreams. He dreams of a day at the beach. Of a lazy morning spent relaxing in bed. Of a Saturday morning stroll down a busy Tel Aviv street with no destination in mind. He plans the little time he has off to the minute. Where he will have his breakfast, lunch, and dinner, and with whom. Of dinner with a romantic interest. Being a soldier, and a man in general, however, his plans are but drawings in the sand.

When we were children, the world was so big, and so open before us. Our drawings in the sand would spring to life. Small piles of sand soared on a moment's thought towards the heavens, and formed spiraling castles; knights in shining armor shot up from the ground. The world was ours and everything in it; all of our dreams were possibilities. I was going to grow up to be a famous baseball player. Everyone would know my name, and kids would imitate my swing in little league for decades to come. When my baseball career ended, I was going to be president. And then G-I-Joe. Nothing was beyond my reach. My biggest concern in life was whether my Mom would be packing Oreos or chips in the following day's lunch bag. But those days are forever behind me, and with their passing, so too has passed my ability to stretch my imagination as I once could. To this day some of my happiest memories were as a child, growing up in that beautiful brick house on Bradford road, with a nice lawn, a white fence, and a pleasant next-door neighbor who we baked cookies for when her husband passed away. Then, being grown up was so far away that in my wildest dreams I could never imagine what it would be like. But unlike the lost boy who shares my name, real people are forced to grow up.

As adults, our plans are like drawings in the sand, hazy in their detail and fleeting in their nature. And if that wasn't enough, they have gotten harder to draw. The pen is not fine enough to draw the picture in as much detail as we would like. The knights in shining armor no longer spring up from the sand. Castles that spiral towards the sky no longer block out the sun.

As any artist will tell you, God is in the details. You can go over the same centimeter of canvas for hours and hours, and yet it still will haunt you. The flower can always be a little bit brighter. The face can always be a little bit more realistic. And this with fine tipped brushes. And so, as adults, without fine tipped brushes, unable to summon the imaginative powers we possessed so strongly as children, and with so much we cannot control, we are left with fuzzy pictures. As children, we controlled everything in our fantasy worlds. But in the real world, some things are beyond our control. Your friends aren't always off base on the same weekend that you are; protests on the borders can cancel your weekend leave at the last minute; the girl who seemed so interested in you the last time you were home can lose interest by the time you're out on your next weekend leave, 21 days later. And in a moment, when we turn our heads away, an incoming wave can wash away our drawing, leaving in its wake no proof that such a drawing ever existed. It becomes a passing dream, remembered only in the mind of its creator. And thus are we destined to keep drawing pictures that are never quite clear enough, that, even when completed to an acceptable degree, will forever be washed away by the incoming waves. But absent alternatives, we draw on, and carry on, and as Fitzgerald wrote, "beat on, boats against the current, borne back ceaselessly into the past."

CHAPTER 37: NAVIGATION BEGINS... AGAIN

When my team began the navigation course, the bunker and I became well acquainted. I spent many hours during those first few weeks perched atop the tower at the far end of the base. Though the shifts were long, I enjoyed the time for quiet reflection that it provided. Unfortunately, I did not always evade the navigations, and there were many nights when I repeated the same navigation I had done a few short months earlier.

The weather had grown colder—the start of our course coincided with the winter season in Israel. Before each week's navigation, we would board the buses bound for the starting point of the first night's navigation, and often, from the comfort of our heated coach bus, we would hear the wind howling furiously outside. Some nights, the landscape was barely visible through the rain-streaked windows, and the only audible sounds were the pounding of rain droplets against the roof and the soothing sound of the windshield wipers. Those nights would have been perfect for throwing some popcorn in the microwave, snuggling underneath the blankets, and putting on a good movie. I was often dreaming about that exact scenario when, suddenly, my fantasy would be torn from me by the awful "pshhhh" sound that signified the imminent opening of the bus's doors. Every combat soldier in the Israeli special forces knows that there is no worse sound than the opening of those bus doors before a navigation or a surprise stretcher march. During the winter, the misery of the physical challenge of navigating long distances on very little sleep while carrying heavy weights is intensified by the weather. While you are exerting yourself, the cold is almost tolerable. But the second you stop, an icy chill overtakes you as the moisture trapped between your body and your cotton uniform serves as a conductor for the cold breeze.

Throughout my training, particularly during navigations, I saw more of Israel in three years than I could have reasonably expected to see in a decade as a civilian. I loved the rolling mountains and the musty smell of forest air on long hikes. I was awed by the spectacular sunsets over the Mediterranean Sea on weekends off in Tel Aviv, as well as the sunrises over the towering hills of Judea and Samaria during weekends of guard duty. I paused often to marvel at the blossoming yellow flowers that sprang up all over our base in early April. I could stare endlessly at the whitecaps that floated gently across the glimmering surface of the Mediterranean Sea, like a sheet being pulled over the bed of a sleeping child. I found wonder in the heavy mist and deep silence that would set over the Golan Heights in the early hours of the morning. Throughout my time in Israel, I was taken by the beauty that surrounded me. The army, in this regard, was a double-edged sword. While it exposed me to much beauty, at times it made that beauty difficult to enjoy. You can't take in the beauty of your surroundings when you are storming a hill and firing a gun at targets, nor can you get the essence of a city and its people when your purpose is to guard its citizens and look out for suspicious behavior.

Throughout my service, I often wished that I could experience the beauty of Israel's landscape without an ammunition belt and a gun. I longed to watch the sunset on a weekday with a whiskey instead of a weapon; to walk the streets of the cities we guarded wearing sandals instead of boots; to watch the children play soccer in the streets, and not from behind a wall of cement. In basic and advanced training, I was constantly dreaming of tropical vacations: of cruise ships and cabins, of physical escape in all its forms. But as I adjusted to the life of a soldier, I reached the conclusion that the place I was searching for was not a tropical island or a mountain cabin but rather a mental place, one that exists inside of each of us. It is a place of inner peace, where we are happy with who we are, what we are doing, and who is with us on the journey. Upon reflection, it occurred to me that my purpose as a soldier was more important and fulfilling than the happiness gained by indulging in the pleasures and beauties of civilian life. After over a year in the military, despite my occasional yearnings for freedom, I was content to be exactly where I was.

My parents and me at my end of training ceremony

With Natan and Ayala in Tel Aviv

With Meema and Poppa at The
Western Wall

The Sirkin 17 family

My certificate of completion of training

A team photo before the final march of training

Team Bashari during an overnight march

Celebrating the end of training with friends and family
(LtoR - Arnold, Rafi, Corey, Mindy, Ellyn, Sydell, Rachel,
Andy, Daniel)

CHAPTER 38: COUNTER-TERROR TRAINING

When our navigation training ended, we began a week of counter-terror training that was reputed to be one of the hardest weeks of the Orev Givati training regimen. On the first day of the training, we were doing *yevesheem* when our instructor called out a command that my teammates had never heard before: "The terrorist fell!" I immediately sprinted towards the cardboard box meant to symbolize the terrorist and (simulated) emptying my magazine into him. We had been taught in Duvdevan to validate the neutralization of a threat. It was not enough to injure someone who might still be able to harm civilians or other soldiers. My teammates looked at me in surprise. The head trainer chuckled. "I guess they taught you well in Duvdevan," he said, visibly pleased. I smiled, satisfied that I had impressed him, but reminded yet again of how much training I was repeating as a result of dropping a training class.

Throughout the week, we were forbidden to speak to one another. We were treated once again like we were in basic training: everything was timed. Twelve minutes to wake up, change into uniform, brush our teeth, clean our room, and stand at attention. Twenty minutes to eat. Four minutes to unload a fully packed bus and organize its contents outside a shooting range 500 feet from the bus. When we failed to complete the task in time, half of the team held the push-up position on our elbows while the other half worked. We spent hours each day at the shooting range working on our form and our accuracy.

Each day also included hours of Krav Maga. One of the most painful drills tested our core strength and mental fortitude. Partnered with someone of equal size, for twenty-second intervals, one of us would stand with his hands over his head wearing minimal padding while the other threw jabs and crosses to his partner's stomach at eighty percent strength. We did not need to be told to keep our arms up at all times while being hit. The shame would hurt more than the bruises if we put our hands down to protect ourselves. While that week pushed us to our limits physically, it also challenged us psychologically.

At the end of the week, we were on our way back to base when our bus came to an abrupt stop. It was shortly before 6:00 a.m., and we were parked in the shadow of a giant mountain. Seconds later, we heard the voice of our officer: "Three minutes, everyone with their gear on, stretchers in the air facing the mountain." There was no time to be upset or tired; we immediately sprang into action. The grueling march took close to three hours, and by the time we reached the summit the temperature was well into the eighties and continuing to rise. Exhausted after a long week and a long march, we trudged down the mountain and back to the buses. When everything was packed up, we loaded ourselves back onto the bus and were all asleep within minutes. Five minutes after the bus had begun to move, we once again felt it come to a stop, and opened our eyes to find ourselves in front of the same mountain. Our officer repeated the same command: "Three minutes, everyone with their gear on, stretchers in the air facing the mountain."

Many of us were sure we were simply dreaming. The rushed movements of those who knew they were not spurred the rest of us to action. After the allotted time had passed, we stood next to the stretchers, now loaded with sandbags, in a mixture of shock and exasperation. On our officer's command, in the absence of any alternative, we ignored our exhaustion and pain, lifted the stretchers upon our already sore shoulders, and repeated the climb once again. At many points during that march, my body threatened to give out under the weight of the stretchers, but somehow my legs kept moving me forward.

While that week was incredibly challenging, with many similarities to counter-terror school, I enjoyed it more than nearly any other week of training. I didn't go to bed each night wishing I was in Tel Aviv or New York or on some distant tropical island. I lived in the moment and enjoyed it for what it was—an opportunity to become a better soldier in the defense of Israel. I looked forward to the challenge of each day, and to the feeling of running on empty and pushing myself that extra step. I can't, as a sane human being, tell you that I enjoyed the pain in the moment. But I enjoyed the knowledge, even in the most painful moments, that I was training to defend something that I believed in so strongly.

As we approached the end of training, the challenges that pushed us to our physical limits grew increasingly frequent, culminating in a week known as Sof Maslool, or The End Of Training.

CHAPTER 39: THE FINAL TEST

I started my training in November 2010 at the Paratroopers training base near Kiryat Gat. In May 2012, nearly a year and a half to the day that I had first become an IDF soldier, that is exactly where the buses dropped us off to begin our final week of training. As a trained soldier, it was strange to go back to the place where I had felt so young and inexperienced at the start of my service. I thought back to all the training I'd been through. The sleepless, bitterly cold nights, blistering hot days, and the weighted marches that never seemed to end. I remembered the despondent feeling of not being able to see the end anywhere on the horizon. And yet, in May 2012, that end was finally in sight.

The final week of training for special forces soldiers is a harder version of the War Week experienced during advanced training. The week was planned by Arik, the man whose interview had landed me in my unit and who was responsible for the oversight of the entire company's training. He was quite qualified to design a week that would simulate a war, having been in several of them.

We started the week on Sunday, carrying enough food in our bags for forty-eight hours. At 21:00, we got a final speech from Arik, a mix of motivation and explanation. The captain of our company decided that the final week required a special send-off, and no sooner had Major Arik finished speaking than were two tear gas grenades unleashed in our direction, which sent us sprinting down the road with full gear on our backs. Unfortunately for us, the wind was at our backs, which meant that for close to ten minutes we were subjected to the lingering remnants of the gas. It was not a pleasant way to begin the week, but as Arik had stressed in his briefing of the week to come, war is not meant to be pleasant. Each night followed roughly the same format: we would walk for about seven miles, execute a drill and then walk for another seven miles before grabbing a few hours of sleep. The drills tested everything we had learned: taking enemy-controlled hills, fighting in close quarters, and even snatching a terror suspect from his car. Towards the end of each drill, inevitably someone would be designated as injured, and for the next two to three miles we would carry him on a stretcher.

As we walked through the barren desert hills each night, every hill looking the same as the last, my eyes fixated on the tiny headlights on the horizon. In a few short days, I would be in one of those cars with my parents and grandparents on the way from my end-of-training ceremony back to Tel Aviv. I drew strength from the approaching conclusion of my training, which, like those headlights, was now visible on the horizon. On our nightly marches, we stopped every hour for a short water break. As soon as our officer motioned to the team that we would be stopping, the silence would be broken abruptly by the sound of twenty exhausted young men simultaneously falling backwards onto the ground, bag first. Though our giant packs made walking difficult, they made excellent reclining chairs. Those ten minutes of rest were so precious that nobody dared waste even a second to bend over and sit, choosing instead to fall backward and attain instant gratification.

One evening, we were ordered to take control of a house from which we were told we had drawn fire. Though it was only a drill, the perils of urban warfare became abundantly clear. The house had multiple rooms, and the walls that separated them were peppered with openings. Loud Arabic music was blasted from a speaker inside the house, and our officers were shouting frantically in Arabic. As blanks were fired all around us, the sound of explosions echoed through the hollow walls of the open structure. The chaos of not knowing where the gunfire was coming from, the darkness, and the difficulty distinguishing combatants from civilians made the situation hellish. The cacophony of gunfire, music and shouting made it nearly impossible to give orders or to hear them. The situation called for lightning-quick decisions to address complex life-threatening situations and efficient delegation of responsibility. We left the exercise disappointed in our performance but with an acute understanding of why casualties are so high in urban warfare.

One of the greatest physical challenges of the week came on the morning of the fourth day in the field. Shortly before sunrise, after marching through the night, we had set up our missile system and gone through the motions of taking out an imaginary enemy supply train. As soon as we achieved our objective, the point at which we assumed we'd be getting a few hours of sleep, we were told to prepare for a march. Sleep-deprived, disappointed, and physically exhausted, we switched to autopilot. We robotically packed up our gear and assisted in securing the team gear. The latter included a missile system that weighed several hundred pounds, which we distributed into several different bags. The training missiles were particularly heavy and awkward. We rotated them around so that no single person had to carry them for too long. By sheer bad luck, my turn to carry the missile came moments before our officer told us to make our gas masks available. After stopping briefly to dig out our masks from our packs, we continued our march through a riverbed. We were exhausted, hot, and at each second expecting to hear the telltale sound of an expiring gas grenade.

About fifteen minutes into the journey, it finally came; the awful hissing noise that accompanies the dispersal of tear gas from the grenade. We quickly put on our masks and continued to walk, our ability to breathe severely diminished in the constricting masks. Several minutes later, two soldiers were designated as injured. After opening the stretchers and fastening the injured onto them, just as we would do on a real mission, we continued our progress towards our objective, a hill several miles away. The officers continued to throw gas grenades at us as we walked, lest anyone think of removing their mask.

We had been tear gassed regularly throughout training, and I knew from experience that my beard would prevent the mask from gripping my face effectively. As the first grenade went off, I silently pledged to myself that I would not let the gas cause me to break or abandon my responsibilities. If the Recon Marines could walk through steady gas for two miles, I reasoned I could walk through three miles with scattered gas attacks.

The missiles I was carrying extended about two feet over my shoulders and weighed a considerable amount. For the first fifteen minutes of the march, I didn't rotate under the stretchers. I stayed in the back with the injured and with others whose bags were abnormally heavy or oddly shaped. By this time, there were a significant number of injured soldiers who were ordered by the doctor not to participate in stretcher marches. Others, like me, believed we couldn't participate due to the equipment we were carrying. We struggled to move forward. Those under the stretchers staggered under their weight with very few replacements. Between the heat, the gas, and the lack of sleep, I drifted between fantasy and reality. My next conscious realization was that I had closed the distance between myself and the stretchers, and I was tapping the shoulder of my friend who was struggling, which was his cue that I wanted to replace him under the stretcher. I had been in serious pain from carrying the missile, suffering silently as my team carried the stretchers, but a switch had flipped inside of me, and suddenly that pain no longer mattered. All that mattered was our collective goal: to finish the march. My body was simply a vessel to achieve that end. I suddenly felt energized by the intermittent gas grenades being thrown at us; the more obstacles we encountered, the more committed I became to succeeding.

After nearly an hour, we made it to the home stretch, a 600-foot hill that appeared to slope upward at a fifty-degree incline. It was without question the steepest slope we had climbed in training, let alone with stretchers. When we reached the base of the hill, I had already been under the stretcher for some time. Though I hadn't raised my fist in the air to signify an imminent need for replacement, I was silently hoping someone would switch me out. As we stood before the intimidatingly steep slope, our officer shouted some brief words of motivation. When we began the ascent, I knew that there would be no relief. Switching people out from under the stretcher on an incline that severe would be both dangerous and ineffectual; the ones who started under the stretcher would be the ones who finished. A short distance from the top, I felt my body folding under the crippling weight of the stretcher and the missiles. But in that last second, right before I was certain that I was going to fall and drop the stretcher, I felt a burst of energy surge through me. Somehow, I found the extra reserve of strength I needed to make it to the top. As we reached the peak and put down the stretcher, I was exhausted but exhilarated by the knowledge that we were less than twenty-four hours from the end of training.

Throughout that week, my sergeant, Togeba, pushed me forward when my resolve faltered. Togeba and I had butted heads often when I began my training in Orev Givati. I had a chip on my shoulder about having to do an additional 6 months of training as a result of switching units, and Togeba had little patience for my attitude. Fortunately, as time passed, I came to appreciate that Orev Givati afforded me a different but equally meaningful opportunity to serve Israel. As training progressed, we grew to respect each other. As a fighter, a status I would attain at the week's end, he would no longer be my drill sergeant; he would be a leader and a friend. We would have to place our lives in each others' hands.

Fifteen hours after finishing the stretcher march up that steep hill, we began the final march of training. Fourteen miles under the stretchers was all that separated us from attaining the status of fighters. The first few miles were the hardest for me. My bag was heavy, my legs were throbbing, and I was exhausted. Each step felt crushing. Just as thoughts of self-doubt began to wash over me, my sergeant looked me in the eyes, as if he was reading my mind, slapped me on the back, and with a big grin yelled, "*Yalla*-Let's go!" His encouragement and the warm look in his eyes as he urged me onward revealed the shifting dynamics of our relationship. I took a deep breath and, with his encouragement, found the strength I needed to keep moving forward.

Nearly four hours and countless tear gas grenades later, our training base finally came into sight, which gave all of us a boost of energy. Our arrival would signify the end of the march and our training. Just as my training had begun with abundant similarities to summer camp, so too did it end that way. When we were a few hundred feet from the end, in an act comically similar to visiting day at summer camp, those who had come to attend our ceremony, who had been held back until that point, were allowed to run towards us and cheer us along as they ran alongside the stretchers. In our exhausted, sleep deprived state, the explosions of colored smoke grenades all around us contributed to a dreamlike atmosphere.

Completing the final march of my training with my friends and family beside me, I was overwhelmed by feelings of pride and accomplishment. It was the achievement of a dream. I had earned my spot on the team with my blood, sweat, and tears. My year and a half of training had tested every ounce of my idealism, motivation and Zionism. I was surprised and humbled to see that in addition to my family, three close friends, Daniel, Jacob, and Bernardo, had also made the three-hour trip south to attend the ceremony. Nearly two years earlier, as the special forces tryouts approached, the three of them trained me, providing me with an advantage that they never had. The guidance and training they gave me were instrumental in my success.

My parents, grandparents and Aunt Amy had all flown in for the ceremony. When I saw my grandmother, I was reminded of a conversation we'd had two and a half years earlier at my kitchen table. She had asked me about my motivations for joining the army. When I explained to her why I was enlisting, she was silent for a few moments, before telling me with conviction in her voice that she understood. She promised that she and my grandfather would attend every ceremony commemorating a milestone in my service. She kept her word.

After we had crossed the finish line and put down the stretchers, everyone who had come to watch was rushed to their seats while we stood in formation facing the podium. Shortly thereafter the ceremony began with

Israel's national anthem. Tears of pride streamed freely down my face. I had finally achieved what had seemed impossible a few short years earlier. I would now be given the honor and responsibility of defending Israel as an active-duty combat soldier. As the ceremony progressed, awards were given out, and we were addressed by various high-ranking officers, including the head of the reconnaissance company, and the head of the Givati Brigade. The end of training marked the beginning of our *regila*, the seven-day leave every combat soldier receives once every four months.

More than a year earlier, when I had finished my beret march, my father brought me a bottle of Johnnie Walker Blue Label in celebration. Unwilling to take my eyes off the prize until I felt I had reached the true finish line, I had given the bottle to my roommate Daniel to hide from me and save for the day I finished training. That evening, I took that bottle and a big Montecristo Cuban cigar to the top-floor lounge of the Sheraton where my parents were staying. Smoking that cigar and enjoying several glasses of Johnnie Walker Blue, with my family beside me and a beautiful sunset view over Tel Aviv beach, I was happier than I'd been in a long, long time.

The week with my family flew by. We hung out on the beach during the day and enjoyed amazing dinners at night. It was hard to say goodbye to my family, but I knew I would soon be given a month off to see them in NY. As I prepared to go back to base, I was excited that I would finally be able to contribute to Israel as an active-duty soldier. The real challenges would now begin.

The mag: my constant companion

Dressed up for Sean's wedding

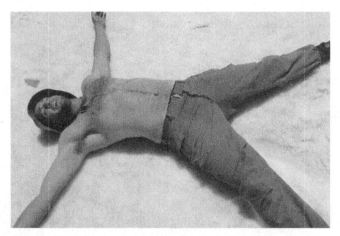

Taking advantge of a rare snowfall

Me and Daniel after a
weekend workout

Tzvika Levi, the "the father of
lone soldiers"

A surprise stretcher march up Mt. Tabor

Carly and me at Oktoberfest

At the range

PART SIX: LIFE AS A COMBAT SOLDIER

CHAPTER 40: THE GAZA BORDER

Our first assignment as active-duty combat soldiers was to Nachal Oz, a small base located less than a mile from the Gaza Strip. While trained combat soldiers in the U.S. military can be deployed to dangerous places, Israel doesn't keep any troops stationed outside the state of Israel. As such, deployments, which seem a world away from the comforts of home, are actually only a few hours' drive and are better termed assignments. After a long day of packing up our gear, we hopped on the bus that would take us from our training base to our new base of operations. Terminally overtired, I drifted off to sleep.

After what felt like seconds, the bus jolted to a stop outside the gates of the base we would call our home for the next six months. The temperature was reportedly just shy of 100 degrees Fahrenheit, and there was no breeze. We were already sweating profusely on the unairconditioned bus, but were ordered to put on our heavy army issued shirts before unloading the team's gear. After lunch, our rooms were unlocked, and our worst nightmares were confirmed: 80 percent of them didn't have air-conditioning. Given our proximity to Gaza (at its closest point, the base was less than 2,000 feet from the strip), we were required to wear full equipment at all times, even when not on patrol. The rooms, which were made of cement, trapped heat to the point where it was often hotter inside than it was outside.

During the previous few months, Hamas had intensified its attempts to kill and capture soldiers. As a result, much of our time was spent in stakeouts a few hundred feet from the border, where we would spend thirty-six to forty-eight hours searching through our missile scope for suspicious activity. Sitting under a camouflaged net in full gear with dozens of flies swarming around our heads in the sweltering heat of the Israeli summer was—and remains—my least favorite activity of all time. During those first few months the days seemed to blend together. We rotated from patrols, to guard duty, to stakeouts. The brutal schedule left little time for anything else.

When we were not on duty, we were assigned workouts and runs to complete on our own. As active-duty special operations soldiers, our officer trusted us to complete our workouts without supervision or babysitting. One evening, on one such run, I rounded the corner of the path that ran parallel to the wall that surrounded the base and found myself temporarily blinded by the rays of the setting sun. As my eyes adjusted, they fell upon an incredible sight. The sun, now looking more like a glowing orange fireball, was retreating behind a backdrop of palm trees. The evening sky radiated with a mixture of orange, red, and pink hues, almost as if a man perched upon the setting sun had thrown buckets of paint across the sky to create the effect. The oppressive heat of the day had finally given way to the cool of the early evening, and a light, refreshing breeze swept across my face as I came around the turn and out from behind the cover of the buildings.

Beyond the palm trees lay the Mediterranean Sea, which would have completed the tropical vista but for one small detail; between that beautiful body of water and myself, among the two million Arabs living in the Gaza strip, were many people who would like to see Israel wiped off the map. Some of them were actively trying to make that vision a reality.

For a second, as I rounded that corner and saw the sun retreating behind those palm trees, I forgot where I was. But just as quickly, I remembered. My eyes followed the tips of the palm trees and traced them downwards, where they fell upon the top of a large cement wall, which served as cover against sniper fire. A big, unsightly reminder of the state of affairs; of young men and women destined for endless conflict along a border that is never really at peace. The army, like a piece of abstract art, is a random mixture of darks and lights, of good and bad. They are intertwined with one another, and one highlights the other just as the shadows in a painting accentuate the light. And every now and then, even in the midst of an oppressive week, of an act of intense physical strain, of an ugly state of conflict, we can be momentarily distracted by a fleeting display of divine beauty. Almost as if sent to remind us that there is always good to be found, even though so much sadness surrounds us.

While on guard duty before sunrise the following morning, I watched a tank roar to life a few dozen feet from my station. The moonlight, already dulled by the rapidly approaching dawn, still enveloped the tank, which seemed to shine even as it was engulfed by a cloud of dust kicked up by its own stirrings. It was strangely beautiful. And yet the purpose of a tank is to seek out and destroy human life. I wondered in that moment, and still wonder, if it is possible for an instrument of destruction to be beautiful. And is it then possible that the beautiful and the ugly are not as easy to distinguish from each other as I once believed? Maybe, as in a painting, there are places where the shadows and the light are intertwined. Things that are simultaneously beautiful and ugly.

As fall approached, and with it Yom Kippur, the day of Jewish atonement, three other soldiers and I learned that we would be spending the holiday asking for repentance in a guard tower along the Gaza border. On Friday night, we sat together looking out over Gaza and recited the Yom Kippur prayers. We ate incremental servings of salted hot dogs and plain white bread in accordance with what the Military rabbi had decreed for soldiers on active duty during the fast. I felt extremely proud to be watching over the people of Israel on such a holy day. As fall turned to winter, the frequency of missile attacks from Gaza intensified, as did terrorist activity along the border. During that period, nearly two years into my military service, I would find myself face to face with a terrorist for the first time.

CHAPTER 41: THE ENEMY

"Rapid-response team from dispatch, we have reports of an infiltration into Israel from Gaza. Over." We were sleeping when the alarm sounded. We jumped out of bed, grabbed our guns, threw on our vests, and within minutes were speeding in armored vehicles towards the suspected infiltration point. We were told along the way that two figures had jumped the fence separating Gaza from Israel at around 4:00 a.m. and were moving in the direction of a nearby settlement. By the time we arrived, the suspects had already been apprehended by a patrol, blindfolded and handcuffed, their knives confiscated.

My officer walked off to discuss the details of the incident with the soldiers who had made the arrest. At that point, I found myself alone with one of the terrorists. I sat in silence with my weapon trained on him. He had crossed into Israel from Gaza with a large knife and the intention to harm Israeli civilians, which made him a terrorist by definition. The problem was that he didn't fit my stereotype of a terrorist. He was skinny and wore sandals and Puma parachute pants. At 14, the same age as my sister at the time, he was tall for his age, but not particularly tall. I could see that he was shaking with fear. My thoughts drifted to my sister and her classmates at Jewish day school, who were taught to respect the religious, cultural, and sexual preferences of others. I remembered her telling me during our last phone call that a speaker had addressed the entire school on the topic of tolerance. Golda Meir once famously said, "When peace comes we will perhaps in time be able to forgive the Arabs for killing our sons, but it will be harder for us to forgive them for having forced us to kill their sons. Peace will come when the Arabs will love their children more than they hate us." As I sat there staring at that scared boy, I thought about her words, and how close he had probably come to being shot by the patrol that picked him up.

The role models in the lives of my sister and her friends were doctors, teachers, rabbis, lawyers, and businesspeople. The role models of the boy sitting before me were radical clergymen and suicide bombers. The public schools in my sister's suburban neighborhood bore the names of generous benefactors and of charitable men and women. Many of the schools in his neighborhood were named after murderers, who had died while taking or attempting to take the lives of soldiers and innocent people. We called them terrorists. On the other side of the fence separating Israel from Gaza, they were called martyrs. I struggled with the cognitive dissonance. On the one hand, he was my enemy. I knew I was supposed to harbor certain feelings towards him, either contempt or at least anger. But as I searched my heart and my mind, I could find neither. What happens when your enemy is not the imposing, remorseless man that you'd dreamed of when you pictured what the first terrorist you encountered would look like? What if he is a scared, blindfolded 14-year-old who has just pissed himself out of fear?

Had we not picked him up, he might very well have made it to the nearby kibbutz and stabbed innocent people before being apprehended or shot. He would not have been the first teenager from Gaza to cross into Israel and kill innocents. After we had dropped him off for questioning, I thought back to photos I had seen published in news outlets like the *New York Times*, of Israeli soldiers with their guns trained on scared, seemingly innocent Palestinian children. I realized that had a reporter been there at that moment, I would have been the soldier on the cover of the newspaper vilified by the international media. Ultimately, stories about villains and victims are far more compelling than the murky area between good and evil that more accurately describes most of reality.

CHAPTER 42: A CHANCE MEETING

We can do everything possible to set ourselves on a path that we believe will lead us to happiness and fulfillment. And yet, it is often the chance meeting of a stranger, who then becomes our partner, possibly for life, which most influences our happiness. There are moments in our lives when we meet people in circumstances that result from factors so unpredictable that it feels as if they are manufactured by a force of nature. The week that began the final year of my service included one such moment.

On Thursday evening, we were happily surprised by the news that we were being given a last-minute weekend liberty. On Friday morning, I excitedly boarded the bus bound for Tel Aviv. After a quick breakfast, I joined my friends on the beach, where we threw around a football and drank a few beers. From there, we headed to my former roommate Daniel's house for an impromptu barbeque. Daniel had a friend from Miami who was spending six months in Israel, and she and her friends stopped by on a last-minute invite. Carly caught my eye the moment she walked out onto the sunny deck of the apartment's balcony. One of my friends, noticing that I couldn't take my eyes off her, asked me how long I was going to stare for before I walked up to her to start a conversation. I glared at him, begrudgingly acknowledged to myself that he was right, and gathered the courage to introduce myself. While the conversation felt easy and unstrained from the start, I felt uncharacteristically shy as I spoke with her. Before I left, I summoned the courage to ask Carly for her number.

The following day, I texted her, asking if she wanted to hang out before I went back to base. Though she declined my invitation, that text began a conversation that progressed from a few texts a day to dozens of texts each day. After several conversations and much convincing, she and her best friend agreed to come camping with a friend and me on our next weekend off base. Thankfully, my friend convinced me that bringing canned tuna and bread from base, which was my game plan for our food, was not what two American girls would be interested in eating on a camping trip. Instead, we stopped to buy real food and a portable grill before picking them up in Tel Aviv. A two-hour scenic drive took us to the shores of the Kinneret, where we parked the car, built our tents, and began cooking dinner. As we ate, drank wine, and exchanged stories, the daylight began to fade. It was a relaxed atmosphere with the sun setting over the Kinneret, the cool breeze, and the muffled conversations of families who had set up their camps in the surrounding area. Far from the commotion and distractions of Tel Aviv, Carly and I got to know each other as we talked and laughed until long after the sun had set. After dinner, the four of us took an evening swim in the Kinneret, finished another bottle of wine, and coupled off into our poorly constructed tents.

Our tent was entirely too small and entirely too hot, but neither of those things seemed to matter as we found ourselves completely immersed in the beauty of the moment and our interest in each other. After talking for twenty minutes in our three-foot-wide tent lying ten inches from each other's faces, she asked me point-blank if I was planning to kiss her. So I did.

Two weeks later, on my next weekend leave, we went out on our first real date. As the hours passed, one bottle of wine became two, and our interest in each other grew. After that first date, we spoke nearly every day and hung out together every weekend I was off base.

Shortly thereafter, I flew back to America for my sister Tara's bat mitzvah. Watching my sister become a woman in the eyes of Judaism was an incredibly special experience. Seeing her so poised and mature as she read from the Torah that morning reminded me that the little girl I had left behind when I'd moved to Israel was turning into a young woman. I was sad that I was not by her side as she grew and matured, nor would I be able to be there for her as she entered the tumultuous teenage years. In the weeks that followed the bat mitzvah, I spent time with family and friends and enjoyed the complete freedom associated with military leave. While it was fun catching up with everyone, I missed Carly, and the deteriorating security situation in Israel left me anxious to return. I didn't know it then, but Israel would soon be involved in a large-scale military operation.

CHAPTER 43: OPERATION PILLAR OF DEFENSE

Throughout the fall of 2012, Hamas militants in Gaza intensified their missile attacks on Israeli population centers. By mid-October, the siren signifying an incoming missile had become a daily routine in Southern Israel, and by early November, we had taken to bringing our mattresses into the bomb shelter before going to sleep. Given the frequency of the nightly sirens, it seemed better to battle the heat and the flies than to run back and forth constantly between our rooms and the shelter. Due to our proximity to the border, there were times when we had only a few seconds between the start of the siren and the telling boom of a fallen Qassam rocket.

One evening in late October, I was on an informational phone interview exploring a future employment opportunity when I heard the *tzeva adome*, the siren signifying an incoming missile. I abruptly interrupted my interviewer, who had just launched into an explanation of her company. "Shit—I'm really sorry. That's the missile siren again. Let me put you on hold for a second." By that point, I had become so desensitized to the missiles that I viewed them as an inconvenience more than anything else. Hearing her shock on the other end of the phone reminded me how remarkably abnormal the situation in Israel was at that time.

On Saturday November 10, 2012, a rocket was fired from Gaza at an army vehicle several hundred meters within Israel. The vehicle was carrying four soldiers from my base on a routine patrol, a patrol I had been on dozens of times before. The rocket hit the vehicle head-on, and every soldier in the vehicle was injured, one critically. From there, things got worse. My team, designated as the first line of defense in the event of incursions across the border, watched helplessly and vulnerably from our semi-fortified vehicle as more than two hundred rockets were fired at Israel over the next several days. Each missile that approached appeared to be coming right at us. Well aware that our lightly armored vehicles would do nothing to protect us if we were hit head-on, we did our best to distract ourselves. We sang songs, exchanged insults—anything to take our minds off the fact that we were sitting in an insufficiently protected armored vehicle a few thousand feet from terrorists shooting missiles at us. Ultimately, Israel's leadership chose to act against the man in charge of Hamas' military wing, who had played a crucial role in the rocket fire as well as numerous terrorist attacks against Israeli civilians over the previous decade.

On November 14, 2012 in the late afternoon, I was sitting on my bed with my headphones on halfway into the movie The Green Mile. I remember the very specific details of the events of that day, just as I can recall exactly what I was wearing, where I was, and how I felt when I was told that two planes had crashed into the World Trade Center on 9/11.

In the middle of a captivating scene of the movie, as I lay comfortably in my bed enjoying the gentle breeze from my small battery-powered bedside fan, the first-responder siren sounded. Over the previous two years, I had been taught to shoot, defend myself in hand-to-hand combat, carry heavy weights for long distances, and various other skills that are essential to a combat soldier. But perhaps the most important thing my training had taught me was the ability to flip a switch in my head and go from relaxing, or even sleeping, to a state of full alert, ready to face whatever challenge might be coming. The moment that siren sounded, that switch flipped.

Those of us on duty rushed to the armored vehicles, arriving fully dressed within the required ninety seconds. As we checked our gear to make sure we had all the necessary equipment, the reason for the siren was revealed to us: intelligence suggested that there was a serious threat of a terrorist infiltration into Israel via a terror tunnel. Our mission would be to defend the kibbutzim and moshavim in our sector and to neutralize any threats that emerged. Seconds later, we were speeding towards the vicinity of the anticipated infiltration point. In retrospect, I believe that the senior ranks of the military, knowing the strike against Jabari was imminent, wanted a strong showing of troops positioned between the border and Israel in the event of cross-border reprisal attacks from Gaza. The threat might have been manufactured to ensure our presence on the border without betraying intelligence about the impending missile strike. I will likely never know for certain.

Shortly after we arrived at the coordinates where the suspicious activity had been reported, we heard a distant explosion. While several months earlier we might have been startled, rocket fire and explosions along the border had become commonplace, and we didn't think much of it. A few minutes later, a teammate who had been reading the news on a phone, which he was not supposed to have, let out a stream of curses. A "Breaking News" alert flashed across his screen. In a solemn voice, he began to read aloud the headline that had caught his eye: "Israel assassinates Hamas military chief Ahmed Jaabari. Hamas: 'Israel has opened the gates of hell.'" Our officer didn't waste even a moment to reprimand my friend for bringing his phone with him. He quickly grabbed the phone out of his hands, since his own phone was still on base, and began calling other officers in the company to try to gather more information.

What happened over the following thirty-six hours was surreal. My team was charged with both reconnaissance and first response. As such, we were required to be in close vicinity to the vehicles, ready to respond to threats to the surrounding Jewish settlements which were a few short kilometers from the border. We also needed to be outside of the vehicles, completely exposed to incoming missiles, in order to successfully carry out reconnaissance of the border, the second and equally important part of our mission.

Later that evening, due to the threat of infiltration and the sheer volume of the shelling that was taking place, our entire base was evacuated. Within twenty-four hours, all of our weapons, gear, and personal belongings had been thrown into bags, loaded onto buses and trucks, and sent east to our training base. In the twenty-four hours immediately following Jabari's assassination, 250 rockets were fired from Gaza at Israel. During that time, six other soldiers from my team, our commanding officer and I were situated in no-man's-land. As the rockets flew overhead, we lay between Gaza and our now-evacuated base, on our stomachs in a divot in the ground surrounded by three earth walls. As the incoming rocket sirens sounded and civilians in the nearby settlements ran for cover, we pressed ourselves against the ground and hoped for the best. With Qassam rockets pounding the surrounding area, car alarms at the nearby kibbutz went off constantly, set off by the impact of rockets exploding in such close proximity.

Three times that day, we heard the screech of a rocket flying directly above where we were lying. Each time, I was certain that life as I knew it was coming to an end. I imagined what it would be like to live without an arm or a leg. Perhaps both. As the sound of each rocket grew louder, I pressed myself as close as I could to the ground, hoping that the ominous whistling that accompanied its approach wouldn't be the last sound I heard on this earth. One of the missiles landed less than two hundred feet from where we were sprawled, on the other side of one of the dirt walls behind which we had taken cover. Dirt and rocks were thrown dozens of feet into the air as the rocket exploded, and as the ground shook, so did our collective sanity. The screech of an incoming rocket is unlike any other sound in the world. It is distinct, it is haunting, and it is one I will never forget.

The assassination of the Hamas military chief spelled the beginning of Israel's offensive. When we weren't taking cover from incoming missiles, we looked on hopefully as Israel finally began to fight back against the terrorists. Shortly after dark, I watched a Blackhawk helicopter fire a missile into the darkness in the direction of what I knew to be the Gaza skyline. Suddenly, a mushroom cloud began to grow on the distant horizon, and seconds later came the sound of the accompanying explosion. Several minutes later, I watched three grad missiles launched in unison in the direction of Be'er Sheva, and I was once again pressed against the ground, my heart pounding so furiously that I feared it would beat right out of my chest. The next day, several Israeli tanks rolled down the road and stopped adjacent to our position. The thundering sound of their firing was deafening, and often left us confused as to whether we had taken fire or received it. For over a year following the operation, every time a door slammed or a siren sounded, I jumped as my body instinctively prepared to enter fight-or-flight mode.

During the two nights we spent in that position, we watched secondary explosions from ammunition storages throw towering orange flames against the darkened Gaza skyline. At dawn, only a cloud of smoke would remain where the house or weapons storage had previously stood. We later learned that in an act unprecedented in its scope in the history of warfare, the IDF had dropped two million leaflets over pockets of Gaza. The leaflets, as well as texts and phone calls, gave residents as much as forty-eight hours' notice of the impending attacks against weapons storages and terror strongholds and urging them to evacuate[14]. When our patrol ended some thirty-six hours after it began, we drove straight to our training base, and new base of operations. There, the preparations for war were already well underway.

On November 14, the army called up 30,000 reservists. Cars were lined up bumper to bumper along the mile-long road leading from the highway to our base. I watched incredulously as an exodus of men and women walked towards its entrance. Most of them had simply left their cars parked on the side of the road. Short of the army boots and pants that they were wearing, most bore no resemblance whatsoever to anything you would imagine when you hear the word "soldiers." And yet all of them, big and small, married and single, some in good physical shape and some most certainly not, had answered the call to defend their country. There was a palpable feeling of patriotism in the air that reminded me why I had decided to enlist in the first place.

As we were waiting for orders, we listened to Galgalatz, Israel's most popular radio station. I distinctly remember sitting in the barracks listening to an Israeli love song that was interrupted three times to announce cities that were under rocket attack and urging residents to seek shelter. In America, radio serves to take us to a different place. We listen on our way to work, or on a long trip out to the country for the weekend. It is a pleasant distraction from the stresses of our normal lives, one that helps us to pass the time and occasionally updates us on traffic patterns or world affairs. But never in America had I heard the radio warning of imminent danger. Hearing Israel's most popular radio station informing citizens in its major cities of direct threats against them was a reminder that despite the strength of Israel's military, given her small size and proximity to hostile neighbors, Israel remains vulnerable.

On Thursday November 15, air raid sirens were sounded in Tel Aviv for the first time in twenty-one years. While the two Iranian-made rockets that were fired towards Tel Aviv made international headlines, the 250 rockets fired at Southern Israel a day earlier did not. Except, of course, for a brief excerpt in the *New York Times* in an article about how Israel had killed civilians. When I heard that a missile had struck Tel Aviv, I knew the stakes had been raised. On Thursday afternoon, word came down the chain of command that we would be entering Gaza the following day. Friday morning, we were briefed by our company commander, who discussed the threats that we would face in the anticipated ground operation. Snipers. Rockets. Improvised explosive devices. Unlike in 2009, he warned, this time they would be ready for us. Over the previous few days, the combination of adrenaline and our preoccupation with the logistics of preparing our gear had left little time for fear. But as our company commander spoke that morning, the fear that had been dormant until that point suddenly came to the surface and could be felt in the silence of the room. We were going to war. Later in the briefing, I heard a few giggles from the back of the room, likely nervous laughter. Our commander was in no mood for it. "I don't know what is so funny," he snapped. "There is a good chance that some of you will be coming back to Israel in boxes." The room fell silent, and after pausing to let his words sink in, he once again addressed the group.

"As long as you have any fight left in your body, you are not to be taken alive," he told us. A chill went through the room as the weight of his words settled in. Several months earlier, Gilad Shalit, a captured Israeli soldier, had been released from his captivity in Gaza in exchange for 1,200 convicted terrorists that were being held in Israeli prisons. In the wake of that deal, Hamas' main objective was to kidnap Israeli soldiers to be used as collateral. Our company commander was clear with us that as special operations soldiers, we were not to become collateral under any circumstances. He stressed the importance of always remaining in groups and looking out for one another, and for sub-teams to constantly check their numbers.

On Friday, I joined a few other soldiers at the operation's staging ground, where we helped to prepare the vehicles we would be taking into Gaza. When we arrived, we saw a line of tanks and armored vehicles stretching to the horizon. A lifetime of war movies had not prepared me for the shocking sight of a real army mobilizing for a ground operation, and the realization that I was going to be part of it. That same morning, though all our phones had since been taken away, word spread that a bomb had exploded on a bus in Tel Aviv wounding dozens and killing one.

My first thought was of Carly, who took a bus each morning to reach her internship. The stress of the previous six months of incessant rocket attacks, the preparations for inevitable casualties in a ground invasion, and the thought that something might have happened to Carly, all bore down on me in that instant, and I felt my breath quicken and my chest tighten. As quickly as I could, without raising suspicions, I ducked behind the back of a tank to avoid being seen and lowered myself to the ground, clutching my chest as my heart beat with such force that I was afraid my teammates would be able to hear it. I felt as though I was observing myself from above, and struggled to think clearly enough to dispel the panic that had washed over me like a wave—today I recognize these symptoms as indicators of psychological shock. Gradually, I was able to compose myself, and as my heart rate slowed, I rose to my feet and made my way towards my team. Our officer allowed those of us with friends and family in Tel Aviv to use his phone to check in on them. After an hour that felt like an eternity, I was able to reach Carly and confirm that she was unharmed, at which point the fear and panic I had felt transformed into anger. At that moment, I knew that there was no price I wouldn't pay to help bring quiet to Israel. The fear I had felt for that hour before I could reach Carly was what the mothers, fathers, husbands, and wives of Southern Israel had felt thousands of times over the previous seven years every time a rocket was fired, as they wondered if their loved ones had made it to safety.

Later that afternoon we were informed that the ground operation would be pushed back twenty-four hours. That evening, like every other Friday we spent on base, those of us not on guard duty sat down together to enjoy the Sabbath meal. As we were singing the Friday night prayers, the siren went off, and we all ran to the bathroom, the nearest designated bomb shelter. Twenty seconds later we heard and felt the telling boom of the exploded rocket, and then, as if it was the most normal thing in the world, we calmly walked back to the table and continued the prayer exactly where we had left off.

The days between Friday and Tuesday were spent in limbo. Each day we went to the operation's intended staging ground in the morning, only to be told in the early evening that the operation had been pushed back twenty-four hours. When people ask me how I felt during that period, I tell them that it was a combination of anxiety and excitement. Looking back on it now, however, there was another emotion that I didn't want to acknowledge at the time, and that was fear. There was the most basic fear of serious injury that all (rational) combat soldiers experience before war, and of the possibility of having to go through life with a permanent disability. But the fear I felt more acutely was that I might not perform to the standards expected and required of me, and that I would let down my teammates and commanders.

On Thursday I had been told I would be the team's heavy machine gunner, despite having never fired the weapon in my life. Though I had since sat with my commander, who attempted to teach me how to aim, fire, and clean the gun, as well as clear blockages that might result from firing hundreds of rounds in a short period of time, there was no substitute for experience. I did not feel any meaningful degree of confidence that I could successfully operate the machine gun whose effectiveness might spell life or death for my teammates. Compounding that anxiety, though I had never carried more than eighty pounds during a training exercise, my bag was now loaded with ammunition for the machine gun, bringing the total weight I would be carrying to over 120 pounds. I wondered how or if I would be able to run with such weight in a war zone.

On Sunday we were back on the buses bound for the operation's staging ground, the third consecutive day that we'd been told that we would be entering Gaza. Today, a ground incursion suddenly felt more likely than it had on the previous days. I asked a female soldier who was non-combat, and thus still in possession of her phone, if I might borrow it for a few minutes. I typed "Psalm 23" into Google, and after reading it over a few times, I gave the soldier back her phone, sank back into my seat, and continued to recite the words in my head:

> "The Lord is my Shepherd,
> I shall not want.
> In gentle pastures he lays me down,
> Beside still waters he leads me.

He restoreth my soul: he leads me
in the paths of righteousness for his name's sake.
Yea, as I walk through the valley of the shadow of death,
I fear no evil. For thou art with me."

Yet again that evening, the ground operation was postponed, and on Tuesday, official word was given that there would be no ground operation. The aerial assault on Gaza's terrorist strongholds had been sufficiently crippling that Israel's leadership felt it would not be worth risking the lives of IDF soldiers in a ground operation, nor the international condemnation that would surely follow. Many of us felt a mixture of relief and disappointment. We felt that, eventually, a ground operation would be a necessity, and we wanted to be part of the fight to bring peace back to our homes and our families. Sadly, history would prove us right in 2014.

After undoing the preparations we had made for war, a process that took nearly twice as long as the preparations themselves—likely a function of the dissipated sense of urgency, the four teams of the company were allowed home in shifts. While we remained on high alert, our officers decided that we all needed a break.

Having spent the past twenty-six days on base, I was excited for a good meal and some good scotch. I was also very excited to see Carly. We had not spoken in over a week, which was the longest we had gone since we'd met.

CHAPTER 44: FROM ME TO WE

When I returned home that weekend, some friends and I enjoyed the long, filling breakfast at Benedict I had dreamt about for weeks. As we ate, we discussed our experiences over the previous month. About an hour after I had returned home from breakfast, Carly showed up at my apartment door unannounced. I vividly remember the bright yellow raincoat she wore, and the look of shyness and affection I saw in her eyes when I opened the door. She held a bottle of scotch in one hand and my favorite ice cream bar in the other. Though I was not very good at expressing my feelings at that point in my life, it seemed to come naturally in that moment. As we embraced, I told her how much I had missed her. We were both relieved to see each other after the intensity of the prior weeks.

Later that weekend Carly and I went to a sports bar called Mike's Place to watch the Ohio State football game with some friends. Observing us together, an acquaintance turned to us during the game and asked us how long we'd been dating. We hadn't yet discussed a title for our relationship, but rather than answer honestly, already a few drinks in and feeling emboldened, I nudged her arm and asked her with a smile, "Are we dating?" She wasted no time in turning the question back on me: "Are you asking me?" I laughed nervously and changed the subject. I was convinced that no girl in her right mind would want to be in a committed relationship with a combat soldier who spent twenty-four days each month on a closed military base.

After the game had ended, Carly and I went to a quiet restaurant nearby for dinner so we could spend some time alone together before I went back to base. At dinner, I again asked her playfully if we were dating, and she again responded with the same question: "Are you asking me?" When her unblinking stare confirmed that she was serious, I took a deep breath, looked her in the eyes, and for the first time since sixth grade, I asked a question I had wanted to ask her for quite some time: "Will you be my girlfriend?"

For the next two years, Carly was my best friend, my constant companion, and at times, my therapist. I was drawn to her values, her patience, her beauty, easy-going nature, and her quickness to forgive my many hiccups as I learned what it meant to be a boyfriend. Though I had little time, money, or control over my schedule, I did my best to make her happy. My life at that time didn't permit me to be the boyfriend most girls envision they will have at 23 years old, but I tried to bridge that gap with spontaneous flower deliveries, surprise weekend getaways, and the occasional romantic dinner. Through our trials and tribulations, I learned that pulling gently, rather than pushing, is the only way to show someone your perspective. I learned that being happy is more important than being right, and that honest, open, and consistent communication is the single most important thing in any relationship. I learned how to open myself up to another person in a way I never had before, and to be honest about my feelings, which up until then I had believed was not something that men did, particularly not combat soldiers.

We shared dozens of amazing experiences during our relationship. From skiing in the French Alps to drinking beer at Oktoberfest, to wine tastings in Mendoza, Argentina. We had some great times, as well as some tough ones. At times, we shared a connection so deep that we knew each other's thoughts without speaking them. And like all couples, we fought and hurt each other, as we often hurt the ones we love most. In the end, life took us in different directions, but I remain grateful for the many invaluable lessons I took from our relationship. Our breakup was hard, but like the hardships I faced in the army, I became a stronger person because of it. My quest to better understand and improve myself, which began with our breakup, is one I have continued to this day.

CHAPTER 45: THE QUIET AFTER THE STORM

In the wake of the Gaza operation, Southern Israel finally experienced a quiet it had not seen in nearly a decade. December 2012 was the first month since 2004 during which not a single rocket was fired on Israel from the Gaza strip.[15] Several weeks later we were reassigned to another base inside a kibbutz on the Gaza border. While we still had routine patrols along the border, the days of running back and forth to the bomb shelter multiple times each day were temporarily over.

The four months we would spend on that base were the most relaxing of our service. We watched movies and TV shows, cooked for ourselves, and got ourselves into great physical shape. Every Tuesday, most of us would gather in the dining hall/makeshift club to watch *The Voice*. The number of stakeouts decreased significantly as we moved further from the end of that winter's operation and the military grew more confident in the temporary stability of the region.

In March, I took my leave from the army to be home for Passover. Attending the Seders was particularly special as an active-duty soldier and, as usual, the time with my family flew by faster than I expected. As we read passages about the hardships the Israelites suffered in Egypt, I couldn't help but chuckle at some of the similarities to army life. I thought back to the year before, when I woke up at five a.m. to Skype with my family for the last part of their Seder. Shortly after thanking G-d for taking us out of slavery in Egypt, I began my shift of guard duty on the Egyptian border. We often joked that the Army treated us like slaves. It was particularly ironic that morning.

Some weeks later I was sent to Course Orev and Course Gil, covering missiles our team was responsible for operating. My team had completed both courses early on in their training while I was still serving in Duvdevan. Though I was approaching the end of my service, doing reserves with my team would require that I be certified in the operation of those missiles. During the six weeks I spent in those courses, I learned the parts and operation of the missiles, as well as how to identify enemy helicopters/tanks/armored vehicles, and which of their parts were vulnerable to our missiles. We did mock operations, during which we would hike several miles in an operational formation, set up the missile in a strategic location, and carry out reconnaissance before eventually "firing" the missile at the mock target.

The soldiers in the course with me had only been in the army for eight months. Though I slept in the soldiers' tent, I socialized with the officers and sergeants, which was a unique situation in the army. I became friendly with Maimon, the officer in charge of those soldiers. Officers within our company shifted around often, and several months later, by chance, Maimon became my officer. Years later, when we were slamming down shots of Arak together in Tel Aviv, he admitted the difficulty of serving as my officer after we had gotten so friendly.

Having completed my certification in the two courses, I returned to my team, which had since been reassigned to a new base of operations in Judea and Samaria. My three-year contract with the IDF was nearing its end, but rather than winding down, the complexity and danger of our missions intensified in our new post.

CHAPTER 46: THE ARREST

Judea and Samaria was called the West Bank in the wake of its nearly unanimously unrecognized annexation by Jordan during Israel's independence war in 1948[16]. It is among the most controversial pieces of land on earth. The 1920 San Remo conference was held with the intention of establishing the precise boundaries for territories captured by the Allies during World War I. At that conference, the Allies officially spelled out the borders of modern-day Lebanon, Egypt, Syria, Israel, Jordan and Iraq, and this area had been designated to be part of Israel, then known as the "Mandate for Palestine"[17]. In 1947, the UN passed resolution 181, which proposed that

Israel, then called Palestine, be partitioned into two states. It should be noted that, per the UN's charter, General Assembly resolutions are simply recommendations, and are not legally binding. While the Jews living in Palestine recognized the significant territorial concessions required by the plan, they accepted it with a mixture of trepidation and joy. The Palestinians living there rejected it, as did all of the surrounding Arab states. Together, they launched a war against the newly independent state of Israel to actively prevent the plan from being implemented[18]. During the course of that war, Jordan seized control of Judea and Samaria. After the annexation in 1948, Jordan began referring to the area as the West Bank, due to its presence on the West Bank of the Jordan river[19].

Since I am neither a lawyer nor a historian, I will keep my observations to my own experience. As Israeli soldiers, we referred to the land as the "area of Judea and Samaria," which is how I regard it in this book. Nearly 70 percent of Israelis living in Judea and Samaria live within five major settlement blocs, which together make up around 4 percent of the total territory of Judea and Samaria. It is commonly accepted that in any two-state solution, these major blocs will remain part of a Jewish State. The status of the areas inhabited by the other approximately 30 percent of Jews living in this area remains hotly contested[20].

A few days after I had signed on my gear, just as I had begun to settle back into the swing of things, we were called into a briefing for a dangerous mission whose objective would be the arrest of a suspected arms dealer. The mission would take place deep within the heart of Area A of Judea and Samaria. According to the Oslo accords, a series of peace agreements made in the 1990s between the Palestinian and Israeli governments, Judea and Samaria are divided into Areas A, B, and C. Area C is entirely under Israeli control and contains the major settlement blocs listed above. Area B is governed by the Joint Administration of Israel and the Palestinian Authority, and Area A is under full control of the Palestinian National Authority. While Palestinian security services enforce the laws in area A and parts of Area B, external security for all three areas remains the responsibility of the IDF.

On the night of the mission, after running through the important points dozens of times, we boarded armored vehicles and sped towards the infiltration point. As we breached the fence and crept down the main roadway, it was impossible not to notice the dozens of posters of Yasser Arafat, former head of the Palestinian Liberation Organization and Palestinian Authority.

According to his wife and many members of the Palestinian Authority, he was also the man responsible for the Second Intifada[21]. Each of us had rehearsed the journey dozens of times in our heads. We knew where the turn was to the street that housed our target, and which position each sub-group was to take around the house.

There is a strange and deep quiet that pervades villages in Judea and Samaria in the dark of night, the kind that seems to hold things within it. As we gradually made our way into the heart of the village, we crept past walls covered in graffiti praising shahids (martyrs). But for the occasional barking of stray dogs, it was eerily silent, and it was hard not to feel that someone or something was constantly watching us. I tightened my grip on my gun as we walked, constantly scanning the buildings above us for signs of movement.

We moved quickly, but we weren't light. We wore bulletproof armor and ammunition vests. Some of us carried semi-automatic rifles, and a few unlucky ones carried bigger automatic ones and all the ammo that went with them. We carried stun grenades, tear gas grenades, and blow-every-thing-and-everyone-to-pieces grenades. We also carried exhaustion; the kind that weighs down both the body and the mind. The kind that comes after hours of briefings and consecutive nights of not enough sleep. The kind that causes your eyes to close involuntarily for a few seconds as soon as you take a knee to await further commands. Some of us carried fear—not just of what was to come, but of how we would react. Would we be able to summon courage if and when it was called for? We carried excitement—blind, ignorant excitement at the prospect of confrontation. The kind experienced by teenagers and young adults that have never been in real combat, and still glorify it, as most young soldiers do. We carried bets; one bet wagered a bottle of vodka on whether or not we'd find the weapons we were seeking.

My role for the mission was to be the commander of the sub-team that was to enter the house directly behind our officer. Should our suspect resist when we entered the house, I would be in charge of "dealing with him," to whatever extent that required. This also meant I would be the first one to be engaged should anything go wrong, which intelligence indicated it might. When all the sub-teams were in place, our officer looked at us, the entry team, and gave us a nod. Bursting with adrenaline, we emerged from the shadows of the street, charged towards the house, and began banging on the front door and shouting in Arabic for someone to open it.

When I reached the door, though my heart was racing, what I felt was not fear but rather a heightened sense of awareness. After a year and a half of training and a year of serving as an active-duty combat soldier, dangerous situations that might have once triggered my flight response, almost always triggered my fight response instead. I was calm, and yet I knew that in a moment I could unleash a burst of aggression should the situation warrant it. As a sheltered New York Jew who had grown up nearly 6,000 miles away from the Middle East, it was hard to believe that I was a soldier in the Israeli Defense Forces about to enter the house of a suspected arms dealer to search for weapons. When I think about holding that loaded gun to the door, ready for a matching barrel to emerge from the other side, I feel now, as I did then, that I'm peering into a dream in which fantasy and reality blend together so seamlessly that it is impossible to discern where one ends and the other begins.

Thirty seconds after my officer had given me the nod, the suspect, eyes filled with sleep and dressed in his pajamas, met us at the door. His front door opened into his living room. Within seconds of him opening the door, we had moved past him and spread out into a straight line with our backs to the wall just as we had been trained. Our barrels faced forward and our eyes scanned the room for potential threats. After we had established that there was no immediate danger to us, our officer asked the man to sit down on his couch while the rest of us remained in position. He sat down next to the man, and politely but firmly asked him for several pieces of information that would confirm his identity. The man confirmed his name, which we already knew, as well as several other details about himself.

Our next order of business was to secure the family in one room so we could search the rest of the house for weapons. We escorted them down the stairs and sat them together in the living room. The children shared a blanket on the sofa, while the suspect and his wife sat inches from one another on neighboring chairs. The IDF had not been in their village in nearly a decade, which was before those children had been born. As they stared at us, bright-eyed and bewildered, it occurred to me that this was likely the first time they had ever seen Israeli soldiers, other than in cartoons demonizing Israel and the IDF. And there we stood, a dozen towering soldiers with bulletproof armor, face paint, helmets, and loaded weapons, standing in their living room. While I felt sympathy for the man's family, evidence suggested that he was providing weapons to terrorists, which if true, meant that he had brought the current situation upon his family.

As I looked around, I was surprised to realize that I felt a certain degree of familiarity. Their house was cozy. It had wooden floors and, in certain places, carpeted ones. Paintings covered the walls and sculptures dotted the rooms. Decorative curtains hung from the windows and contributed to a feeling of serenity and quiet. For years I had seen articles in major U.S. newspapers peppered with photos portraying the entirety of Judea and Samaria as a refugee camp. Though I knew better, I was still surprised to find myself in a house that might have been pulled out of Westchester County, New York.

Despite the beautiful interior of their home, I was not naïve. I knew that regardless of how well they might appear to be living, Palestinians living in Area A face severe economic hardships due, in part, to the security fence and the hundreds of military checkpoints throughout Judea and Samaria. I feel terrible that innocent people are suffering, but I believed then, as I do now, that the Israeli government is responsible for keeping its citizens safe. Both the fence and the checkpoints were established in response to the Second Intifada, during which hundreds of Palestinians crossed into Israel and carried out terror attacks that killed almost 1,000 Israeli civilians and injured another 5,600[22].

As a soldier, I could not and did not want to understand the perspective of the Arabs of Judea and Samaria as acutely as I do today. Nonetheless, I always recognized the humanity of the people with whom I interacted, and I did my best to act with respect and kindness whenever possible. As we stood in the living room that night, I noticed the suspect's wife begin to shiver. Instinctually, I fetched her a blanket from the other room, as I believe another one of my teammates would have done had I not done it first. Our kindness would have no impact on the man's answers.

After we had searched all the bedrooms, we got down on our hands and knees with forty pounds of gear and loaded weapons around our necks, and we folded the clothes that we had displaced from the dressers and closets during our search, and re-made the children's beds. During my time in the IDF, the one thread that connected the overwhelming majority of the soldiers I served with was their sense of humanity; they were people as well as soldiers.

Though intelligence suggested there would be a struggle at the door on the night of that mission, thankfully, nothing happened. On the one hand, we were relieved. The man was taken into custody peacefully, and nobody was harmed. But on the other hand, as embarrassing as it is to admit, we were slightly disappointed. Serving as a soldier in a peacetime army comes with many contradictions. You are trained constantly for war and combat, and to be aggressive, and then you are put in situations that require restraint and sensitivity. As a soldier representing the IDF, I did my best to act with compassion and with the self-discipline demanded by the complicated relationship between Arabs and Israelis living in Judea and Samaria.

CHAPTER 47: THE BEGINNING OF THE END

Shortly after that mission, I left my team for a two-month course called Nativ, which is offered to all soldiers that are either not Jewish and wish to become Jewish or have lived less than ten years in Israel before drafting. Hebrew school was the extent of my formal Jewish education, and the course provided a great opportunity for me to further my understanding of Judaism and the history of Israel and the Jewish people. In addition, as a combat soldier used to six days off a month, it wasn't bad to have every night free to see Carly. Those two months were the most intellectually stimulating of my service. We traveled to museums throughout the country, dove into questions of morality, and learned not only about Judaism and the Bible, but about the history of the land of Israel. At the end of the course, I was humbled to be chosen by my fellow soldiers to receive the award for Outstanding Cadet.

After the course, I once again returned to my team to complete the two months that remained until the end of my service. We were stationed in Eshkelot, a Jewish settlement within Area B of Judea and Samaria. For the most part, we carried out routine patrols along the border to prevent illegal crossings into Israel.

At around that time, on the weekend of the third anniversary of my moving to Israel, I thought it would be fitting to visit the kibbutz that was my first home in Israel when I made *aliyah*. Kibbutz Yiftah is among the northernmost points in the country, and the bus ride from Tel Aviv, where I had stopped to pick up Carly after arriving from base, took close to three and a half hours. When we arrived at the designated junction, a friend was waiting for us with his car, as there was no public transportation that could take us directly to the kibbutz.

After the long, scenic drive up the winding mountain road, we finally entered the gates of the kibbutz and pulled up to the two rows of rooms that twenty-four boys and girls had called home in the summer of 2010 when we had first arrived in Israel. As I stepped out of the car, the sight of our rooms was simultaneously familiar and foreign. I had been back only once since joining the army. Then, two years earlier, the rooms had still been occupied. On that visit, there had been laughter in the air, and the joy of soldiers enjoying their weekend leave. Now, save for the sound of the wind rustling through the leaves, all was quiet.

The rooms were no longer occupied, and nature had begun to take over. The nearby trees were no longer well groomed. Weeds had begun to grow, and empty bottles of Arak had integrated themselves into the landscapes, as weeds, flowers, and grass grew around them and, in some cases, over them. An eerie silence and emptiness now occupied the space that was once so vibrant, fueled by our excitement and anticipation. Everywhere I looked were memories. The hammock, which sat between the two rows of rooms, where I used to relax in the afternoons and call friends and family back home. The tree with the red flowers, under which Alon, Eitan, and I had done hundreds if not thousands of sit-ups. The stone benches where we sat and discussed our futures over beers and the occasional hookah pipe.

As I walked down the row of rooms, finally arriving at the end, I found myself face to face with room number six. This was the room Eitan and I had called home during that tumultuous, uncertain three-month period before we drafted, wondering in what units and with whom we would be spending the next three years of our lives. Though all were supposedly locked, I tried the door out of habit.

Surprisingly, the knob creaked and the door pushed open. As I entered the room, clearing away the cobwebs that had formed in the doorway, I was taken back in time. My eyes fell firstly upon the sink, which sat immediately to the left of the room's entrance. We had used our kitchen sink to clean the five or so dishes that we owned. It had also doubled as our bathroom sink since we tried to avoid our bathroom as much as possible given the state of wildlife that dwelled within it. Our beds and dressers were still in place, just as we had left them. I searched for some memento from the past, perhaps a letter from a loved one, a draft notice, some piece of my old life, but I found none. There was no physical trace that we had been there; only my memories remained.

Carly's voice snapped me back to reality, and as my eyes met hers, she understood that I was lost in my memories. Silently, she took my hand, and together we left the room and the past behind us and walked slowly up the hill of the kibbutz. That evening, we had dinner with my adopted kibbutz family and caught up on all the changes in our lives. I had already begun planning my post-army trip, and they were very interested to know where I would be traveling. As always, their hospitality was gracious, and the food was delicious and abundant.

We allowed ourselves a few hours to digest before heading to a party on the kibbutz. We drank Goldstars, caught up with old friends, and made some new ones. Shortly after midnight Carly and I wandered away from the party towards a dark field on the edge of the kibbutz where I used to lie and watch the stars. As we walked, the sound of the music faded and finally dropped off to a whisper. Above us were the glimmering stars of the Milky Way, unobscured by city lights, and all around us a quiet that seemed to demand a reverence from those that dwelled within it. After lying in silence for some time, mesmerized by the stunning view of the sky, we rose to our feet and walked to the room that Nissan had prepared for us to spend the evening.

I lay in bed that night lost in memories that, like a receding tide, pulled me back towards the ocean of my past. When I first stepped foot on the kibbutz in the summer of 2010, I was a bright-eyed youth with dreams of grandeur, convinced of the absolute nature of right and wrong. Nearly three years later, I had become a man, and my youthful idealism had tempered into optimistic realism. As it turned out, the world was not perfect. Working hard for the things you want, though a good habit, does not always get you those things. Good and evil are not as easily distinguishable as I once believed; there is a little bit of both within each of us, and it's up to each of us to decide which guidance to follow. Eventually, aided by the soothing sound of chirping crickets and the spinning of the fan's blades, I drifted off to sleep.

CHAPTER 48: ROCKS

When I returned to base that Sunday, we began briefings for another mission that would take us into the heart of Area A, which was under the complete administrative control of the Palestinian Authority and off limits to Israeli civilians.

As dusk gave way to nightfall on the chosen date, we were picked up by a *Yas'ur** helicopter from a staging point near our base. As with the C-130 transport plane, the sound of the Yasur is deafening. Hand signals were the only way to communicate as we boarded the bird. We could feel the floor

*The Hebrew designation for the Sikorsky CH-53 Transport Helicopter.

vibrating under our boots as the powerful blades lifted us off the ground and into the night sky. We watched as yellow lights below us turned to green ones, signifying to us that we had entered Palestinian territory. Eventually, all light vanished as we soared over the mountains of Judea and Samaria in complete darkness. Though we knew our pilots were equipped with night-vision goggles, that knowledge did not mitigate the strange sensation of hurtling through the air at 150 MPH in complete darkness. Minutes later, we reached a field several miles from our intended destination. We filed off the chopper, which quickly took off again, flying a different route than the one it had taken to avoid being targeted by small arms fire or surface-to-air missiles. Shortly after midnight, after the officers had reviewed the mission, we pulled black masks over our faces and began the journey to our intended infiltration point. It was about two miles away, and we needed to move quickly; as soon as the dogs caught our scent, the village would know of our presence. Half a mile away, we stopped, each chambering a bullet in our guns, and continued our march towards the village.

The main road, which ran along the side of the village, was well lit and would have exposed us. Rather than risk being detected before reaching our destination, we took a circuitous route that led us up a steep mountainside. As the adrenaline from our ride in the Black Hawk wore off, we began to feel the weight of our gear and the steep incline of the ascent. Our pace slowed as we progressed up the mountain and towards the village.

Finally, we arrived at our entry point. As we moved from the shadows to the edge of the road, we crouched down, awaiting orders. On our officer's signal, we crept quickly and quietly towards the cover of the shadows on the far side of the main road, where we silently broke into two groups and began to move towards our intended houses. Suddenly and without warning, the silence was shattered by the sound of a single rock smashing against the wall several feet to our left. Despite the precautions we had taken to avoid detection, we had been spotted, and whoever had seen us was not pleased by our presence.

What began as a few rocks thrown intermittently quickly intensified. A few short minutes later, we were pressed against the sides of houses as rocks the size of baseballs flew past us at deadly speeds and with terrifying accuracy. As I positioned myself to keep eyes on the growing crowd, a rock flew a foot over my head and shattered against the concrete wall behind me. I imagined what that rock would have done to me if it had hit me, and

I pressed myself closer against the house while continuing to scan the road for potential threats.

Above the sounds of shattering rocks, voices charged with adrenaline shouted orders and exchanged information. Our officer ordered several tear gas grenades be thrown to disperse the large and building crowd that now separated the two teams of our company. While the tear gas was effective at first, it left no lasting deterrent, and as each gas grenade dissipated, the crowd would return, often larger than before. Our chief weapon that evening had been the element of surprise. Once we had been discovered, without any shields or vehicles, we were completely exposed to the rocks. Rather than risk injuries to our soldiers, a decision was made to abandon the mission. The instigators of the riot posed a greater immediate threat than the people we had set out to find that evening.

The group that had been trapped by the rock throwers executed a daring but effective move. Though we knew our comrades were vastly outnumbered, their position was covered and the rioters could not be sure of their numbers. Using their information advantage, they fired several tear gas grenades in the direction of the crowd, followed immediately by several live-fire shots into the air, after which they shouted and charged the crowd that had cut them off, which succeeded in forcing them into a retreat. In the commotion that followed, my teammates were able to grab two of the more prominent rock throwers, whom we brought back with us for processing in Israel.

With the company finally united, we began the two-mile journey down the road to the entrance to the village where IDF transport vehicles would be waiting for us. The crowd of rock throwers followed at a distance and continued to hurl rocks, checked only by tear gas grenades, which deterred them only until the gas dispersed. There were several near misses, and our company commander, furious at the situation, ordered me and five others to try to grab more of the ringleaders.

As we were coming down the road, I saw a small rock wall that looked as though it would provide sufficient cover, and silently motioned to the others to follow behind me. We threw a tear gas grenade in the direction of the crowd and took advantage of the temporary commotion it caused to dive behind the wall, hoping we had not been noticed. Our plan was to wait until the crowd was parallel to our position and then grab the instigators. Unfortunately, we were not as sneaky as we thought we'd been, and within a minute there was a concentration of rocks flying directly over our heads; someone had seen us duck behind the wall.

After another minute passed, I realized there was a legitimate danger that we could be overrun. Slowly, I lifted my head above the wall to take stock of our situation. A split second after my eyes had cleared the wall, a rock the size of an orange slammed into the front of my helmet, stunning me, and knocking me straight onto my back. Had I come up a few milliseconds quicker, the rock would have hit my face rather than my helmet. Two inches had changed the course of my life.

Despite his actions, the rock thrower was not harmed or even pursued. As per IDF guidelines at the time, as soon as the rock left his hand, he ceased to be an enemy combatant and was considered an unarmed civilian. My friend Noah grabbed me by the vest and pulled me against the wall so that I wouldn't be hit by the barrage of rocks that continued to fall. Rather than expressing any concern for my well-being, seeing that I was alive and functioning, Noah's first words to me as I regained my senses were, "Dude. You got smoked!"

Without the element of surprise, we had no hope of grabbing the ringleaders and thus decided to focus our energies on rejoining our team. After throwing several tear gas grenades to create distance between us and the crowd, we took off towards the bottom of the hill where the rest of our company was waiting beside the armored vehicles that would extract us from the village. While the gas bought us several moments of respite, the rock throwers quickly regrouped and took advantage of our exposure to shower us with rocks before we could reach the safety of the armored vehicles. I was hit several times and would later discover that one of the rocks had chipped a bone in my wrist, though at the time the pain was masked by adrenaline.

When we reached the vehicles at the base of the hill, our pursuers decided it was not worth taking on armored trucks. They lingered for a few minutes at a safe distance before ultimately dispersing. As we stood around awaiting clearance to leave the village, I watched as one of the soldiers on my team cut the zip-tie that bound the hands of one of the rock throwers we had apprehended and handed him a cigarette. A few of my teammates lit up cigarettes and began to make small talk with the two young men we had taken into custody, who only an hour earlier had been the ring leaders of a mob that almost killed us. As pleasantries turned to talk of soccer, a few jokes were made, and everyone laughed, not so much at the jokes, but at diffusing tension. The lines that divided Arab and Israeli, soldier and enemy, began to break down and were replaced by the recognition of our common humanity.

I thought again about the place between the dark and the light, where the lines between right and wrong could blur, where something could exist that was simultaneously beautiful and ugly. For me, this moment was the embodiment of such a place.

The next day, as usual, we went out on patrols, guarded the company's gear, and dropped off the rock throwers at the police station. By then, they had smoked an entire pack of cigarettes which were given to them by the same soldiers they had spent the previous evening trying to injure or kill. At the station, they were questioned by the local authorities. Since they were first-time offenders, they were returned to their homes a few days later without punishment.

CHAPTER 49: THE LAST PATROL

On a warm afternoon in late October, I went out on the final patrol of my military service. Several minutes after we had left the gates of the base, we received an urgent transmission over the radio alerting us that a hole had been cut in the border fence through which dozens of people were illegally crossing into Israeli territory. Typically, Palestinians that crossed in such a fashion came in search of jobs, but there was always the risk that there were some crossing with more sinister motives. More importantly was the element of deterrence; the radical elements within Judea and Samaria took notice of everything the army did and did not do. If they determined that it was easy to cross the fence into Israel in our sector, it could create security issues. The breach site was directly in front of a field several hundred meters wide, which those who made it through the fence would have to cross before reaching the main road that separated them from Israel.

We sped towards the edge of the field. The border crossers could see us coming and decided that they no longer liked their odds. They spun on their heels and began to run back towards the fence. Official army regulations dictated that every soldier leaving an armored vehicle within a half-mile of the border fence must wear a bulletproof vest and a helmet. But I knew I couldn't make up the lost distance if I was wearing my armored vest. I also knew that those who had crossed the fence in broad daylight likely posed little threat. As soon as our vehicle screeched to a halt, I kicked open the door, grabbed my gun and helmet, and took off towards the fence, leaving my vest behind me in the vehicle. The distance separating me from the fence was approximately the length of a football field—a sizable distance to cover at a sprint.

Adrenaline took me through the first few hundred feet, and though I was starting half a field-length behind, I was beginning to close the gap. By the time I had crossed the halfway mark, only about ten of those who had crossed the fence still remained in Israeli territory. As I got within three hundred feet of the fence, three Palestinians were still struggling to make it back to their side. By this point, we had become a spectacle. Adrenaline surged through my bloodstream, and my senses heightened; I became aware of the sounds of clapping and cheering. As my eyes registered the scene before me, it became clear that the noise was coming from the hundreds of Palestinians who dotted the hill on the other side of the border. They were cheering for their guys, just as you might expect the home team crowd to do at Yankee Stadium when the runner on first takes off to try and steal second base.

When I was twenty feet from the fence, there was only one man left. The terrain was covered with small hills and holes and was quite difficult to traverse. As I closed in on him, he fell several times, jumping back onto his feet each time and continuing his laborious run towards the Palestinian side of the fence. On one such fall, which would turn out to be the last, his backpack became dislodged, and as he rolled to his knees, he glanced backward and saw that I was only several feet behind him and closing in fast. Leaving the bag behind, he closed the final distance between himself and the border in a manner that could best be described as a four-limbed gallop, presumably because he didn't want to waste the time to stand up fully. His scurry culminated in a head-first dive through the small hole in the fence just as I flung myself forward towards him, touching but failing to grasp onto his shoe.

The Palestinians erupted in applause. We both sat up slowly on our respective sides of the border, panting like racehorses and looking at each other through the fence. As he well knew, soldiers were not permitted to cross the fence without a very good reason, and certainly not by themselves. I grabbed his backpack and examined its contents. It was full of clothes. As I might have guessed, the man had come in search of work and had brought a change of clothes with him. I took the bag in my hand, rose slowly to my feet, and approached the hole in the fence, still panting heavily from my run. The man's eyes flashed with fear, and I could see that for a moment he believed that I might be crazy enough to pursue him across the fence. Instead, I flashed him a smile and tossed his bag through the fence. "Nice effort," I said in Hebrew.

I turned around and walked back to the armored vehicle. For several minutes, I endured the jokes of my friends about how I was far too old to run after anyone, and that it was about time I got released. As the banter died down and I was left to my thoughts, it occurred to me that my interaction with that man was the last interaction I would have with a Palestinian during my military service. I couldn't help but reflect on the irony. I had spent a year training for one of the top counter-terror units in the world, six months of training for a specialized reconnaissance unit, and a year and a half of active duty peppered with missions and dangerous patrols. And yet, the final act of my military service was throwing a "Hello Kitty" backpack through a hole that had been illegally cut into Israel's border, and congratulating a man who had crossed through it for his effort.

Regardless of one's ethnicity, religion, or politics, we are all human beings who just want what's best for ourselves and our families. In retrospect, I believe the recognition of that fact was the most fitting end for my final IDF patrol.

CHAPTER 50: THE FINAL SUNRISE

A few days later was my last night as an IDF soldier. On the evening of October 1, 2013, soldiers from the other team in our company switched out everyone on my team from their posts to give us an hour to spend together before my release. Because of the various missions we were charged with carrying out, it was very rare that all of us were together in one place at one time. I took advantage of the opportunity to read some words I had written about each of my teammates, and the impact they had on my service and my life. After some hugs and reminiscing, those who had been switched out went back to their posts. I settled in for an eight-hour shift at the front gate. I had volunteered to take an extended shift so that my teammates, who still had another six months of service, could catch some extra sleep. As the morning sun crossed the horizon and the Israeli flag waved in the foreground atop the pole on the front gate of the base, I was both relieved and saddened that the coming day would mark the end of the most significant chapter of my life.

When my shift ended, I gathered my belongings and caught the bus to our unit's training base, Mishar HaNegev. I was joined by Noah who was also being released that day. We arrived in civilian dress, carrying with us the final items we were ordered to return before being released. These included two pairs of dress uniforms, a towel, an army bag, and a few other small items. Noah had all of them. I had none of them. When we arrived at the base, we headed to the personnel office to get the form we would need signed from various departments before being released. My first stop was the gear station. I begged the sergeant in charge to look the other way and sign my form, despite all the things I was missing. He was unwavering in his insistence that I would need to stand trial for the gear I lost before I could be released. This would force me to travel to a different base. After an hour of back-and-forth negotiation, a more senior NCO (non-commissioned officer) yelled at the sergeant to sign my form.

After acquiring the various signatures I needed to confirm that I had returned (or allegedly returned) all of my gear, uniforms, etc., I arrived at the moment every Israeli soldier fantasizes about at some point during their service: the cutting of the IDF ID, the unofficial recognition of the completion of military service. When the time finally came for that ceremonious moment, as I had come to expect in the IDF, there were logistical problems. Somehow, there were no scissors in the office. After locating a pair in an adjourning office, I did what I was both sad and ready to do: I cut my blue army ID in half. Ironically, over three years, I carried thousands of pounds over thousands of miles, yet it took only a minuscule amount of pressure applied by my index finger and thumb to cut my last link to the IDF. For three years, the IDF had owned me and defined me, tortured and rewarded me, testing my limits at every turn, while simultaneously giving me a sense of purpose.

Three years of ups and downs, heartaches and realized dreams, failures and achievements; three years of blood, sweat, tears, stretcher marches, and unforgettable experiences, of pain and of triumph. With one pound of force on the grips of a scissor, it all swiftly and abruptly came to an end. Then, with the click of a mouse, I watched the liaison officer change my status from "active duty" to "reserves".

It is not often that one cuts up a contract with an employer in front of his face on completely good terms. But if the army is anything, it's a place of "first times" and strange occurrences. Most soldiers leave the army at the same time as their teammates. But because I dropped down a training class when I switched units, and the rest of my team had drafted six months after me, they still had six months left in their service. As my thoughts drifted to this reality on the long bus ride home, I was saddened to be leaving behind a family that would continue, in my absence, with business as usual.

Jokes would be made, missions carried out, and stretcher marches endured, but I would not be there to curse, laugh, participate, or lend a hand. I thought back to the beginning; long nights training on the kibbutz for unknown tryouts to come, the waiting, the fear, the acceptance, the disappointment. It all washed over me like an avalanche. I thought back on my service, and the time when my sole job was to train my body and mind to defend Israel. My army experience was a double-edged sword. I struggled physically and emotionally through long sleepless nights and endless marches with heavy weights. I longed for the company of my family, and the comforts of civilian life. Yet my job was the defense of the country I loved, and I had felt immeasurably proud to wear the IDF uniform.

Arriving in Tel Aviv as a civilian, free of all military responsibilities, and accountable to nobody except myself, I felt strange. In a mere six days, I would be on a plane to Amsterdam to begin seven months of traveling. That night I went out to celebrate with my friends, and as the whiskey began to dull my senses, and my head went light from the flavorful Cuban cigar, I felt the burden of army life slowly rolling off my shoulders.

Six days later, three hours before I was to leave for the airport, and two minutes after getting back from dinner, I realized that there was an important travel detail I had neglected—I needed to pack. I desperately tried to fit everything I had acquired over the last three and a half years into my luggage without exceeding the airline's baggage limits. I was exhausted, physically and emotionally, from all the goodbyes of the prior week. While sad to be leaving the country I loved so much, I was simultaneously excited about my upcoming travels.

When my bags were finally packed, I kissed Carly goodbye and jumped into my friend Rudy's car. He sped me to the airport and towards the next chapter of my life—this time armed not with a rifle but with curiosity and excitement for the adventures to come.

PART SEVEN:
LOVE AND WAR

CHAPTER 51: THE WEDDINGS

In July 2014, I returned to Israel for the weddings of two close friends. It was my first trip back to Israel since the end of my military service. During the months leading up to that summer, terrorists in Gaza intensified their campaign of rocket fire aimed at the towns of Southern Israel. The mood was tense, and throughout the country sirens warning of incoming rockets had once again become daily occurrences. One of the weddings I had returned to Israel to attend was Rudy's. Prior to the wedding, Rudy and Yael, both Sephardic Jews from France, held their Henna* party on a beach in Haifa, a city sixty miles North of Tel Aviv. It was a beautiful summer day, and we danced and drank by the beachside bar while enjoying the sunshine and the warm Mediterranean breeze.

The wedding planner had brought a large selection of traditional Moroccan garments for the guests, and a few of us, by then several drinks in, dressed up and participated in the ceremony. As the heat of the midday sun began to subside, we continued to celebrate the soon-to-be-married couple. Suddenly and without warning, the peaceful atmosphere was shattered by a sound that had become a daily occurrence in Israel over the prior months: the unmistakable cry of the siren signifying an incoming terrorist rocket. The Gaza strip was more than 100 miles away, which meant that whatever was coming towards us was a serious missile, not a simple grad rocket like those that were routinely fired at the towns surrounding the Gaza strip.

Rudy's entire group of friends had served in combat units of the IDF and were acutely aware that, without a concrete shelter, there was no sense in hiding. Since we were on a beach with no shelter in sight and little else to do, we stood our ground and hoped for the best. The staff working the party did not see things the same way, and a few of the waitresses immediately dove under the plastic tables where they remained trembling in fear even after the siren had stopped. While my first instinct was to laugh at the drastic difference

---

* Ashkenazi Jews, those whose ancestors are of European descent, perform a ritual known as a Bedeken at their wedding ceremony. The groom places the veil on the bride, recalling the story of our patriarch Jacob who did not realize that he was married to Leah, and not her sister Rachel, until it was too late. The Bedeken is meant to assure the groom that he is marrying the right woman. At a Sephardic wedding, which denotes Jews from the Sephardic tradition, there is a separate celebration held a few evenings before the wedding in which the bride and groom have Henna (a type of ink) applied to their palms. The Henna does not come off for quite some time, so at the wedding a few days later, the couple is easily identified.

in our reactions, my grin turned to a grimace as I realized the tragedy of my cavalier attitude and their gripping fear.

When the party ended, we boarded buses bound for Tel Aviv, where we continued the celebration. Revisiting the bars we had once frequented as soldiers on leave, now with slightly bigger incomes, naturally led to slightly bigger hangovers the following day.

A few days later, Rudy and Yael were married. The wedding took place at Gioia Mia, a beautiful venue in Kibbutz Nahshonim forty-five minutes southeast of Tel Aviv. Shortly before the couple exchanged their vows, a rocket was fired from the Gaza strip and could be seen clearly in the distant sky. A few short seconds later, to our collective relief, it was shot down by the Iron Dome, the missile defense system employed by Israel to protect its civilian population against terrorists' rockets.

In the tradition of Judaism, before a couple becomes man and wife, the man breaks a glass with the heel of his shoe, shattering it into dozens of pieces. Among the explanations given for this unusual act of destruction is that it induces the couple to remember, even during the happiest occasion of their lives, the suffering the Jewish people have endured since the fall of the Second Temple. Almost all of the Jewish weddings I had attended until that point had been in America, far from the perils of war. At those weddings, that part of the ceremony had seemed a remnant of a bygone era. As I watched two close friends moments from becoming husband and wife endangered by a terrorist's rocket, I was reminded that for Jews in Israel, the danger of lives being shattered like glass is not just a historic memory. It is a present reality.

Happily, the wedding continued without further incident, and we celebrated late into the night. During our time in the army, Rudy and I had supported each other through the hard times. His wedding marked a new chapter in his life, as well as a new chapter in our friendship. While we would still push and support each other, as we had done as soldiers, now we could also share in the happy occasions in each other's lives.

The next weekend was the wedding of Eitan's older sister, Yasmin, and her fiancé, Ben. Yasmin, Ben, Eitan and I had all lived together in Tel Aviv during the final year of my army service. Ben and Yasmin were like older siblings to me during my time in Israel, which made their wedding especially important to me. The ceremony took place on Kibbutz Urim, where Ben had grown up. Over the previous week, rocket fire from Gaza had intensified. As the big day approached, we were guardedly hopeful that the wedding would be unaffected by the mounting tensions on the border that lay less than three miles from the kibbutz. Most couples spend the week before their wedding agonizing over table arrangements, last-minute invites, and weather. In stark contrast, though dozens of friends and family had flown to Israel to help celebrate, Ben and Yasmin were rightfully concerned, even until the final hour, that they might have to postpone their wedding due to rocket fire.

Fortunately, as the dawn broke on Thursday, everything was still set to take place as scheduled. That afternoon, chartered buses pulled into the Central Train station of Tel Aviv to take us to the wedding. The July heat was oppressive, and the moment the buses pulled up we practically tripped over each other to board them and collapse into the comfortable, air-conditioned seats.

We arrived several hours before the ceremony began, so my friends and I happily passed the time reminiscing, while of course sampling the various quality scotches that were stocked behind the bar. As the hours passed, a cool breeze blew in from the west, taking with it the oppressive heat of the day. As day turned to evening, and evening to night, the beautiful, dynamic colors of the plants, trees and flowers dulled as the light waned, almost as if to show their deference to the beautiful bride and her groom, whose night it was to shine.

Ben and Yasmin had invited one of Ben's closest friends to officiate, and his words were so eloquent and impactful that there was barely a dry eye left when he had finished speaking. Unfortunately, as night fell, so too did Katyusha rockets. Five times during the wedding ceremony, rockets fired from Gaza landed in the vicinity of the kibbutz, shaking the ground and our nerves for a few terrifying seconds. An hour after the ceremony ended, soldiers from an adjoining base arrived at the kibbutz and informed the father of the groom that the central command had canceled all public gatherings within six miles of the border due to the threat of rocket fire. Due to this order, they would have to shut down the wedding.

Unwilling to see his son's special day marred, and intimately familiar with the inefficiency of the army, Ben's father kindly asked that the soldiers return with that order in writing, after which, he assured them, he would happily comply. After a brief period of confusion and protest, the puzzled soldiers pledged to return with the documentation he had requested. Nearly ten hours later, when the soldiers finally returned with the written order, there was no longer a party to interrupt.

Those of us in attendance were kept blissfully unaware of how close the party was to being canceled, and the night flew by as the drinks flowed and the band played. When the band stopped playing at midnight, a DJ took its place, and the party continued. As the first rays of dawn began to illuminate the morning sky, a group of us took a break from dancing to sit in one of the many beautiful cabanas that had been set up on either side of the field, adjacent to the dance floor. Looking around that circle at nearly all my closest friends, whom I had come to love as family, in the country I had learned to call home, I could not have imagined a place I'd rather be. Less than two miles from where we sat, celebrating love, Hamas terror operatives were stockpiling thousands of Katyusha rockets in preparation for war.

CHAPTER 52: OPERATION PROTECTIVE EDGE

Shortly after the wedding, in response to the continually increasing rocket fire from the Gaza strip, the Israeli Air Force launched Operation "Protective Edge" with the dual mission of restoring security to the civilians of Israel and dismantling Hamas' rocket stores. Prior to the operation, it was reported that Hamas held approximately 12,000 rockets in the Gaza Strip. Before the end of the operation, Hamas would fire over 3,000 of those rockets, most of them at Israeli civilian centers.

Friends and family back home had begun to ask me if I knew of some way for them to help the soldiers stationed on the border and the people of Southern Israel. Both had been subjected to an incessant barrage of rocket fire over the prior weeks and months. By that time, schools and all public gathering places along the Gaza border had been closed indefinitely by order of the Central Command due to the increasing threat of rocket fire. Children accustomed to running around outside were now confined to bomb shelters for days and weeks with little to do to stave off boredom and fear.

My reserve commander had put the company on notice that we would be called up in the coming weeks. In the meantime, I was determined to do whatever I could to raise money and deliver supplies to the people in Southern Israel. Throughout the summer of 2014, the country of Israel came together as one. Restaurants advertised free meals for soldiers in uniform, and stores donated portions of their proceeds to buy apparel for troops on the border. People showed up at bars that had been transformed into makeshift sorting centers, where they helped organize supplies that had been donated for delivery to military bases. People's generosity was so immense that nearly every brigade of combat soldiers reported that they had more food and basic apparel than they knew what to do with; I routinely arrived at bases in the South to scenes of boxes stacked eight feet high, full of underwear, socks and snacks.

One of the more gratifying experiences during that period was bringing clothing and equipment to my former unit in the Givati Reconnaissance Company. Two friends, Sam and Brittany and I began the long drive towards the Gaza border in the late morning of July 17th. We arrived in the Southern District of Israel just as the latest cease-fire had ended. Unsurprisingly, the bombardment once again resumed, and police closed the roads that lead towards the Gaza strip to all nonessential military personnel. Fortunately, I had prepared for this possibility and dressed in my military pants and boots. Carrying my reserve card, I assured the police at the roadblocks that I was a reservist that had just been called up, and that my friends were dropping me off. By the time we arrived at Mishmar HaNegev, the base where I had spent nearly a year in training, we were starving. We had spent a full day packaging and loading donations and navigating roadblocks. We made a quick stop at Moti's shakshuka stand right outside the gates of my old base, where we ate what I am still convinced is the best shakshuka served anywhere in the world. From there, we continued south to a major training base called Tze'elim, where most of the company was undergoing urban warfare training in preparation for the imminent ground operation in Gaza.

Since we were unable to bring a civilian vehicle onto the base due to security concerns, a military jeep and a driver were sent to meet us in the parking lot. We transferred the donations from the car to his jeep, and drove through the base, which was abuzz with activity. Finally, we arrived at Mala, which at 7.4 square miles, is the largest urban warfare training center in Israel. The center is used by many of the world's most elite military units as a training ground for operating in densely populated urban environments.

When we reached the area where my company was training, it was nearly dark. Working quickly to take advantage of what light still remained, we hopped down from the jeep and began unloading the boxes of donated supplies, which contained food and over 400 pairs of socks and underwear. Soldiers nearby immediately rushed over to help us take the boxes down from the jeep. When all the donations had been unloaded, the company commander gathered the soldiers in a circle so we could share a few words of encouragement and appreciation on behalf of the donors.

Once the formalities were behind us, I snapped a few photos and joked around with old friends. As we laughed and reminisced, it was easy to forget that Israel stood on the brink of a dangerous ground operation. Quite suddenly, the company was called to attention, and we were asked to step away for security considerations. There was complete silence as the company commander spoke. I didn't need to hear the words to know what was happening. His tone was solemn, and I could see from the expressions on my friends' faces that the green light had been given for a ground operation. The company would be entering Gaza. When the commander dismissed them, I returned to say goodbye. None of us mentioned what we all knew would be happening in the coming hours. I told them how proud I was of them, and how united the people of Israel and the entire global Jewish community was behind their efforts to bring lasting peace to the people of Southern Israel.

I took back the food that they told us they wouldn't have time to eat or room to carry, and Sam and Brittany and I made our way back to Tel Aviv. As we reached the highway, we heard news over the radio that the ground operation had begun. Israeli troops had officially entered Gaza, among them my friends whom I had just left.

Over the next two weeks, generous friends and family members wired me nearly $20,000, which I used to purchase supplies for soldiers who had spent weeks on the Gaza border without respite. With the help of a few friends, I made several trips to the South to deliver the supplies. One of those trips brought me to Sderot, a city that had seen more shelling over the previous decade than any other major population center in Israel.

CHAPTER 53: THE BOMB SHELTER CAPITAL OF THE WORLD

A visit to Sderot, nicknamed "The Bomb Shelter Capital of the World," is not like a typical visit to a new city. Ordinarily, upon arriving in a new city, one would check a map to get a sense of the surroundings, or ask a friend where to get a bite to eat.

When you get off the bus in Sderot, the first thing you do is locate the nearest bomb shelter. Even during times of relative peace throughout the rest of Israel, Sderot is the constant target of Qassam rockets from Gaza. When a rocket is fired from Gaza, just over a half mile away, you have fifteen seconds, at most, to find cover. I say "at most" because after speaking to several Sderot residents, I learned that many times the missile lands before the siren goes off, or as little as seven seconds thereafter. Seven seconds to run for your life.

As I got off the bus that morning, I imagined what my life would be like if I lived in Sderot. What would I wear if I lived in Sderot? Sandals in the summer, or running shoes, which might spell the difference between reaching shelter before the rocket hit or not. How would I sleep at night? Would I ever know the relief of resting my head on a cool pillow, burrowing under the covers, and falling into a deep, peaceful slumber after a long day at work? What would it have been like to grow up as a child in Sderot? A study, published in 2011, found that approximately 75 percent of the city's children have symptoms of post-traumatic stress disorder (PTSD) as a result of the constant rocket fire[23]. As a child with ADHD, I often struggled to concentrate during exams. How much harder would it have been to focus if I knew that at any moment I might have to run for cover from an incoming missile? As a parent, would I allow my children to play outdoors in Sderot? One parent, faced with this problem, helped build the world's first bomb shelter playground. A 30-foot-long caterpillar built of reinforced concrete wraps around the side of the playground, so that young children are never more than a few seconds from cover. One child in Sderot, when asked why turtles had shells, replied confidently, "To protect them from Qassams."

I thought then about the elderly. How would I feel if my grandmother lived in Sderot? The elderly are not quick enough to run for cover in fifteen seconds, let alone seven. As I ate lunch that afternoon, a siren went off while two men in their eighties were playing checkers at a café across the street. I fought my initial instinct to run for cover and sat there observing them. Their stress was palpable as they shifted their bodies around uncomfortably within their chairs, flicking their eyes towards the sky every few seconds, but continuing to play their game. They knew that they could not run quickly enough to make it to a shelter in time.

When we think of casualties of war, we think of physical casualties, of which there were many during the Gaza war. Tragically, during that operation, in addition to civilian losses suffered in Israel, many innocent civilians in Gaza were injured and killed. This was in no small part the result of Hamas firing rockets from schools, hospitals, and even a UN building, turning their civilians into human shields[24]. But physical wounds are not the only type of wounds. I thought about what it would be like to spend decades living in fear of missiles, of jumping every time a door slammed or a glass broke. I thought about the pain of a son who found his father doubled over and clutching at his pacemaker after three consecutive rocket sirens, wondering how many more sirens his father's fragile heart could handle. I thought about pregnant women—how could they move quickly enough to seek shelter when the siren sounded, and what about the effects of stress on their pregnancy? A study in the *Journal of Bio-Behavioral Medicine* found that exposure to rocket attacks increased the risk of miscarriage by 59 percent[25]. As I left Sderot that evening, I did so with a renewed commitment to Israel's defense; the people of Southern Israel deserved to live free of terror. I pledged to intensify my efforts to do whatever I could to help the soldiers on the front lines of the war, and hoped that my company would be called up so that I could do my part to defend our country.

CHAPTER 54: RESERVES

Several days before we were called up to the reserves, on the night of July 29, 2014, I drove down to the operation's staging ground to deliver camel-baks and portable chargers to my company. They were making their final preparations for their third entry into Gaza. I left Tel Aviv shortly after 10:00 p.m. and began the long drive down the mostly deserted Highway 6. Though my thoughts wandered as I drove, I was snapped back to the present several times with the realization that the projectiles moving towards me were not fireworks. They were rockets fired by terrorists at the civilian population of Israel.

Shortly after midnight, I reached my unit. The staging ground was a con-glomeration of tanks, armored vehicles, soldiers, and tents, the likes of which I had not seen since the Gaza operation in 2012, when I was an active-duty soldier. Some of the men I had served with back then had remained in the army and become officers. They were now the commanders who would be charged with leading their soldiers into Gaza. Those soldiers were the ones I had joined for six weeks during Course Orev in the spring of 2012. At that point, they had only been in the military for seven months. Now, two years later, they had lost the naivety of youth. I saw in their eyes the exhaustion that only soldiers know. It's the kind that comes from weeks without sufficient sleep and from being constantly on edge in fear of ambush, rocket fire, or a bullet from a sniper. In Gaza, there was no letting your guard down.

When I was satisfied that all my friends and their soldiers had working camel-baks and at least one portable charger, I reached out to Benaya Sarel. He was the commanding officer of another unit within my company, and I wanted to give his soldiers the remaining gear. We had a brief but friendly conversation in which he thanked me for the donations, and put me in touch with one of his subordinate officers to facilitate the distribution of the donations. Less than seventy-two hours later, he was killed in action, along with two other soldiers from the company. The morning that Benaya was killed, he and two of his soldiers were surveying a terror tunnel that Hamas had dug to launch terrorist attacks into Israel when a suicide bomber detonated his vest. I still think about the conversation we had that night and the kindness and exhaustion I could hear in his voice.

Before heading back to Tel Aviv that night, I went to see my friends and the soldiers they commanded one last time. Some were sitting together in a circle, while others slept directly behind them. Not wanting to disturb those trying to catch a few minutes of sleep, I said my goodbyes to those still awake and wished them well. As I walked back towards my car, I said a silent prayer that they would all return home safely. Sadly, not all of them would. During Operation Cast Lead, sixty-seven IDF soldiers were killed.

Among the fallen was Jordan Bensemhoun, a lone soldier from France who was killed when an anti-tank missile fired by Gazan terrorists struck his vehicle. Though (I later found out) his family had asked that only close friends and family attend his funeral, as a fellow lone soldier, I felt a special bond with Jordan and decided to attend and pay my respects. As it turned out, I was not alone in feeling a strong connection to Jordan. Tens of thousands of Israelis showed up that morning to see Jordan off to his final resting place, and in so doing sent a strong message to the IDF and to the world: The nation of Israel is one family, united behind our soldiers. Jordan's officer spoke of his commitment to Israel, and of his bravery. The noted Soviet dissident Natan Sharansky spoke for all of us that morning as he addressed Jordan's family: "Your son is our son. Your brother is our brother."

As the funeral procession passed by, I saw his devastated teammates with their heads down, a casket blanketed with the flag of Israel balanced gently on their shoulders. My thoughts drifted back to a military funeral I had attended earlier in my service, that of another lone soldier from France with whom I had trained prior to drafting. At 21 years old, with a lifetime of opportunity and promise in front of him, his life had also been cut tragically short. He left a comfortable life in France, and came to Israel to join the IDF to defend our Jewish Nation. As he endured the grueling physical and mental training of the IDF's special forces, he felt alone, far from his home and the warmth of his family. To those who have never been lone soldiers, no matter how great your support network might be, the loneliness that sometimes overwhelms you is impossible to describe. The losses we suffer in the defense of Israel are incurred not only during training and on the battlefield, but also in the psychological wounds that remain long after the bullets stop flying.

There is nothing sadder than the looks of grief on the faces of parents who have lost their son; there are no poems, no songs, and no words that can fully capture that pain. As my thoughts returned to the present and the scene unfolding around me, I watched as the funeral procession approached Jordan's immediate family. A piercing cry left his mother as she was handed the flag that had been draped over her son's coffin, her pain so deep and unadulterated that it penetrated my soul. As long as I live, I will never forget that sound. A three-volley salute was fired, each shot rattling our nerves and shattering the solemn silence. And while the sound of exploding gunpowder pierced the air, the pained cries of Jordan's mother pierced our hearts.

Days later, on August 4, my wish to be back in uniform came true. With a military operation already underway, the IDF mobilized 83,000 reservists. During the three weeks we spent in uniform, we took over the responsibilities of the soldiers who, until that point, had been stationed on a kibbutz adjacent to the Gaza border. We set up our center of operations in the kindergarten, which was underground in a makeshift bomb shelter. The bunker was dark and cool, both the result of its depth beneath the ground, which made it a welcome respite from the heat for combat soldiers sleeping during off hours. Despite the comfort it provided, it was impossible not to note the tragedy of kindergarten classes that were permanently held in an underground bomb shelter.

Eight times during the operation there were cease-fires, during which we were permitted, in small groups, to visit the bar on the kibbutz. Despite the absurdity of soldiers walking around a civilian bar wearing semi-automatic rifles, several of the patrons in the bar approached us to thank us for being there. Given their proximity to Gaza and the infiltrations of the previous few weeks, they could seldom let their guards down. In an underground bomb shelter surrounded by armed soldiers, they finally felt they could relax, if only for a little while. One night during the cease-fire, with little to do but sleep and guard, some friends and I decided to try to raise awareness about what was happening in Gaza. Taking inspiration from the ALS "ice bucket challenge" we created the "Hamas vs. Hummus challenge". We spoke tongue-in-cheek of the difference between Hamas and hummus, noting that Hamas was a terrorist organization that threatened the lives of Palestinians and Israelis, whereas hummus was delicious. We then smeared hummus on our faces and nominated three friends to do the same, or to donate money to the FIDF. Before I went to bed I sent the video to a few people, all of whom told me I was an idiot. I woke to a phone call at 7:00 a.m. the following morning from a reporter for Arutz-2, Israel's most popular television network. Our video was aired later that day on national television and seen by millions of Israelis. EliteDaily posted an article about the video, as did the pro-Israel advocacy group StandWithUs, where it garnered millions of views.

Each night we rotated through shifts of guard duty atop the tallest building on the kibbutz. Seated in a beach-chair provided by a resident, and armed with night-vision binoculars, we watched over the area between Gaza and the kibbutz. We would be the first line of defense in the event of a terrorist infiltration, of which there had been a dozen over the prior few weeks. Intermittently throughout my watch each night, rockets soared overhead in the direction of Israel. Even Human Rights Watch, which has been a consistent critic of Israel, acknowledged that Qassam rockets are too inaccurate and prone to malfunction to be used against specific military targets in or near civilian areas. That same report concluded that, "The absence of Israeli military forces in the areas struck by the rockets, as well as statements from the leaders of Hamas and other armed groups, indicate that many of these attacks are deliberately intended to strike Israeli civilians and civilian structures."[26] I tried to comprehend how people could lash out with such blind hatred toward other human beings.

At night, I often heard the powerful blades of Apache helicopters hovering overhead. This was inevitably followed by the sounds of explosions as their missiles struck their targets in Gaza, and the weapons stores they had been targeting exploded. On August 25, after seven long weeks, the war finally came to an end. As in all wars, there were no winners, and many innocent people were killed.

While nothing can justify, or lessen the tragedy of innocent lives taken, intention matters, and I took pride in the measures taken by Israel to prevent civilian casualties. Many of Israel's actions during the operation were unprecedented in the history of warfare. This included dropping pamphlets, sending texts, and making phone calls warning civilians of impending strikes. This was done even though it gave terrorists time to flee with the weapons caches the Air Force had intended to destroy. In 2009, Richard Kemp, former Commander of British Forces in Afghanistan, observed the Gaza operation from the ground. In his assessment he noted that, "Israel did more to safeguard the rights of civilians in a combat zone than any army in the history of warfare." In his testimony to the UN, he confirmed that view as it related to the 2014 Gaza operation.[27] At that time, I was serving as a reservist on the Israel/Gaza border. Though the IDF's advanced notice gave terrorists an opportunity to move their rockets, increasing the danger that I faced, I was proud to serve in a military that holds itself to high moral standards.

Shortly after the war ended, I returned to New York and began working for Taboola, an Israeli founded digital media company. As I sought to settle into civilian life, one of the hardest challenges I faced was reconciling my new perspective with that of my old friends. Their perspectives were informed by the paths they had taken after college, which were neither better nor worse, but drastically different than mine. The result was a distance between us that would take much time and mutual effort to overcome.

For months, I jumped whenever I heard slamming doors, fireworks, or the scream of an ambulance. I often thought about that Gaza operation. At times, I struggled to ground myself in the present. My new reality seemed trivial when compared to all that I had experienced as a soldier in a warzone. Those feelings gradually subsided, and I grew accustomed to the working world and my new life. Not a day goes by, however, when I do not think about the brave men and women who defend Israel. I am grateful to have had the privilege of serving in the IDF.

Tomer and me on a rainy night
of training

"Welcome" to nowhere. Reserves
in the desert

Hanging out before a company BBQ during
reserve training in the Negev

With Amit and Yona (LtoR) on a break
from a drill

The boys at Nuri and Eden's
wedding

Sar and Me before an overnight drill

Drinking coffee with Eyal before a
company briefing

Reunited at Rudy and Yael's wedding

Training in the desert

Preparing for a simulated
urban warfare operation

In the midst of an evening exercise

Arutz 2 (Channel 2 news) playing the
Hammas vs. Hummus challenge

EPILOGUE

On the day of my release from the IDF, after signing off on my gear and cutting up my military ID, I walked out the gates of my training base as a civilian. My life was now my own; there was nobody to report to on Sunday morning except myself.

On the bus ride back to Tel Aviv, I had a flashback to the moment I first realized I would one day become an IDF soldier—when Danny Ben-Farahan had looked me in the eyes and told me that I hadn't tried on his beret because I wanted to earn it. Danny was only 28 years old when he died, leaving behind a fiancée, loving family and friends, and a bright future. Danny was a hero to me, as he was to many others. I thought back to the night I met him in Jerusalem. I remembered the thrill of listening to the stories of a real-life IDF Paratrooper. I remembered his poise and his confidence and the look of his neatly pressed uniform, his silver Jump Wings, and his M-16. A few months into my service, I went with a close friend and fellow soldier to a synagogue in Jerusalem to speak to a Birthright group. As I stood there in my uniform and spoke about why I left my life in America to come to Israel and enlist, I realized that I was echoing many of the sentiments that Danny shared with me four years earlier. I felt a powerful connection to him in that moment, as I did each time I reached a milestone in my service.

In the months immediately following my release, I enjoyed my newfound freedom. I traveled. I slept late. I skipped workouts. But as the months turned to years, despite the intensity and difficulty of life as a combat soldier, I realized that there was a lot that I missed. The profound simplicity of my purpose—to defend a cause I believed in. The physical and mental challenge of training. Most of all, I missed my friends.

Serving in the IDF, I learned lessons that shaped me as a person. I learned to be selfless and to think about my teammates as an extension of myself. To take a friend's shift of guard duty so that he could catch an extra half hour of sleep. To do an extra round under the stretcher to help a struggling comrade, confident that he would do the same for me. I learned that my supposed physical and emotional limits were, in fact, arbitrary boundaries. I learned what it meant to be humbled, and to be broken. To contract hypothermia after carrying a leaking jerrycan through a cold desert night while insufficiently clothed against the elements. To hold the push-up position on my knuckles for the better part of three hours. To navigate eighty-five miles while carrying seventy pounds on my back with a slightly torn meniscus in my knee. To say goodbye to friends on their way to war, knowing that they might not come back.

I learned the meaning of exhaustion, the kind so overwhelming that you fall asleep while you're walking. I learned the meaning of hunger, the kind that wakes you up in the middle of the night. I learned how to fight through pain. In the first year of training, I sprained my ankle three times, partially tore the meniscus in my right knee, broke a bone in my hand, contracted hypothermia, damaged the tissue in my shoulder, and had a parasite enter my leg in the field, which had to be carved out with a scalpel.

But through it all, I persisted and persevered because as much as it hurt at times, and as much as it may cost me in perpetual medical issues down the line, Israel is worth it. Over the course of my IDF service, what started as a blind love for Israel grew into measured admiration for the tiny country the size of New Jersey that is home to the Jewish State. Israel, I came to realize, is not the "City Upon a Hill" that we who love her sometimes fantasize that she is, and that her founders dreamed she might one day become. But neither is she the tyrant that the international media often portrays. Despite her shortcomings, in a Middle East dominated by dictatorships, subjugation of minorities, and fanaticism, Israel remains a lone beacon of democracy, tolerance, and reform. Though I set down the path of military service with the intention of giving back to the country that means so much to me, in the end, my contribution was far eclipsed by all that I received and all that I learned.

ACKNOWLEDGMENTS

I first want to thank the former lone soldiers who were my family in Israel during the four years that I lived there. Through good and bad times, they were with me, as they are to this day, to lend an ear, a helping hand, and a bottle of scotch, when necessary. Assaf, Ben, Bernardo, Daniel, Eitan, Eric, Gal, Jacob, Jason, Joel, Josh, Liron, Nuri, Omer, Rafi, Rudy, Shar: Thank you for everything over the years.

To Nissan, Liza, and Tom – without your help, I could never have navigated the IDF's bureaucracy. Thank you for going above and beyond to help me.

I want to acknowledge my team, Tsevet Bashari/Dekel/Maimon, who made my service meaningful. It was an honor to serve alongside you for two years, and I hope that one day you all learn enough English to understand some of what I've written here.

To Duvdevan: Thank you for teaching me to never quit on myself, no matter how great the pain. I am forever grateful for the year I spent in training, and the brotherhood I formed with Tsevet Avi/Flor as we learned together what it meant to be soldiers.

To the teachers of The Windward School: Thank you for empowering me and helping me to overcome my learning disabilities. If not for the invaluable lessons you taught me, neither attending college nor publishing a book would have ever been possible. I am forever grateful.

To Ayala, Natan, Shoshanna, Danny, Orit, Noam, Maya, Gal, Yuval, Tomer and Yifat, my relatives who wrapped me in the warmth of family while I lived in Israel: I will always be grateful to you for the great efforts you made to make me feel at home.

To Ellyn Gutman, Beebie Michael, my father, and the many others who helped me edit my story, and transform it into a book: Thank you for your time and hard work, and for your belief in me.

Yasmin and Ben: Thank you for supporting me as roommates, but more importantly, as the older siblings I always wanted and you never asked to be—now you are stuck with me.

Lastly and most importantly, I want to thank my family. To my Mom and Dad, Mindy and Andrew, my siblings, Russell, Jackie, and Tara, and my other brother, Eitan: Your support gave me the strength I needed to persevere through the many difficult periods of my service. To Meema, my remaining grandparent who so gracefully represents them all: You have been a beacon guiding my Jewish values and a love of Israel, and supported me with unconditional love and unwavering confidence in my every endeavor. I am lucky to have you in my life. To the rest of my family and friends: Thank you for helping me find the strength to live out my dream of serving as a combat soldier in the IDF.

ABOUT THE AUTHOR

After receiving his bachelor's degree in political science from the University of Pennsylvania in 2010, Corey Feldman left his home in Westchester, New York, and moved to Israel to enlist in the Israeli Defense Forces. In 2013, he completed his three years of IDF service in a specialized combat unit within the Givati Brigade. He holds the rank of staff sergeant, and proudly returns to Israel each year to serve alongside his team in the IDF Reserves.

Corey currently lives in Manhattan. He is an Erickson certified professional coach, holds an Executive MBA from the Quantic School of Business and Technology, and is currently pursuing his Masters in Healthcare Innovation from The University of Pennsylvania. Corey is a volunteer EMT, and works as an entrepreneur in the digital healthcare space. His website and blog can be found at TheExaminedLife.NYC. His podcasts, "The Lone Soldier Podcast," and "Healthcare Reimagined," can be found on Spotify and Apple podcasts.

ENDNOTES

1   Lipman, Dov. "The Second Intifada: Israeli Society Terrorized." HonestReporting.com

2   Finn, James. letter to the Earl of Clarendon, Sept, 15, 1857; British Foreign Office Documents 78/1294 (Pol. no. 36).

3   Twain, Mark. 1869. The Innocents Abroad [by] Mark Twain. London: Collins Clear-type Press. Chapter 56.

4   Stanley, Arthur Penrhyn. Sinai and Palestine. London: John Murray, 1881, p. 118

5   Netanyahu, Benjamin. A Durable Peace: Israel and Its Place Among the Nations. New York, NY: Warner Books, 2000. Page 44.

6   According to the IDF's website, the KABA is determined from several components:
    1. Psycho-technical test station - A series of computerized tests on various subjects.
    2. The personal data verification station – The Army notes the candidate's education level and other relevant personal details.
    3. Personal Interview Station – A psychologist determines the candidate's suitability for combat roles.

7   "Hebron: History & Overview." Jewish Virtual Library. Accessed November 20, 2020. https://www.jewishvirtuallibrary.org/history-and-overview-of-hebron.

8   Kamisher, Eliyahu, and Adam Rasgon. "Hebron: The Conflict in a Nutshell." The Jerusalem Post, September 24, 2017. https://www.jpost.com/Magazine/Hebron-The-conflict-in-a-nutshell-490446.

9   Tikkanen, Amy. "Hebron." Encyclopædia Britannica. Accessed November 20, 2020. https://www.britannica.com/place/Hebron-city-West-Bank.

10   Avi-Yonah, Michael; Shapira, Moshe; Orni, Efraim; Rubinstein, Daniel "Hebron." Encyclopedia Judaica. Encyclopedia.com. October 16, 2020 https://www.encyclopedia.com/places/asia/west-bank-and-gaza-political-geography/hebron.

11   Lipman, Dov. "The Second Intifada: Israeli Society Terrorized." HonestReporting, March 3, 2020. https://honestreporting.com/the-second-intifada-israeli-society-terrorized/

12   Bard, Mitchell. "West Bank, Gaza and Lebanon Security Barriers: Background & Overview." Background & Overview of Israel's Security Barriers. Accessed November 20, 2020. https://www.jewishvirtuallibrary.org/background-and-overview-of-israel-s-security-fence

13   The Gatekeepers. Directed by Dror Moreh. Tel Aviv: Sony Pictures Classics, 2012.

14   Lappin, Yaakov. "Dealing with Hamas's Human Shield Tactics." The Jerusalem Post | JPost.com, November 20, 2012. https://www.jpost.com/Defense/Dealing-with-Hamass-human-shield-tactics.

15 Rosen, Armin. "All Quiet on the Gaza Front." The Atlantic. Atlantic Media Company, February 4, 2013. https://www.theatlantic.com/international/archive/2013/02/all-quiet-on-the-gaza-front/272794/.

16 1948-1967: Jordanian Occupation of Eastern Jerusalem. CAMERA - Committee for Accuracy in Middle East Reporting and Analysis. Accessed December 12, 2020. http://www.sixdaywar.org/content/jordanianocuupationjerusalem.asp.

17 "Conference of San Remo." Encyclopædia Britannica. Encyclopædia Britannica, inc. Accessed December 12, 2020.

18 "United Nations Resolution 181." Encyclopædia Britannica. Encyclopædia Britannica, inc. Accessed December 12, 2020. https://www.britannica.com/topic/United-Nations-Resolution-181.

19 1948-1967: Jordanian Occupation of Eastern Jerusalem. CAMERA - Committee for Accuracy in Middle East Reporting and Analysis. Accessed December 12, 2020. http://www.sixdaywar.org/content/jordanianocuupationjerusalem.asp.

20 Katz, Yaakov and Myre, Greg. "The Consensus settlements." Jewish Virtual Library. https://www.jewishvirtuallibrary.org/the-ldquo-consensus-rdquo-settlements. Updated January 1, 2020.

21 Marcus, Itamar, and Nan Jacques Zilberdik. "Arafat Planned and Led the Intifada: Testimonies from PA Leaders and Others: PMW Analysis." Palestinian Media Watch. Palestinian Media Watch, November 28, 2011. https://palwatch.org/page/3297.

22 Lipman, Dov. "The Second Intifada: Israeli Society Terrorized." HonestReporting, March 3, 2020. https://honestreporting.com/the-second-intifada-israeli-society-terrorized/

23 "Relentless Rocket Attacks Take Psychological Toll on Children in Sderot." The New Humanitarian, January 27, 2008. https://www.thenewhumanitarian.org/news/2008/01/27/relentless-rocket-attacks-take-psychological-toll-children-sderot.

24 Mshasha, Sami. "UNRWA Condemns Placement of Rockets, for a Second Time, in One of Its Schools." UNRWA, July 22, 2014. https://www.unrwa.org/newsroom/press-releases/unrwa-condemns-placement-rockets-second-time-one-its-schools.

25 "Rocket Attacks in Israel Significantly Increase the Likelihood of Miscarriages, According to BGU Researchers." AABGU. American Associates, Ben-Gurion University of the Negev, September 18, 2014. https://aabgu.org/rocket-attacks-in-israel-significantly-increase-the-likelihood-of-miscarriages-according-to-bgu-researchers/.

26 "Rockets from Gaza." Human Rights Watch. HRW, August 6, 2009. https://www.hrw.org/report/2009/08/06/rockets-gaza/harm-civilians-palestinian-armed-groups-rocket-attacks.

27 Harkov, Lahav. "Former British Commander in Afghanistan: No Army Acts with as Much Discretion as IDF Does." The Jerusalem Post, September 4, 2014. https://www.jpost.com/Arab-Israeli-Conflict/Former-British-commander-in-Afghanistan-No-army-acts-with-as-much-discretion-as-IDF-does-374382.

Made in the USA
Las Vegas, NV
03 July 2022

51055869R00136